Unsilencing Gaza

"Roy is humanely and professionally committed in ways that are unmatched by any other non-Palestinian scholar."

—Edward W. Said

"Roy is the leading researcher and most widely respected academic authority on Gaza today."

—Bruce Bennett Lawrence, Nancy and Jeffrey Marcus Humanities Professor of Religion at Duke University

"A compelling study that continues the author's investigation of the dehumanizing and destabilizing effects of the Israeli occupation on Palestinian politics and society. Essential reading for those intent on understanding both the causes and the consequences of this conflict."

—Irene Gendzier, Professor Emerita, Boston University and author of *Development Against Democracy*

"For several decades, Sara Roy has been bringing her unique moral authority to bear on the searing injustice that continues to be Palestine. This indispensable collection confronts us all with the inhuman conditions of life for the people of Gaza, tempered by the courage with which Roy explores it, her insistence on the unbreakable link between Jewishness and justice, and her ultimate faith in the resilience of the Palestinian people."

—Jacqueline Rose, Professor of Humanities, Birkbeck Institute for the Humanities

Unsilencing Gaza

Reflections on Resistance

Sara Roy

PLUTO  PRESS

First published 2021 by Pluto Press
345 Archway Road, London N6 5AA

www.plutobooks.com

Copyright © Sara Roy 2021

The right of Sara Roy to be identified as the author of this work has been
asserted in accordance with the Copyright, Designs and Patents Act 1988.

British Library Cataloguing in Publication Data
A catalogue record for this book is available from the British Library

ISBN   978 0 7453 4136 1   Hardback
ISBN   978 0 7453 4137 8   Paperback
ISBN   978 1 7868 0825 7   PDF
ISBN   978 1 7868 0826 4   EPUB
ISBN   978 1 7868 0827 1   Kindle

Typeset by Stanford DTP Services, Northampton, England

Simultaneously printed in the United Kingdom and United States of America

In memory of

Peter Gubser, Augustus Richard Norton and Hilda Silverman

Contents

List of Abbreviations

ACTA—Anti-Terrorism Clarification Act
AIPAC—American Israel Public Affairs Committee
ANERA—American Near East Refugee Aid
BDS—Boycott, Divestment and Sanctions
CMWU—Coastal Municipalities Water Utility (Gaza)
COGAT—Coordinator for Government Activities in the Territories
EU—European Union
FAO— (UN) Food and Agriculture Organisation
GMR—Great March of Return
GRM—Gaza Reconstruction Mechanism
ICAHD—Israel Committee Against Home Demolitions
IDF—Israel Defense Forces
IFRI—Institut français des relations internationales
MB—Muslim Brotherhood
MEPP—Middle East peace process
MERIP—Middle East Research and Information Project
MFA—Ministry of Foreign Affairs (Israel)
MMUP—Materials Monitoring Unit Project
MOH—Ministry of Health (West Bank)
NIS—new Israeli shekel, currency in Israel and Palestine
OPE—Operation Protective Edge
PA—Palestinian Authority
PCBS—Palestinian Central Bureau of Statistics
PEP—Paris Economic Protocol
PHRI—Physicians for Human Rights–Israel
PIJ—Palestinian Islamic Jihad
PLA—Palestine Liberation Army
PLO—Palestine Liberation Organization
PWA—Palestinian Water Authority
RAO—Refugee Affairs Officer
UN—United Nations
UNCTAD—United Nations Conference on Trade and Development

UNDP—United Nations Development Program
UNICEF—United Nations Children's Fund
UNOCHA—UN Office for the Coordination of Humanitarian
Affairs
UNRWA—United Nations Relief and Works Agency for Palestine
Refugees in the Near East
USAID—United States Agency for International Development
WFP—World Food Programme
WHO—World Health Organization

Acknowledgments

Over the many years of research and writing represented in this book, there have been more people than I can mention—teachers, mentors, colleagues, friends and students throughout the world—who deserve my profound thanks for their commentary, counsel and constant support. I shall always be in their debt.

I do want to acknowledge just a few, each of whom, in their own way, played a significant role in my research: Elaine Hagopian, Herbert Kelman, Martha Myers, Irene Gendzier, Lani Frerichs, Norman Finkelstein, Marc Ellis, Walid Khalidi, the late Fr. Vincent Martin OSB, Denis Sullivan, Noam Chomsky, William Granara, Lenore Martin, Susan Kahn, Brian Klug, Afif and Christ'l Safieh, Husam Zomlot, Salim Tamari, Desmond Travers, Karam Dana, Nubar Hovsepian, Alexandra Senfft, Brigitte Schulz, Ellen Siegel, Paul Aaron, the late Thomas Mullins, the late Allen Bergson, Deirdre Bergson, the late Edward Said and Roger Owen, the late Russell Davis and Donald Warwick, the late Haidar Abdel Shafi, Huda Abdel Shafi, the late Hatem Abu Ghazaleh, the late Eyad el-Sarraj and Naseer Aruri, the late Alya Shawwa, Talal Abu Rahme, Amira Hass, Ruchama Marton, the late Dan Bar-On, Ibrahim Barzak, Raji Sourani, Omar Shaban, Adnan Abu Hasna, Charles Shammas, Hiromu Odagiri, Takanori Hayao, Mari Oka, Thomas and Patricia Neu, Marilyn Garson, Brian Moore, Chris Gunness, Linda Butler, Michelle Esposito, Deena Hurwitz, Hilary Rantisi, Susan Akram, Sherman Teichman, Anne Joyce, Rhona Davies and the late Peter Johnson, the late Ellen Greenberg, Kim Burnham, Leticia Pena, Lisa Majaj, Nancy Murray, Angela Bader, Souad Dajani and Marie Francis.

The late Augustus Richard Norton, Peter Gubser and Hilda B. Silverman to whom this book is dedicated, were pivotal to my learning and thought, dear friends and cherished colleagues who are deeply missed.

A special note of gratitude to Roger van Zwanenberg for his years of support and friendship.

Just as I was completing this manuscript, Meron Benvenisti passed away at the age of 86. I am especially grateful to Meron who, more than anyone, set me on a trajectory that would become my life's endeavor. As a young doctoral student, I read a report that he had written on US economic assistance to the West Bank and Gaza as part of the West Bank Data Base Project, which he founded and directed. I was struck by his argument, which was both compelling and courageous especially at that time (1984). His paper and our many subsequent conversations helped me formulate my doctoral research and was the seed of all my future work. Meron was prophetic, brilliant and principled, among the most decent human beings I have known. He spoke truth to power throughout his life. He was consistent and unafraid. I shall always be grateful to him.

A special note of thanks to the superbly talented staff at Pluto Press: my editor, Neda Tehrani, Melanie Patrick, Robert Webb, Dave Stanford, Jeanne Brady, Tania Palmieri, Emily Orford and David Shulman.

I also want to extend my sincere thanks to the following individuals and publications for permission to reprint the articles contained in this book (the original source is cited in each chapter). They are:

Center for Contemporary Arab Studies, Georgetown University
Christian Science Monitor
Counterpunch
Foreign Policy
Informed Comment
Institut français des relations internationales (IFRI)
Jamie Stern-Weiner
Journal of Holy Land and Palestine Studies
Journal of Islamic Studies
Journal of Palestine Studies
London Review of Books
Middle East Policy
Middle East Research and Information Project (MERIP)
Olive Branch Press
OR Books
Postcolonial Studies
Professor Juan Cole
Professor Nubar Hovsepian
The Nation
The United Nations Palestine Committee, Division for Palestinian
    Rights

A final note of loving appreciation to my wonderful family—Jay, Annie and Jess—without whom my accomplishments, such as they are, would be far less.

The truly civilized man is marked by empathy.

Malcolm Kerr
The Arab-Israeli Confrontation of June 1967: An Arab Perspective

Introduction: "I can't eat my lights"

Gaza is central to the Palestinian–Israeli conflict and to its ultimate resolution. This has always been the case and it will remain so. Its small size belies its far greater significance. This is why Israel has worked to marginalize Gaza politically and economically in an attempt to remove it from any form of serious consideration particularly as it regards the resolution of the conflict, let alone a future Palestinian state (no matter what form it may assume). As this book will show, the assault against Gaza has been consistent and relentless.

The latest iteration of this policy, which of course is directed at Palestine as a whole, is the "peace" agreement signed in 2020 between Israel and two Gulf states, the UAE and Bahrain.[1] While the term "peace" is a misnomer since Israel was not at war with either country, the agreements represented a diplomatic and political coup for Israel, demonstrating that it was possible to make "peace" with Arab countries and normalize relations with Israel—without ending the occupation and before the establishment of a Palestinian state.[2] Reflecting the diminishing role of the Palestinian issue in regional politics (at least at present), a senior Likud official stated:

> The Israeli and international left always said that it is impossible to bring peace with Arab nations without peace with the Palestinian people. That there is no other way except from withdrawing from the '67 borders, clearing out the settlements, dividing Jerusalem and establishing a Palestinian state. This is the first time in history that Prime Minister Netanyahu broke the paradigm of "land for peace" and brought "peace in exchange for peace."[3]

Yet, as this book will show, Gaza alone proves this wrong.

My first trip to Gaza occurred in the summer of 1985 and at the time I could not have imagined that Gaza (and Palestine) would be as diminished and compromised as it is now, 35 years later. This book of my selected writings over the last 14 years attempts to explain why and to articulate a possible way forward. It continues where *Failing Peace: Gaza and the Palestinian–Israeli Conflict* left off. Together, these two books are informed by over three decades of my research and writing on Gaza.

Unsilencing Gaza analyzes Gaza's imposed and rapid decline over the last decade in particular—then as now, the majority of Gazans remain dependent on humanitarian assistance to survive—and some critically missed opportunities that might have initiated a meaningful response. One understanding—which remains outside the analytical boundaries of many observers—that emerge from the pages that follow is the ways in which Israeli policies have further and more dangerously constrained and delimited life in Gaza and the particularly ruinous impact of these policies politically, economically and socially.

For example, in the context of Israel's relationship with Gaza, the use and purpose of collective punishment needs to be understood differently. Here collective punishment is not only (or even principally) meant to inflict harm as it typically does in other contexts. In Gaza it is meant to prevent any kind of normal environment from emerging, institutionalizing in both practical and psychological terms a form of abnormality that resists change the longer it is allowed to exist and take root. In Gaza this abnormality has assumed many forms. One that is visible and well documented is Gaza's near-total dependence on humanitarian aid and other sources of external financing, a dependence created by long-standing Israeli policies (notably closure, which began in 1991, and siege) which are deliberately aimed at shattering Gaza's economy and, by extension, its society. Within this imposed construct, it perhaps should come as no surprise that today, some people in Gaza are searching for food in trash piles.

The economic ruination that has resulted also reflects the absence of sovereign laws in Gaza that obligate the ruling power to protect the people it is ruling over. Instead, the only laws that truly apply in Gaza are those of war where the sovereign power, Israel, can inflict violence without accountability or any reference to law. The withdrawal of law—and with it, justice—in Gaza, combined with economic collapse, has not only necessitated humanitarian intervention but also has situated Gaza between periodic conflict and potential catastrophe, where violence is used not so much to inflict death as debility.

Israel's objective in Gaza, therefore, is limited and contained: to avert any large-scale disaster such as starvation, and nothing more. Gaza is controlled by the threat of wholesale catastrophe be it hunger, institutional destruction, or total economic demise, where Israel rules by maintaining a liminal, indeterminate state, and where the sites of resistance are narrow and ineffective. Israel governs by how near to the disaster threshold Gaza is allowed to go. Within this mode of rule, Palestinians are regarded as charity cases or terrorists. In this way Israel uses scarcity as a form of control, creating conditions that increase the need for humanitarian aid. As one young man said when Gaza's acute electricity crisis improved, "I can't eat my lights."

Another example of Israel's strategic objective in Gaza concerns its handling of the coronavirus. As I write this (Fall 2020), the Covid-19 crisis in Gaza has taken a dangerous turn with the discovery of community transmission—once believed contained—that threatens the Strip's 2 million people. The impact on Gaza's already disabled economy has been disproportionately damaging (see Chapter 25). Yet, this crisis is unfolding within a context of punitive measures imposed on Gaza beyond its 14-year siege. According to the Israeli NGO, GISHA, which monitors human rights conditions in Gaza:

> Starting August 11 [for example], Israel had barred entry of con- struction materials to Gaza and from August 13, it had banned entry of fuel, including for Gaza's power plant. As a result, the plant shut down on August 18, leading to a further reduction in the overall supply of electricity. On August 16, Israel imposed a full maritime closure, and from August 23 until this morning [September 1, 2020], it was limiting entry of goods to food and medicine only. During this period of time, the first cases of community transmission of coronavirus were discovered in the Strip ... Power supply was down to less than six non-consecutive hours daily. The power shortage was a source of great concern, particularly for Gaza's healthcare system and civilian infrastructure and services such as water distribution and sewage disposal [see Chapter 20].[4]

Under growing international pressure, the Israeli authorities sub-sequently reversed their ban on the entry of fuel and other needed supplies and eased the maritime closure, but the siege remains in place.

What exists now to unify Palestinians and encourage them forward, particularly when compared to the past? Without a political horizon or clear direction, without effective leadership or independent civil society agents in Gaza or the West Bank, the situation on the ground will continue to be fragile and volatile, where survival is the principal unifying force (see Chapter 24). As one Gazan put it: "In the '90s there was Oslo, in the 2000s there was Arafat's fight, from 2007 until now there is nothing, so we live day to day." Yet, as this book will also show, Gaza's people have continually resisted and have found creative ways of doing so, refusing any notion that what they must endure is the result of what they have done.[5]

ORGANIZATION

This book is divided into eight parts and 25 chapters. Each part begins with a quotation(s) that sets the tone for the chapters that follow. Parts I–VII consist of selected articles arranged according to a specific theme, with the themes organized chronologically (similar to *Failing Peace*). The writings included in this book occurred largely during the two Obama administrations (2009–16); as such his admin-istration's approach to the conflict is critical for understanding the US policy context, which was (and remains) defining for Palestinians generally and Gaza, in particular. The writings selected for Part I, "Setting the Stage for Conflict in Gaza: US Policy Failures Redux," examine certain critical political dynamics in the wake of the 2011 Arab uprisings, which key actors to the conflict—the Palestinian leadership and people, the US and Egypt—hoped, and feared, would alter the trajectory of a failing peace process. For Palestinians and their renewed struggle for a state, this entailed, among other things, a shift in strategy from negotiable to non-negotiable rights and the adoption of peaceful, non-violent resistance as the defining political strategy for dealing with Israel. For the leadership, it meant securing recognition of a Palestinian state on 1967 borders, admission to the UN as a state in some official form, and a unity agreement between Fatah and Hamas.

The dynamics reshaping the Palestinian political landscape had implications for US foreign policy and many hoped, incorrectly, that these changes would push the Obama administration into a more balanced approach to the conflict, particularly as it regarded Israeli settlements. There was a sense, propagated by the US administration, that Obama's foreign policy toward Israel/Palestine represented an important, albeit cautious, departure in US foreign policy. This "departure" was cast in different terms but the two most striking were: the willingness of the Obama administration to confront Israel on the occupation and insist on meaningful change; and a possible openness to engaging politically and diplomatically with Hamas as the power in control of Gaza, which this book argues is a necessary component of a sustainable peace. Depending, of course, on where one stood politically, the administration's supposed foreign policy departures were either threatening or welcome. I argue that, semantics aside, Obama's foreign policy was no different in substance from that of his predecessors, never going beyond long-observed and well-defined political constraints. Hence, I ask, if "the paradigm for negotiations since 1967 has been land-for-peace ... what happens when there is no land?" (see Chapter 2).

However, given the emergence of a far more draconian policy toward Gaza following the election of Hamas and its subsequent takeover of Gaza in 2007, the continued failure of US foreign policy to challenge occupation policy imposed an even greater toll on Gaza's already weakened and compromised economy and society. What emerges is not only the failure of the US (and the international community more broadly) to resolve the conflict when it could have, but also its complicity—through omission and commission—in the oppression of Palestinians.

"The Marginalized Center: The Wars on Gaza and their Aftermath," is the title of Part II, which examines in some detail the defining and ruinous economic, social and political impact of two of Gaza's most destructive wars: Operation Cast Lead (December 2008–January 2009) and Operation Protective Edge (July–August 2014). The selected writings in this chapter further analyze the dissolution of a coherent Israeli policy toward Gaza, replaced by a series of punitive approaches meant to destabilize yet contain Gazans and the Hamas regime and, in so doing, marginalize them from the larger Palestinian collective and body politic.

What emerges, particularly after Operation Cast Lead, are some new and altogether unprecedented political and socioeconomic dynamics. They include: the elimination of occupation as an analytical or political concept in favor of annexation and imposed sovereignty; the transformation of Palestinians into intruders and perpetrators and the reduction of Palestinians from a political to a humanitarian issue; dispensing with the concept of an economy in Gaza; the provision of aid outside an economic context and its use as a punitive measure, and, finally, the almost complete separation of the Gaza Strip and West Bank and with it, the particularization and narrowing of Palestinian life. These dynamics, among others, have since altered Gazan society and the very nature of the conflict and its possible resolution (and set the stage for the more profound paradigmatic shifts examined in Parts III and IV). These dynamics are critical yet have been continually ignored by Israel, the divided Palestinian leadership, and the donor community—notably the United States and the European Union. The longer these forces are allowed to persist and deepen institutionally, the more disabling the socioeconomic and political erosion will become.

Part III, "Toward Precarity: Exceptionalizing Gaza," and Part IV, "Undoing Attachment: Creating Spaces of Excess," examine the ways in which Israel (with the assistance of the US, the EU and certain Arab states) transformed Gaza into a wholly humanitarian issue, depriving it of any political claim, agency, or aspiration, and positioning Gaza as exceptional (and arguably illegitimate) to the Palestinian cause. This paradigmatic shift is examined along with several others that are unprecedented, such as the ruination of a functional economy spurred by the elimination of normal trade relations and the almost total destruction of Gaza's middle class, massive unemployment, widespread impoverishment and increasing homelessness, and rising levels of youth migration. Both parts examine the intensification of Israeli approaches (in the continued absence of a coherent policy) aimed at making Gaza an aberration (and by extension, the larger Palestinian project) and their impact on daily life and political organization. This intensification moves beyond imposed impoverishment and debility to a form of invalidation or nullification of the Palestinian "other," undoing, to the extent possible, all forms of attachment between

Israelis and Palestinians in Gaza. In this way, I argue that Israel has redefined the colonial distinction between self and other, the space that Israelis and Palestinians inhabit. In this redefined space, which is most acutely expressed in Gaza, there is no engagement, reciprocity, or redemption. Palestinians are simply erased from Israel's emotional and political landscape. Attention is also paid to the ways in which ordinary Palestinians in Gaza resist these attempts to make them anomalous, insisting on their place in the world.

"A Jew in Gaza: Reflections" is the title of Part V. Over the last decade, more of my writing has turned to the impact of my Judaism and personal history as a child of Holocaust survivors on my research and thinking. I included some earlier writings on this theme in *Failing Peace*, but here I explore and interrogate the impact of my family history on my work in greater detail and depth. I reflect on a range of issues including Israel's assault on Lebanon in 2006, continuing repression and dispossession of Palestinians, the last three wars on Gaza, over a half-century of occupation, and the abuse and weaponization of anti-Semitism. In one selection, "Tears of Salt," written specifically for this book, I write, "For Israel (and by extension, perhaps, the larger Jewish community), the politics of inevitability is taking us toward an 'unchangeable hegemony' where seeing—into the past or the future—occurs only through the scope of a rifle, and where our security—and humanity—are ensured by denying the same to others." The other selections build upon this theme in different ways and at different times.

In Part VI, "The Passing of a Generation: Commemorating Courageous Palestinian Voices," I write about the death of two Palestinian intellectuals, Eyad el-Sarraj and Naseer Aruri, who were close friends and colleagues and who had a profound impact on my work and thinking from the beginning of my research as a young doctoral student. I met Eyad during my first visit to Gaza in the summer of 1985. He was then the director of mental health services in Gaza's Department of Health (which was under Israeli military control) but would go on, years later, to found and direct the Gaza Community Mental Health Programme, which became one of the principal institutions in the Occupied Territories treating the mental health needs of Palestinians.[6] Eyad was also an activist and humanitarian, advocating courageously for the human rights of his people not only with the Israeli military authorities but with the Palestinian authorities as well.

Naseer was a prominent Palestinian academic whose scholarship was among the first I read as I began my own research. I had heard of Naseer and studied his work long before we met, and his writings had a profound impact on me. As I say in my tribute, he showed me that it was possible to be a serious and rigorous scholar and human rights advocate at the same time. In fact, he taught me that the two were inextricably linked, each deriving power from and sustaining the other. Naseer was a gentleman scholar in the truest sense of the word, a dignified individual of immense integrity who, through his lived experience, demonstrated the importance of speaking truth to power. The loss of these two remarkable people is not only mine. Their passing represents something far greater for the Palestinian cause and for human rights work going forward.

In Part VII, "The Past as Future: Lessons Forgotten," I look back to life in Gaza *before* and *during* the first Intifada and both chapters are informed by my personal experiences living and working in Gaza during these historical periods. I argue there are lessons from the past that are strikingly relevant for the present. The first piece, published in 1987 in French, was co-authored with a friend, Gary Taubes, now a prominent science writer, and describes life in Gaza after two decades of occupation before the first Intifada. The English version appears here for the first time. This piece was written at the beginning of my research work in Gaza. By current standards, the conditions Gary and I describe appear benign but only in a relative sense. In fact, they laid the foundation and provided the context for the uprising that erupted just a few months after this article was published. Rereading the article, I was struck by how different—and diminished—life in Gaza is today. I do vividly remember being shocked by the many damaging and unjust ways the occupation impacted life in Gaza early in my career, but could not know then nor could I possibly have envisioned the kind of destruction and injustice that has befallen Gaza since. The reality that we depict over thirty years ago is unknown to most Gazans today; in fact, it is unimaginable. For despite the restrictions and discrimination described, this was a time when Palestinians and Israelis were able to engage each other beyond mythology and abstraction, a time when Palestinians could move more freely, work, and provide for their families.

The second piece, "When a Loaf of Bread Was Not Enough," is taken from a slogan of the first Intifada, *Ragheef al-Khubz La Yakfii*, and was written specifically for this book. It is drawn from nearly 300 pages of field notes I kept when my husband Jay and I lived in Gaza during the second year of the first Intifada (1988–89). I was in Gaza to do fieldwork for what became *The Gaza Strip: The Political Economy of De-development* and Jay, who had just completed his residency in general surgery at the Brigham and Women's Hospital in Boston, Massachusetts, volunteered as a surgeon at the Ahli Arab Hospital, which was then, I recall, the only private hospital in the Gaza Strip. It was an extraordinary period in our lives. This chapter is not a literature review of the first Intifada or a formal academic study of that period. A copious literature on the Intifada has long existed. Yet, this literature fails in some measure to address some of Gaza's distinct experiences with the Intifada despite similarities with the West Bank. My aim, therefore, is narrower and more specific. By drawing from selected parts of my field notes and giving voice to those who spoke to me, I want to reflect on that period, how it changed the Palestinian struggle and national definition of self, how it was crucial for shaping where Gaza and Palestinians finds themselves today, and how the lessons derived from that period—long forgotten or unknown by most Gazans today—still remain relevant and inspiring. I try to present a broad range of world, individual and situational views from across the Gaza Strip and the people given voice—many of whom have since died—were selected for the power of their ideas not because I agreed (or disagreed) with their position.

Part VIII, "Between Presence and Absence: Palestine and the Antilogic of Disposability," concludes the study by examining where conditions in Gaza stand at present. I underline a theme that runs through my decades of research in Gaza and the West Bank and that is the notion of the *indefinite* or *transitional* as a state imposed on Palestinians with the promise of something better and permanent that is never achieved. Instead, the undefined or indeterminate itself becomes permanent, leaving Palestinians, especially in Gaza (where it finds its most acute expression), in a state of exception. This chapter addresses Gaza's imposed exceptionalism and continued economic decline, accelerated by the impact of the Covid-19 crisis, and the pivotal social and political changes that have resulted. It ends by reflecting on what is possible for Gaza.

Despite the considerable literature that now exists on the Israeli–Palestinian conflict generally, and the occupation more specifically, the human dimensions of the occupation still demand deeper examination. The resulting gap is often filled by essentializing conceptualizations of Palestinians, by a belief—sometimes stated, sometimes not—that Palestinians belong where Israeli Jews have put them, making the occupation—the unbroken site of Arab suffering—acceptable, even legitimate. I decided to add an Epilogue to my concluding reflections, entitled "On the Falseness of Distinctions—'We are no different than you,'" that, quite simply, addresses the vilification and demonization of Palestinians especially in Gaza and in particular those associated with the Islamic movement—in my long experience, this denunciation has never been so extreme. I therefore close this book with a story that challenges such appalling and deeply misguided views that, in effect, consider Palestinians undeserving of protection, as people who are disposable and of no consequence. It speaks to the urgency of placing ourselves into other lives and realities, to understand Palestinians as we understand ourselves. As Edward Said put it: "The best corrective … is to imagine the person whom you are discussing—in this case the person on whom the bombs will fall—reading you in your presence."[7]

The plea—tragically, still necessary—is to humanize a part of the world few of us will ever know and to aspire to a "shareable world,"[8] that is slipping beyond our reach.

PART I   SETTING THE STAGE FOR CONFLICT IN GAZA: US POLICY FAILURES REDUX

For, although we merely know, but do not yet understand, what we are fighting against, we know and understand even less what we are fighting for.

Hannah Arendt
Mankind and Terror

The West in general should stand up more for its own values. It is not always worthwhile to compromise.

Imre Kertesz
Recipient of the 2002 Nobel Prize in Literature

Yes, You Can Work With Hamas: The US Approach to the Palestinian Territories is Inviting Disaster[*]

The Bush administration's approach to the divided Palestinian territories is inviting disaster. By favoring the "good" Fatah over the "evil" Hamas, it is letting a dysfunctional ideology trump a good opportunity to bring progress to the Palestinians—and to the larger quest for peace with Israel. There can be no peace process with a Palestinian government that excludes Hamas.

Here are specific steps that President Bush can take to correct course:

- Announce support for a Hamas-Fatah dialogue to revive a unity government and quietly open diplomatic contacts with Hamas.
- Commit serious diplomatic muscle to restarting substantive Palestinian-Israeli negotiations.
- In cooperation with its Quartet partners—the European Union, Russia and the United Nations—convene a peace conference informed by the US commitment to a two-state solution.

How did the US end up in its current predicament? In January 2006, Palestinians in the occupied West Bank and Gaza cast their ballots. Voting for the first time in ten years, and resentful of corruption and arrogance in the Palestinian Authority, they decided for Hamas, described by many in the West as a terrorist group. Blindsided by its legitimate victory, the Bush administration faced a stark dilemma. If it accepted the result, a group that has launched terrorist attacks against Israel would be permitted to enjoy power. However, since the

---

[*] Originally published with Augustus Richard Norton, *Christian Science Monitor*, July 17, 2007.

US had strongly backed the elections, rejecting the outcome would be hypocritical.

Seasoned diplomats urged a middle path: Work with Hamas and foster a pragmatic dialogue with Israel. But the US rejected this. Instead, it campaigned to isolate and financially undermine the Hamas government, while working secretly to overthrow it.

That policy prompted derision of US claims to foster democracy in the Arab world. And it upheld the radical Islamists' claim that democracy is a sham.

Despite its history of anti-Israeli terrorism, Hamas has effectively suspended suicide bombings since its 2006 political victory. Ironically, groups affiliated with Fatah have recently claimed more Israeli victims than Hamas.

Soon after the elections, Hamas sought to form a broad coalition government. Non-Hamas politicians committed to a two-state solution did consider joining a unity government with Hamas.

But they were warned off by the US, which subsequently led to the political and economic boycott against the Palestinian government and people. Israel, for its part, confiscated taxes and duties that it collected on behalf of the Palestinian Authority to drain the Hamas coffers.

These decisions deepened Palestinian suffering. According to the UN, a family of four must earn over $2 per day to stay above the poverty line. Because of the US-led boycott, the number of Gazans living in poverty increased from an already high 65 percent to 80 percent. Among West Bankers, the percentage of poverty-stricken rose from 30 to 55.

The White House reacted to the Hamas conquest of Gaza by expediently supporting a rump Palestinian government under the elected president, Mahmoud Abbas.

Meanwhile, the defining fact of Palestinian life among Gazans and West Bankers is dispossession and humiliation under the continued Israeli occupation.

Despite the dangerous division of the Gaza Strip and West Bank, it is unlikely that Palestinians will cede their desire for a state with East Jerusalem as its capital. Hamas voters overwhelmingly support a two-state solution, and the Hamas leadership has declared it would honor any agreement ratified by popular referendum.

Hamas has proposed a long-term truce with Israel but both sides must demonstrate a real commitment to end attacks against each other. Hamas continues to recognize the legitimacy of Mr. Abbas and calls for renewed cooperation with Fatah.

Can it truly be to America's or Israel's benefit to support a fractured Palestinian government that needs dictatorial powers to survive? The electoral and military success of Hamas was a verdict on the failure of the Fatah old guard. A smarter policy would work toward broadening the scope of Palestinian politics—not blessing a Fatah administration that is rapidly becoming a useful instrument of American and Israeli interests.

2

US Foreign Policy and the Israeli–Palestinian Conflict: A View From Palestine*

In the near twenty years since the Oslo peace process began, Palestinians have had to confront an extremely adverse reality marked by continued loss and dispossession of land and other resources. This is seen most dramatically in the massive expansion of Israeli settlements and infrastructure and the building of the separation barrier; territorial and demographic fragmentation, cantonization and isolation, and economic fracture and decline. More than anything, these factors reflect the continued failure of the political process and the American-led negotiations which largely define them. This in turn has given rise to some new and unprecedented strategies and policies, both at the official level and at the level of civil society in Palestine, that should be understood not as a coup or revolution but as a transformational and evolutionary model.

It should be said at the outset that the situation within Palestine is uncertain and, at times, internally contradictory but it is dynamic in a way it has not been since the first Palestinian uprising in 1987 and, arguably, since 1967. The terrain is undeniably changing although the future is unclear and impossible to predict. What follows is a brief examination of some key dynamics and changes.[1]

ESTABLISHING A NEW FRAMEWORK: THE END OF NEGOTIATIONS AS DEFINED BY THE US UNDER OSLO— FROM NEGOTIABLE TO NON-NEGOTIABLE RIGHTS FIRST

The failure of the US-led political process and the illegitimacy of the Palestinian political system were powerfully underlined by the release

---

* Originally published in *Note de l'Ifri*, Institut français des relations internationales (IFRI), September 2011.

of the Palestine Papers, which some observers regard as a critical turning point in Palestinian politics. These documents underlined the bankruptcy of the negotiation process as it had existed since the Oslo period (characterized by open-ended negotiations with no terms of reference, no conditions and no neutral referee, and in which the Palestinian side offered concessions that went well beyond the national consensus and were rejected by Israel).[2] The Oslo negotiation model focused on *negotiable* rights, i.e. borders, land, water (issues of statehood), before addressing *non-negotiable* rights, i.e. right to work, travel, move, build a house, market goods, and plant a tree, which were largely ignored under the Oslo framework.[3] Furthermore, negotiable rights such as land were gradually reframed and redefined in adverse ways.

The post-2006 split between the West Bank and Gaza, eventually pitting Fatah and Hamas against each other, introduced yet another complication: the negotiation process as defined by Oslo would not proceed should the two factions reconcile. In this way, political negotiations precluded inter-Palestinian reconciliation and were actively positioned against it, further delegitimizing the US-led negotiation model over time. As Prime Minister Netanyahu recently stated, "The Palestinian Authority [PA] has to choose between peace with Israel and peace with Hamas."[4] According to Professor Joel Beinin, Netanyahu "seems incapable of understanding that in addition to responding to popular Palestinian and regional Arab pressures, it was necessary for Abbas to seek an agreement with Hamas because the Palestinian Authority could not reach a peace agreement with Israel on terms any Palestinian would accept."[5]

Given the enormous losses incurred over the last 18 years and the corruption of the political process and those engaged in it, the Oslo model of "partners" around the negotiating table has been largely if not totally discredited especially following the release of the Palestine Papers. Simply put, "Even those Palestinians most supportive of American-led negotiations with Israelis cannot bring themselves to negotiate anymore while Israel builds settlements."[6] There is a growing consensus that absent a new strategy for securing their rights, Palestinians will be consigned to a form of indefinite occupation. Hence, it was impossible for the political leadership in the West Bank to re-engage Israel through the existing negotiation structure and be seen as legitimate. Even before the revolutions in the Middle East, it was extremely unlikely that the Palestinian people would have accepted such a re-engagement.

As articulated to the author by some Palestinian officials and analysts, there appear to be two new and complementary strategies taking shape among Palestinians—one at the level of civil society and the other at the official level—in their renewed struggle for independence.

CIVIL SOCIETY: A RIGHTS-BASED APPROACH— THE UNITY OF PEOPLE OVER UNITY OF LAND

The shift in strategy from negotiable to non-negotiable rights can be seen at the level of civil society. Even before the March 15 demonstrations in Gaza and the West Bank—which called for popular unity and the end of internal divisions—Palestinian civil society organizations had embraced a new strategy informing the popular struggle against occupation that had as its core imperative the unity of people over the unity of land (the latter being a practical impossibility at least in the near term). There has been a growing consensus that as long as the Palestinian struggle for independence remains focused on land—which of course remains important—it cannot be won (particularly given the gross asymmetries in power between Israelis and Palestinians and the latter's virtual abandonment by the US and other members of the international community).

According to this argument, it is not a state per se for which Palestinians should be fighting, but for their rights within that future state: human, political, economic, social and civil rights, which others, Israelis and Americans among them, possess. The assumption informing this strategy assumes that occupation will remain, precluding the establishment of a Palestinian state in the short to medium term. This strategy does not require a political movement but smaller, more decentralized groups that organize around specific issues—such as housing rights or access to international markets—attempting to forge linkages and alliances with Palestinians inside the West Bank and Gaza, with Palestinians and other groups regionally and internationally, and with Israelis who support the Palestinian struggle.[7]

This points to another critical strategic component that has taken root in Palestinian civil society: the adoption of peaceful non-violent resistance as the dominant Palestinian strategy for dealing with Israel going forward (which aims to reframe the conflict on the same terms that brought down Ben Ali in Tunisia and Mubarak in Egypt). Although this strategy has a long history among Palestinians, it gained renewed momentum in 2005 with the emergence of the Boycott, Divestment and Sanctions (BDS) movement, which arose in response to world inaction around enforcement of the 2004 International Court of Justice decision on the illegality of the West Bank Wall.

Massive non-violent resistance explicitly rejects continued accommodation to the status quo in favor of peaceful confrontation, and has assumed a prominent role in the collective struggle. This was clearly seen on Nakba Day when hundreds of unarmed Palestinians in the West Bank, Gaza, Lebanon and Syria approached the border with Israel; in the Syrian case, many actually crossed the border and "without so much as a sidearm, penetrated farther into the country than any army in a generation."[8] When the Palestinian Authority goes to the UN in September in its bid for statehood and membership, thousands of Palestinians are planning peaceful marches to Israeli settlements, checkpoints and the Wall.

OFFICIAL LEVEL: RECOGNITION OF A PALESTINIAN STATE ON 1967 BORDERS AND UN ADMISSION AS A MEMBER (OR NON-MEMBER) STATE

The shift to non-negotiable rights in Palestinian strategic thinking is also reflected in changing policies at the official level. This fall will mark the twentieth anniversary of failed Israeli–Palestinian negotiations.[9] In a conversation I recently had with one Palestinian official, he captured the bankruptcy of the political process for Palestinians: "We already have two states," he said, "Israel within 1967 borders, and a state of settlers with Palestinian cities on the periphery." Since the Oslo period, Palestinian officialdom has sought international political legitimacy, which led to continued losses, greater disenfranchisement, and deepening defeat. According to Professor Mushtaq Khan:

The Oslo Accords were based on the assumption that Israel's self-interest would rapidly result in the creation of a viable Palestinian state. But the accords bound the Palestinians to agreements, which significantly reduced their bargaining power *vis-à-vis* Israel and allowed the creation of new Israeli facts on the ground after the signing of the Accords. This resulted in a vicious cycle of diminishing legitimacy of the Palestinian leadership, their diminishing ability to deliver vital "state" functions like security, which in turn allowed Israel to create further facts on the ground and increase its bargaining power in successive rounds of negotiations. The ultimate result was the rupture of the Palestinian movement in 2007–08.[10]

And in all this, the US played a direct role.

Indeed there are specific factors which have weakened the US position among Palestinians over time and they all emanate from the almost seamless fusion of the Israeli and American positions: the insistence on the Oslo "peace process" framework of open-ended, bilateral negotiations which defer final status issues to some indeterminate point; the argument that the Palestinian bid for statehood on 1967 borders is illegitimate while refusing to acknowledge Palestinian losses, and the unwillingness to accept a reconciliation agreement between Fatah and Hamas by insisting that there be no Palestinian unity government unless Hamas agrees to renounce violence, recognize Israel as a Jewish state, and abide by previous agreements.

Furthermore, the February 2011 American veto of the UN Security Council resolution condemning Israeli settlements as illegal—a veto of its own official position and the only "no" vote cast—only underscored the futility of continuing to participate in a US-led process. With this veto, the US strikingly demonstrated that it is unable to deliver a just solution to the conflict. The US veto, the author was told repeatedly, was a defining event in official Palestinian thinking. One highly placed Palestinian official close to the leadership confided that the US—while the vital political actor—is increasingly regarded by the Palestinian leadership as handicapped (for structural reasons) unable to implement its own policies, having nothing to offer but a diplomatic dead end.

Consequently, the Palestinian leadership decided to pursue an alternative strategy that appears to be informed by two key factors:

an acceptance that the US will not abandon Israel whose interests are paramount, and a change in strategy from acceding to US partisanship to challenging it. This new strategy appeals to international institutions rather than to Israel and the US primarily, adopting a multilateral approach, and is seen in the upcoming UN initiative for "international recognition of the State of Palestine on the 1967 border" and admission "as a full member of the United Nations."[11] This new strategy, in effect, aims to set "borders of a two-state solution along internationally recognized lines and determines the endgame for a political resolution of the conflict."[12] It seeks international *legal* (not just political) legitimacy, an "internationalization of the conflict as a legal matter"[13] that will establish a term of reference that will improve Palestine's bargaining position.

According to Michael Sfard, who is the legal advisor for the Yesh Din human rights group in Israel: "The significance of a Palestinian state joining the UN is that, for the first time, it will be the Palestinians who will decide what the international legal framework is that is binding in their territory." Sfard demonstrates that a UN acceptance will create the legal jurisdiction of a sovereign, what he calls a "legal tsunami":

If indeed Palestine is accepted as a full member of the UN in September, the button controlling jurisdiction over events that will take place in the West Bank and Gaza Strip will, to a large extent, be transferred from Jerusalem to Ramallah, from Benjamin Netanyahu to Mahmoud Abbas—because the significance of accepting Palestine as a member of the UN is that the new member will be sovereign to sign international treaties, to join international agreements and to receive the jurisdictional authority of international tribunals over what happens in its territory.[14]

Palestinian officials are well aware of the problems surrounding this policy (particularly American and Israeli objections which argue that such a move undermines peace negotiations, which should only occur between the two parties[15]), but view it as a necessary though insufficient step in the process of liberation. It will not end the occupation nor create a viable state, but it is hoped that it will create a new basis for negotiations characterized by greater parity with Israel in a state that is internationally recognized.

Reflecting Israeli concerns, Barak Ravid of *Haaretz* writes:

> The Palestinians are hoping that if the General Assembly votes in favor of a Palestinian state in the 1967 borders, they will then be able to take up a seat as a full member of the United Nations. This will change the situation into a conflict in which Israel is occupying another country, which may result in severe international sanctions against Israel.[16]

The concern in Israel also extends to the fear that the Palestinian state, post-reconciliation, would be a Hamas state. The Israeli analyst Ami Isseroff writes that the declaration of a Palestinian state is more serious than a settlement freeze because

> ... [the] Palestinians would be free to pursue the "liberation" of *Palestina irrendenta* with the blessings of Mr. Solana and the UN, since East Jerusalem as well as all settlements would be considered "occupied territory" and an incursion into the territory of the Palestinian state. Both rockets and UN resolutions initiated by the Palestinian state would rain down on Israel, until Israel was forced to bow to all Palestinian demands including "return" of refugees. At the very least, the plan is a device to force Israel to agree to all Palestinian demands, since almost anything is less bad than a unilaterally declared state that has no treaty of any kind with Israel.[17]

Netanyahu also has questioned whether Hamas will take control over the West Bank as it did Gaza.[18]

Ravid, quoting sources close to the prime minister, further reveals that Netanyahu is worried about Israel's isolation and delegitimization that could result from the impending declaration but still "is not willing to negotiate on 1967 borders with exchange of territory, and in the end he will be faced with a UN decision on a Palestinian state in the 1967 borders, without territorial exchanges."[19]

The unilateral declaration of statehood via the UN also has its Palestinian critics and their criticism focuses on the fact that the occupation will remain as will the siege of Gaza and could generate even more frustration and anger among people if expectations remain unmet.[20] They argue that the UN strategy represents an act of desperation from a leadership that has lost its legitimacy with an attendant risk that the leadership will not pursue the initiative seriously. Consequently, what does it mean to recognize a Palestinian state under continued Israeli occupation where the PA does not have control over most of the West Bank or Gaza (despite an uneasy and troubled reconciliation) or its presumed capital in East Jerusalem?

These critics argue that certain individuals and classes will have their power protected and solidified while the majority of Palestinians will continue to suffer under the occupation. Borders may continue to be violated without much international condemnation. Settlement expansion and land confiscations can be expected to continue under an Israeli threat of de jure annexation.[21] Rather, Palestinians will remain financially and politically dependent on the goodwill of the international community, particularly the US and EU, and will find it extremely difficult to resist external pressure. A UN resolution will likely force the US to oppose it (economically as well as diplomatically) particularly in an election year and will provoke Israeli responses on the ground.[22] Furthermore, the rights of Palestinians outside the West Bank and Gaza are entirely neglected.[23] Indeed there is criticism from diaspora Palestinians who fear that the declaration of a state in the UN "limits Palestinian aspirations to the West Bank and Gaza Strip and excludes their voices from Palestinian political decision-making."[24]

OFFICIAL LEVEL: FATAH–HAMAS RECONCILIATION— THE AGREEMENT ON UNITY

Another critical dynamic reshaping the Palestinian political landscape is a stated commitment to Palestinian unity. There can be no doubt that the uprisings in the Middle East and popular pressure demanding unity as seen in the March 15th movement played a critical role in pushing both sides to an agreement to form an interim government,[25] which was also propelled by the September 2011 deadline for Prime Minister Fayyad's state-building program.[26] The unity agreement caught the Obama administration by surprise, while Netanyahu stated that it will end the Israeli-Palestinian peace process. The Egyptian government played a crucial interventionist role in the unity talks.

Critically, the PA's continued failure to reach an agreement with Israel and most importantly, the US's failure to promote serious two-state negotiations converged with internal popular pressure, compelling the parties to seize the initiative and compromise because "the alternatives were worse ... and nothing is guaranteed anymore."[27] "The region will not reverse itself," said a Fatah official, "and this is a new and constant variable"[28] that greatly influenced political thinking regardless of US or other reactions. There also can be no doubt that for Abbas and the Ramallah PA the removal of Mubarak was the loss of an important patron and source of support.

The pressures on Hamas were similarly strong. For example, Hamas has come under enormous pressure from its population in Gaza for its economic and political failures including: the futility of armed resistance and the firing of rockets; the loss of 1,400 lives during Israel's 2008–09 assault; the lack of economic improvement, change, or reconstruction; the continued siege and sealing of the borders; rising unemployment now approaching 50 percent and unrelieved impoverishment with 80 percent of the population still dependent on humanitarian assistance to survive, and the lack of political legitimacy domestically and internationally. Hamas cannot continue to rule Gaza indefinitely under a state of constant siege.[29] Similarly, the turmoil in Syria has placed Hamas in an increasingly tenuous position (see below). In fact, the Syrian regime apparently demanded that Hamas take a position on the political turmoil in Syria. The international Muslim Brotherhood (MB) apparently came out in support of the protestors while Hamas kept silent, which did not satisfy the Syrian government.[30]

A Palestinian colleague and analyst from Gaza who recently met with the leadership in Ramallah and Gaza and the Egyptian Ambassador to the PA about the reasons for the reconciliation wrote the following after his meetings:

It was clear that the three bodies ... involved (Egypt, Fatah and Hamas) [were] bored by the lack of progress on the reconciliation file. The internal and external factors which pushed both parties to reach an agreement in a few hours while they spent [over] 1,500 hours of talk throughout the past three years [include the following]: The PA and president Abbas have become hopeless with [i.e. lost hope in] Israel and the US [with] regard to the peace talks. For four years, [the] PA got nothing from Israel except more settlements and roadblocks [among other restrictions]. The US veto at the UN [over the settlement resolution] made Abu Mazen [even more] disillusioned with US mediation. [Also] the new regime in Cairo wants to get rid of this file as it doesn't have the luxury to [enter] into [an] endless process of talks and mediation.

[Furthermore], [the Cairo government] wanted to increase its popularity among the Egyptians by solving this hard file and to prove that the previous regime of Mubarak wasn't sincere in its efforts to finish this file. Hamas, the youth movement, the growth of Salafist groups in Gaza, the development[s] in Syria and the rise of the Muslim Brotherhood in Egypt created new elements and [additional sources of] pressure on Hamas, [pushing it toward] compromise. A key Hamas leader said to me, "We cannot neglect the new developments in the Middle East. We are part of this world [and] we should understand the new reality." The Hamas leadership in Syria is [not] in a good position these days due to the Syrian revolutions. There [is] some news that [the] Hamas leadership was asked to leave Damascus and to find [a] new place, either Jordan, Qatar, or even Gaza.[31]

What is particularly intriguing about this assessment is the role of the Muslim Brotherhood in Egypt as a source of pressure on Hamas. This was intriguing because, weeks before, various Palestinian analysts were predicting that Hamas would not enter into any reconciliation with Fatah because Hamas believed that the forthcoming Egyptian elections would bring the MB to power and thereby strengthen Hamas's position *vis-à-vis* Fatah in any future reconciliation negotiations. When the author queried her informant more on this point he said that the Egyptian Muslim Brotherhood played a vital role in pushing Hamas toward reconciliation. With their decision to form a political party and become part of the political system, the Egyptian MB argued that Hamas, as a branch of the MB, must do the same. The first step toward this end was to reconcile with Fatah and prepare for elections within the year. Hamas was told that it could no longer ignore changing developments in the region, meaning it must seek other, new alliances that would mitigate its dependency on Syria and Iran.[32]

The unity agreement also is seen as a victory, albeit a cautious one, for all sides of the Palestinian equation. For Hamas, its survival and continued role as a political actor able to impose some of its key conditions is regarded as a significant achievement given ongoing attempts to destroy it. For Fatah, the victory lies, at least for now, in the fact that it is challenging its manipulation and co-optation by Israel or the US. For the Palestinian people, victory lies in the fact that the unity agreement addresses, in some measure, one of the most formidable internal crises confronting their struggle for freedom.[33] And despite the many obstacles to unity and challenges that remain to be overcome, a key feature of the unity agreement is the return of Gaza to the conflict, to the struggle and to the Palestinian cause after five years of separation and isolation.

However, given past failures and the clear lack of confidence and trust among Palestinians in their leadership and political system, popular skepticism remains high, particularly with regard to reforming institutions such as the security forces and those classes and elites who have benefited greatly from existing divisions and stand to lose from any reform. Other problems include freeing of political detainees, reopening of closed (social and political) institutions, and reinstituting human rights and civil liberties. Half of Palestinian society is said to belong to either Fatah or Hamas while the other half is not mobilized,[34] leading some Palestinians to ask whether the reconciliation agreement aims to unify two political factions or all segments of the Palestinian people?

It is important to understand that people are truly fatigued and fragmented and less able to be spontaneous than in other Arab countries where there are no viable political parties or movements.[35] They are also angry and frustrated. The majority of young Palestinians in the West Bank have never been to Gaza and their counterparts have never been to the West Bank, let alone anywhere outside these territories. There is no exposure and no mixing.

This leads to another emerging and critical dimension of change, particularly at the civil society level (and a potential source of conflict with the leadership): the revitalization of a common national identity and "reunified body politic with representative mechanisms and political and intellectual pluralism"[36] that aims to incorporate all sectors of Palestinian society, including Palestinian citizens of Israel and the refugee communities outside of Israel/Palestine. As one Palestinian activist explained:

> Our roof is the occupation and our floor, the political factions. In Gaza, nearly all political demands have been associated with one party or the other. If you demand elections you are accused of supporting Fatah and if you support ending Oslo you appear to be supporting Hamas. So, in order to maintain neutrality and establish a popular position, we have demanded an end to the division.[37]

Popular pressure, particularly among Palestinian youth, is building and being mobilized around demands that transcend borders, as seen in a renewed campaign around the refugee right of return, publicly demanding "a right that is recognized under international law and by UN resolutions but has not been implemented for 63 years,"[38] and in calls to hold elections for the Palestinian National Council in order to "reconstruct a Palestinian national program based upon a comprehensive [and non-violent] resistance platform."[39] The aim is not only to "memorialize the past but also to demand a new future"[40] that is characterized by the absence of factionalism and incorporates the "entirety of Palestine before 1948."[41]

Despite the emerging potential for real change, a critical and more immediate question remains: How can a joint Palestinian government function without Israeli and US cooperation? Historically any agreement with Hamas would have threatened if not ended American (and European) funding. In fact, on July 7, 2011, the US House of Representatives "overwhelmingly passed a resolution ... urging ... Obama to consider suspending economic aid to the Palestinian Authority if it continues to pursue statehood outside of direct negotiations with Israel."[42]

IS US POLICY BECOMING LESS RELEVANT?
A CHANGING PARADIGM

According to Geoffrey Aronson of the Foundation for Middle East Peace in Washington, the almost two-year diplomatic effort on the part of the Obama administration "to build a solid foundation for final status negotiations by winning meaningful concessions from Israel on settlement expansion has now been declared a failure by the administration itself."[43] In December 2010, Hillary Clinton called for the resetting of US policy away from temporary reductions in settlement expansion toward final status issues, despite Netanyahu's reluctance to engage in a process that addresses final status issues.

Aronson further argues that the administration has been unwilling to meaningfully confront Israel on the issues of settlements, notwithstanding the ten-month settlement construction moratorium that ended in September 2010. Since the end of the moratorium, Israel has begun construction on 1,500 new settlement units in the West Bank on both sides of the separation barrier. Although East Jerusalem was not included in the moratorium, the government announced last November that it would begin construction on an additional 2,085 new housing units.[44]

Furthermore, Netanyahu's rejection of the US's "unprecedented package of incentives aimed at moving diplomacy beyond a short-lived settlement moratorium," effectively forced the US to declare an end to the settlement freeze initiative, which is no longer a "key weapon in the arsenal of American and international peacemakers."[45] On December 7, 2010, President Obama decided to abandon his policy, suspending American efforts to resume direct negotiations between Israel and the PA. The Palestinians remain opposed to restarting direct negotiations as long as Israel continues to build settlements and as long as the construction moratorium excludes East Jerusalem.

According to Fayyad:

> Each one of these guarantees and undertakings [offered by the US] is more dangerous and worse than the issue of settlements … Let us consider the issue of keeping an Israeli security presence in the Jordan Valley: The Israelis want to keep their army in that area for decades. What sovereignty would a Palestinian state enjoy when it is hemmed in by Israeli troops on all sides? What is even more serious is that these US guarantees are preventing us from internationalizing the problem, which is one of the few tools we have in our hands … All these guarantees were given in the hope that Netanyahu would extend his moratorium by two months, which in any

case does not include Jerusalem or the major settlement blocs. This is nonsense and we reject it completely.[46]

The paradigm appears, in fact, to be changing. American power (and unilateralism) to shape regional events in its own interests is weakening particularly with regard to preventing outcomes the US government does not want. This is seen, for example, in America's failure to secure a settlement freeze from Israel even with the offer of incentives and the inability to coerce Palestinians to the negotiating table without preconditions.[47] The Palestinian and Arab peoples are not willing to rely as heavily on the US as they once did or take their lead from the US, another sign, perhaps, of declining influence. How will the US respond to, and deal with this new, emerging sense of political empowerment?[48]

PRESIDENT OBAMA'S SPEECH OF MAY 19, 2011

In his speech, Obama made it clear that the US role will remain largely unchanged. A transformed role would have included, for example: ending a policy of double standards regarding sanctions; ending America's military, economic and diplomatic support for Israel's occupation; support for popular, grassroots-based democratic initiatives throughout the Arab region, and respect for local decision making.[49]

Rather, Obama embraced the same two-state formula of direct, bi-lateral negotiations that proved such a failure for the last twenty years, despite a more explicit and firm reference to 1967 borders in his speech, which is fundamentally in line with the US position since the 1990 Madrid peace process. The entire post-Madrid process was explicitly based on UN Resolution 242 (land for peace), which does not reference 1967 borders explicitly but territories acquired in the 1967 conflict; both Clinton and Bush referenced 1967 borders/1949 armistice lines (albeit accounting for current realities).

Furthermore, in calling for a resumption of the peace process based on US diplomacy and Israeli demands as a formula for negotiations—which should also be understood as an attempt to derail the UN initiative in September—Obama failed to break any new ground and perhaps most important of all, did not reflect in any measure the repressive reality on the ground for Palestinians, let alone offer any practical recommendations for addressing it. In fact, "the illegit-imacy of Israel's repression of [Palestinian] basic human rights never enters Obama's lexicon,"[50] nor does Israel's well-documented obstruc-tionism of earlier negotiation efforts. This is particularly striking for another reason: by invoking a new peace process in terms that remain unchanged, the president is situating Israeli policy toward Palestinians and Palestinian non-violent challenges to that policy *outside* the revo-lutionary changes taking place in the region. In effect, the US is saying that it will not hold Israel accountable to the standards demanded of other countries in the region, placing it in a category of exceptions reserved for Saudi Arabia and Bahrain.[51]

Obama's address was problematic in some other important respects. First, references to the 1967 borders with territorial swaps (which is not new) likely translates now, as before, into an acceptance of Israeli settlement blocs and Israeli control over vast swaths of West Bank lands unilaterally determined by Israel. Now as before, this reduces the Palestinian state to a group of disconnected territorial enclaves. Second, Hamas remains excluded from the process, a tacit rejection of the recent Fatah-Hamas unity agreement, which is essential if the Palestinian side is to deliver meaningful change. Third, calls for a demilitarized Palestinian state is how Obama defines a viable Pales-tinian state. The only reference in his speech to security was for Israel, not Palestine. Obama did call for a contiguous state, a call made by previous American presidents which continues to ring hollow, given US acquiescence to Israeli settlement expansion. Fourth, silence about the illegality of Israeli settlements is tacit acceptance of their presence. Fifth, deferral of Jerusalem and refugees' rights—perhaps the most contentious issue of all—to a later stage reveals the same lack of seri-ousness and commitment to a fair resolution of the conflict that characterized the Oslo process. For one thing, it ignores the fact that Netanyahu's Israel has refused even to discuss final status issues until his list of preconditions (e.g., recognizing Israel as a Jewish state) is met in full. And sixth, implying equivalence and parity between Israel and the Palestinians (a characteristic feature of the Oslo negotiations) as Obama did, is seriously flawed and misleading given the gross asym-metries in power between the two actors. Such equivalence assumes, as it long has, that the Palestinians are terrorists and the Israelis require security to protect them from Palestinian terrorism.

SOME REFLECTIONS ON THE US POSITION

The paradigm for negotiations since 1967 has been land-for-peace but what happens when there is no land? Because it is becoming less tenable for the US to explain the lack of political progress, the fiction of two states continues to be pursued and in order to pursue it, the US emphasizes continued negotiations over real outcomes, which are, in effect, already predetermined—a Palestinian state that is weak and lacking real sovereignty. It is clear that Obama and his administration want to preclude any possibility of a UN vote on Palestinian statehood and admission as a (non-member or member) sovereign state. One informant, a high-level State Department official, stated that American officials are "besides themselves" with worry and concern about the impending vote.

A United Nations vote on Palestinian statehood and admission would isolate the US and Israel, and humiliate the US, especially in a changing regional context where Arab peoples are fighting and dying daily for their freedom and liberty, further eroding America's public image if not its influence.[52] But there is another, less obvious but critically important dimension to the US position, one that is characterized by anger over losing control of the political process. In some private meetings between US and Palestinian officials, the Palestinians expressed their desire to pursue a more autonomous policy as seen in the UN initiative, and engage more directly with other actors be they regional, European, or multilateral. They were met with considerable hostility from some (but not all) American officials.

The impression that one high-level Palestinian negotiator was left with was described as follows: the US wants to maintain control over, and leadership of, the process and should a void be created, as it now has, it will be filled with more process since no credible alternative to the status quo was presented. Any attempt by the Palestinian leadership to break out of the US-defined framework will be opposed if not punished.[53] It was also made clear to the author that key members of the Palestinian leadership are now unwilling to tolerate past approaches and are prepared to bear costs and consequences unthinkable just a few years ago. This may, of course, change, but for now it appears to be a new and striking dynamic.

While it may be that the US desires a peaceful settlement with security for Israel and a state for Palestinians, US policymakers do not possess the will to do what is necessary to ensure that outcome—i.e., challenge Israeli policies. There are many reasons including the oft-cited influence of the Israel lobby that treats Israel and its security as a domestic (and structural) issue. But as one American official confided, "This explanation, while real, is too simplistic and categorical. It's like pushing against an open door [which] is characterized by a predisposition toward Israel that derives from sympathy over the Holocaust, the rise of Arab terrorism, and the rise of anti-Muslim sentiment especially after 9/11."

A State Department official with 15 years of experience working on the Israeli–Palestinian issue, provided the following assessment:

It should come as no surprise that key decision makers and Congress generally find Israeli arguments persuasive and can readily imagine that Israel is dealing with legitimate security concerns such as those they genuinely believe will arise from a unity agreement between Fatah and Hamas. Personal threats to Israel are seen as real and are felt. There is little acceptance that Israel is a large part of the problem and is the stronger party. Similarly, there is a belief that the West Bank territory that Israel wants to retain is not a big deal, poses no serious problem even if it degrades the territorial contiguity of a Palestinian state. The US does not fundamentally understand or care about the issues of injustice that form the Palestinian reality. It does not catch the attention of the US. Like their Israeli counterparts, US policymakers fundamentally believe that the existence of the State of Israel is predicated on the denial of Palestinian nationhood. Palestinians are seen as intruders. Palestinians do not matter and have little to offer the US, especially when viewed against our strong alliance with Israel economically, militarily, and politically. They are not respected and are considered weak and reactive, easily pushed around. We can't move Israel but we can move others.

Despite official rhetoric, the Arab Spring is seen by many inside the administration as a threat to Israel. When Palestinians crossed the Syrian border into Israel, administration officials saw them as barbarians coming over the border. It apparently is a deeply held belief among US policymakers that the Arab people are not mature enough for democracy and there is a real fear that the Muslim Brotherhood will take over in different Arab countries. [Hence, for many inside the administration] Israel is right when they say there is no reliable partner to deal with.[54]

Eric Cantor, the majority leader in the US House of Representatives, echoed these sentiments in his address to the annual conference of the American Israel Public Affairs Committee (AIPAC) on May 22, 2011: "Sadly, it [Arab culture] is a culture infused with resentment and hatred. It is this culture that underlies the Palestinians' and the broader Arab world's refusal to accept Israel's right to exist as a Jewish state. This is the root of the conflict between Israel and the Palestinians. It is not about the '67 lines."[55]

A CHANGING DISCOURSE AROUND 1967 BORDERS IN ISRAEL

In calling for a return to 1967 borders, the Palestinian leadership is not without its supporters in Israel. It is also important to highlight the changing dialogue around 1967 borders within Israel itself, which opposes Netanyahu's position.[56] Strikingly, key figures in Israel's security establishment including former chiefs of Israel's main security services—Mossad, Shin Bet and the Israel Defense Forces (IDF)—are calling for a two-state agreement with the PA based on 1967 borders similar to the 2002 Arab League peace initiative, in addition to ending all calls for an attack against Iran. In fact on May 6, 2011, Shaul Mofaz, a former IDF chief and ex-defense minister (and now Chairman of the Knesset's foreign affairs and defense committee) called for an immediate recognition by Israel of a Palestinian state "followed by negotiations between the two states over borders [and] security arrangements." He also stated that the unity pact between Fatah and Hamas was an "opportunity" for Israel, "predicting that if Israel seized the initiative now, it might well push Hamas into accepting Israel and swearing off terrorism."[57]

Furthermore, on April 1, 2011, there was a petition signed by the so-called Israel Peace Initiative consisting of Israeli notables—former security officials, ex-diplomats, academics, artists, celebrities and business leaders (including Yitzchak Rabin's children who are part of the Initiative's leadership)—supporting a two-state solution based on the 1967 borders (with mutually agreed upon adjustments), which is more significant than it may first appear.[58] For years, talk of returning to the 1967 borders has been unacceptable in the general discourse (except for the extreme left), but it is increasingly becoming the norm in certain social and political sectors in Israel. Similarly, the Quartet members refer to 1967 borders with increasing frequency as a point of reference and have proposed their own peace plan which consists of "a two-state solution based on the 1967 borders with an exchange of territories; a fair, realistic and agreed-on solution to the Palestinian refugee problem; Jerusalem as the capital of both states; and security arrangements that safeguard Israel while not compromising Palestinian sovereignty."[59]

Hence, although Israel has succeeded in winning international legitimacy within the 1949 armistice lines, it is unlikely that it will win legitimacy—including from a growing segment of Israelis—for the Greater Israel project, despite the facts on the ground and despite US support. Whether one believes the two-state solution is possible or not, there is a strengthening international consensus about the need for a return to 1967 borders as a solution to the conflict.

Will the US continue to remain outside this consensus increasingly alone except for Israel (and despite the tensions between Obama and Netanyahu)? Aaron Miller, former advisor on Arab-Israeli negotiations, answers, in effect, yes:

No matter how artful and skillful the UN campaign is, the United States will almost certainly oppose it. Washington will veto the resolution in the Security Council. While it can't block resolutions in the General Assembly, the United States won't concede either the principle of declaring statehood outside of negotiations or marshaling international pressure against Israel ... To say that the Obama administration won't risk spending political capital on an international campaign to isolate Israel in the UN General Assembly the year before a presidential election is probably the understatement of the century. And if the campaign pressuring Israel gets serious, Congress will be only too ready to restrict critical aid to the Palestinians and perhaps to Egypt as well if it helps lead the effort.[60]

IS EGYPT BECOMING MORE RELEVANT?

The raising of the Palestinian flag in Tahrir Square in front of the Israeli embassy in Cairo was an important reason why the recent [March 2011] aggression on the Gaza Strip stopped, after it became clear to the Israeli government that Egypt, its leadership and people, reject any Israeli aggression on Gaza. Also the role played by the Egyptian Foreign Ministry in curbing the attacks was very important as well as the decision made by the Arab League asking the UN Security Council for a no-fly zone over Gaza.[61]

So said a friend of the author's in Gaza, also a highly respected analyst. He later wrote that during the latest offensive on Gaza, Egypt sent a message to Tel Aviv through the EU, which stated the following:

Gaza is the backyard of Egyptian national security. Therefore we consider any attack on Gaza now as a direct threat to Egypt. We can't stop any among the 80 million Egyptians from voicing his/her anger against Israel and we don't have any means to stop any protest in Cairo or anywhere simply because such protests reflect the ... attitude of the army and the government. War on Gaza is not allowed anymore.[62]

Palestinian officials visiting the Egyptian foreign ministry in March 2011 were told that the siege of Gaza is criminal and will be lifted, and those people in the former Egyptian government who participated in it will be prosecuted. Clearly, in deciding its future policy including toward Gaza, the new Cairo government will have to weigh its relationship with Israel and the US and the powerful (military and economic) ties that define it against the need to normalize its border with Gaza and normalize relations with Iran, among other policies. However, unlike its predecessor, the current Egyptian regime appears less concerned that opening a channel to Egypt in the absence of free movement between Gaza and the West Bank will solidify Israel's separation policy. Indeed, the fact that only 36 percent of Egyptians would maintain Egypt's peace treaty with Israel and 54 percent want to annul it no doubt influences official thinking.[63]

As stated above, the Egyptian government played a critical role in forging the unity/reconciliation agreement between Fatah and Hamas. Indeed, in private negotiations, Egypt stated that it would consider opening the Rafah crossing—both for people and goods—if Palestinian reconciliation was achieved, a unity government was created, and Gaza's special status within the Occupied Territory was terminated. Perhaps the Egyptians were attempting to catalyze a new Arab-Israeli peace initiative with Palestinian unity as a vital precondition.[64] Although the role of the Egyptian government is evolving and is impossible to predict accurately, it appears that it is seeking to reestablish its credibility and legitimacy within the Arab world and possibly reclaim some form of regional leadership. It also is filling a growing void, in Palestinian eyes.

A CONCLUDING THOUGHT

The question, of course, remains, how will the US respond to the changing Palestinian and Arab paradigm? Will it try to reduce the deepening gap between American policy as it has historically been defined and new Palestinian and Arab aspirations? Will the US be willing to work with those countries that support policies it does not, such as the Fatah-Hamas unity agreement?[65]

And perhaps most importantly, is the US capable of asking, what role do the Arab people want us to play?[66]

PART II THE MARGINALIZED CENTER: THE WARS ON GAZA AND THEIR AFTERMATH

I am living in minutes. I need one more minute.

From a friend in Gaza
Summer 2014

3

If Gaza Falls ...*

Israel's siege of Gaza began on November 5 [2008], the day after an Israeli attack inside the Strip, no doubt designed finally to undermine the truce between Israel and Hamas established last June. Although both sides had violated the agreement before, this incursion was on a different scale. Hamas responded by firing rockets into Israel and the violence has not abated since then. Israel's siege has two fundamental goals. One is to ensure that the Palestinians there are seen merely as a humanitarian problem, beggars who have no political identity and therefore can have no political claims. The second is to foist Gaza onto Egypt. That is why the Israelis tolerate the hundreds of tunnels between Gaza and Egypt around which an informal but increasingly regulated commercial sector has begun to form. The overwhelming majority of Gazans are impoverished and officially 49.1 percent are unemployed. In fact the prospect of steady employment is rapidly disappearing for the majority of the population.

On November 5, the Israeli government sealed all the ways into and out of Gaza. Food, medicine, fuel, parts for water and sanitation systems, fertilizer, plastic sheeting, phones, paper, glue, shoes and even teacups are no longer getting through in sufficient quantities or at all. According to Oxfam, only 137 trucks of food were allowed into Gaza in November. This means that an average of 4.6 trucks per day entered the Strip compared to an average of 123 in October this year and 564 in December 2005. The two main food providers in Gaza are the UN Relief and Works Agency for Palestine Refugees in the Near East (UNRWA) and the World Food Programme (WFP). UNRWA alone feeds approximately 750,000 people in Gaza, and requires 15 trucks of food daily to do so. Between November 5 and November 30, only 23 trucks arrived, around 6 percent of the total needed; during the

* Originally published in the *London Review of Books*, Volume 31, Number 1, January 1, 2009.

week of November 30, it received 12 trucks, or 11 percent of what was required. There were three days in November when UNRWA ran out of food, with the result that on each of these days 20,000 people were unable to receive their scheduled supply. According to John Ging, the director of UNRWA in Gaza, most of the people who get food aid are entirely dependent on it. On December 18, UNRWA suspended all food distribution for both emergency and regular programs because of the blockade.

The WFP has had similar problems, sending only 35 trucks out of the 190 it had scheduled to cover Gazans' needs until the start of February (six more were allowed in between November 30 and December 6). Not only that: the WFP has to pay to store food that isn't being sent to Gaza. This cost $215,000 in November alone. If the siege continues, the WFP will have to pay an extra $150,000 for storage in December, money that will be used not to support Palestinians but to benefit Israeli business.

The majority of commercial bakeries in Gaza—30 out of 47—have had to close because they have run out of cooking gas. People are using any fuel they can find to cook with. As the UN Food and Agriculture Organisation (FAO) has made clear, cooking-gas canisters are necessary for generating the warmth to incubate broiler chicks. Shortages of gas and animal feed have forced commercial producers to smother hundreds of thousands of chicks. By April, according to the FAO, there will be no poultry there at all: 70 percent of Gazans rely on chicken as a major source of protein.

Banks, suffering from Israeli restrictions on the transfer of banknotes into the territory were forced to close on December 4. A sign on the door of one read: "Due to the decision of the Palestinian Finance Authority, the bank will be closed today Thursday, 4.12.2008, because of the unavailability of cash money, and the bank will be reopened once the cash money is available."

The World Bank has warned that Gaza's banking system could collapse if these restrictions continue. All cash-for-work programs have been stopped and on November 19, UNRWA suspended its cash assistance program to the most needy. It also ceased production of textbooks because there is no paper, ink, or glue in Gaza. This will affect 200,000 students returning to school in the new year. On December 11, Israeli Defense Minister Ehud Barak sent $25 million, following an appeal from the Palestinian prime minister, Salaam Fayad, the first infusion of its kind since October. It won't even cover a month's salary for Gaza's 77,000 civil servants.

On November 13, production at Gaza's only power station was suspended and the turbines shut down because it had run out of industrial diesel. This in turn caused the two turbine batteries to run down, and they failed to start up again when fuel was received some ten days later. About a hundred spare parts ordered for the turbines have been sitting in the port of Ashdod in Israel for the last eight months, waiting for the Israeli authorities to let them through customs. Now Israel has started to auction these parts because they have been in customs for more than 45 days. The proceeds are being held in Israeli accounts.

During the week of November 30, 394,000 liters of industrial diesel were allowed in for the power plant: approximately 18 percent of the weekly minimum that Israel is legally obliged to allow in. It was enough for one turbine to run for two days, before the plant was shut down again. The Gaza Electricity Distribution Company said that most of the Gaza Strip will be without electricity for between four and twelve hours a day. At any given time during these outages, over 65,000 people have no electricity.

No other diesel fuel (for standby generators and transport) was delivered during that week, no petrol (which has been kept out since early November) or cooking gas. Gaza's hospitals are apparently relying on diesel and gas smuggled from Egypt via the tunnels; these supplies are said to be administered and taxed by Hamas. Even so, two of Gaza's hospitals have been out of cooking gas since the week of November 23.

Adding to the problems caused by the siege are those created by the political divisions between the Palestinian Authority in the West Bank and the Hamas Authority in Gaza. For example, Gaza's Coastal Municipalities Water Utility (CMWU), which is not controlled by Hamas, is supposed to receive funds from the World Bank via the Palestinian Water Authority (PWA) in Ramallah to pay for fuel to run the pumps for Gaza's sewage system. Since June, the PWA has refused to hand over those funds, perhaps because it feels that a functioning sewage system would benefit Hamas. I don't know whether the World Bank has attempted to intervene, but meanwhile UNRWA is providing the fuel, although they have no budget for it. The CMWU has also asked Israel's permission to import 200 tons of chlorine, but by the end of November it had received only 18 tons—enough for one week of chlorinated water. By mid-December, Gaza City and the north of Gaza had access to water only six hours every three days.

According to the World Health Organization, the political divisions between Gaza and the West Bank are also having a serious impact on drug stocks in Gaza. The West Bank Ministry of Health (MOH) is responsible for procuring and delivering most of the pharmaceuticals and medical disposables used in Gaza. But stocks are at dangerously low levels. Throughout November, the West Bank MOH was turning shipments away because it had no warehouse space, yet it wasn't sending supplies on to Gaza in adequate quantities. During the week of November 30, one truck carrying drugs and medical supplies from the MOH in Ramallah entered Gaza, the first delivery since early September.

The breakdown of an entire society is happening in front of us, but there is little international response beyond UN warnings which are ignored. The European Union announced recently that it wanted to strengthen its relationship with Israel, while the Israeli leadership openly calls for a large-scale invasion of the Gaza Strip and continues its economic stranglehold over the territory with, it appears, the not-so-tacit support of the Palestinian Authority in Ramallah—which has been co-operating with Israel on a number of measures. On December 19, Hamas officially ended its truce with Israel, which Israel said it wanted to renew, because of Israel's failure to ease the blockade.

How can keeping food and medicine from the people of Gaza protect the people of Israel? How can the impoverishment and suffering of Gaza's children—more than 50 percent of the population—benefit anyone? International law as well as human decency demands their protection. If Gaza falls, the West Bank will be next.

4

Endgame in the Gaza War?*

Although diplomatic discussions about a ceasefire between Hamas and Israel have begun, the Gaza war will continue for days, maybe even weeks to come. The US and Israel insist on a "durable and sustainable" ceasefire, in the words of Secretary of State Condoleezza Rice. This means that Hamas must not only stop the firing of rockets into Israel, but also re-subordinate itself to the West Bank-based Palestinian Authority (PA) headed by Mahmoud Abbas whose silence while Gaza burns is astonishing.

Israel will stress its acceptance of a ceasefire in principle but will continue to pummel Gaza while the US stiff-arms growing calls for an end to the war. Hamas will on principle refuse any ceasefire that denies its political role or demands its surrender. Meanwhile, the toll in civilian victims escalates in densely packed Gaza, which is already suffering an immense humanitarian crisis ludicrously denied by Israel.

Hamas' strategic miscalculation in rejecting an extension to a six-month truce with Israel was a gift on a "golden platter" to Israel, as Egyptian Foreign Minister Ahmed Aboul Gheit wryly noted. The Israeli security establishment has been intent since its flawed 2006 war in Lebanon to reassert Israel's hegemony and its deterrent power. But the attack on Gaza may also have deeper causes. Lost in most of the coverage is the fact that the Israel-Hamas truce was working—a fact fully acknowledged in a recent intelligence report released by Israel's Ministry of Foreign Affairs (MFA). According to that report, "Hamas was careful to maintain the ceasefire." Furthermore, "the lull was sporadically violated by rocket and mortar shell fire carried out by rogue terrorist organizations in some instances in defiance of Hamas."[1]

Yet on November 4, when the world was focused on the US presidential election, Israel effectively ended the "period of relative quiet"

* Originally published with Augustus Richard Norton, *Informed Comment: Global Analysis* (Parts I, II, III), January 4, 2009 (slightly edited).

to which the MFA report refers by attacking Gaza, killing at least six Palestinian militiamen. Hamas responded to the killings with salvos of rockets. Israel believed that the group was planning to abduct Israeli soldiers through a tunnel it was digging near a border security fence, but whether Hamas wished to risk a successful truce and the possibility of political progress in order to abduct Israeli soldiers is debatable.

The extensive report released by the MFA acknowledges that most of the rockets and mortar shells fired at Israel during the six-month lull fell after November 4.

Why would Israel want to end the truce? The success of the Israel-Hamas truce tacitly legitimized political dialogue with the Islamists, something that Israel (as well as the US and Egypt) vehemently rejects. Equally important, while the truce was holding, there was greater talk internationally about possible negotiations and freezing illegal Israeli settlement expansion and moves to boycott products made in those settlements. There were also growing calls for compromises that successive Israeli governments have been unwilling to make. Despite recent comments from outgoing Prime Minister Ehud Olmert linking Israel's survival to withdrawal from the occupied West Bank, Israel has consistently rejected a viable two-state solution because it insists on maintaining control of the West Bank.

The periodic rain of rockets from Gaza into Israel since November 4 provoked broad public support for military action against Hamas. With President Bush soon packing his bags for Texas, there was also a strong incentive on Israel's part to capitalize on support from a predictably pliant White House.

In rhetoric reminiscent of the Israeli campaign in Lebanon in 2006, Israeli officials, including Foreign Minister Tzipi Livni, have denied that the Palestinians of Gaza are facing a humanitarian crisis. The evidence shows otherwise: as of January 2, according to a report by the UN Office for the Coordination of Humanitarian Affairs (UNOCHA):[2]

> 80% of the [Gazan] population cannot support themselves and are dependent on humanitarian assistance. This figure is increasing. According to the World Food Programme, the population is facing a food crisis [with] food shortages of flour, rice, sugar, dairy

products, milk, canned foods and fresh meats. The imports entering are insufficient to support the population or to service infrastructure maintenance and repair needs. The health system is overwhelmed having been weakened by an 18-month blockade [and] utilities are barely functioning: the only electric power plant has shut down [leaving] some 250,000 people in central and northern Gaza [without any] electricity at all due to the damage to fifteen electricity transformers during the air strikes. The water system provides running water once every 5–7 days and the sanitation system cannot treat the sewage and is dumping 40 million liters of raw sewage into the sea daily. Fuel for heating … and cooking gas are no longer available in the market.

Yet Livni, the Kadima party candidate for prime minister in the February elections, refers to the Israeli battle with Hamas as a struggle between moderates and extremists, and portrays the war as a chance to strike a blow against Islamist radicals in the Arab world, not least the venerable Muslim Brethren. She suggests that Israel is finding common purpose with "moderate" Arab regimes.

A recent *Jerusalem Post* article by veteran journalist Herb Keinon argues that Israel's objective in Gaza is to undermine and delegitimize Islamist power by creating a state of chaos that will make it impossible for Hamas to rule, hence, the destruction of Gaza's infrastructure. This state of chaos will have the added benefit of weakening Iran's influence. Other Israeli analysts have suggested that by devastating Gaza and Hamas, Israel may provoke an attack by Hezbollah or Iran, which would justify an Israeli counterattack.

For the fighting to end on Israel's terms, Hamas must accept blame for provoking the Israeli assault without winning any acknowledgement of the humanitarian crisis that has been unfolding in Gaza ever since Hamas won the US-promoted elections in January 2006. For almost two years, a concerted effort to isolate and overthrow Hamas and to undermine the Gaza economy has been encouraged by the US government and the European Union and implemented by Israel and the PA. Hamas leaders were told they could lift the siege only by abstaining from anti-Israeli violence, acknowledging the legitimate existence of Israel, and accepting the agreements signed between Israel and the PA.

Hamas has consistently refused, arguing that recognition of the peace agreements with Israel would be equivalent to recognizing occupation, particularly against a history of Palestinian concessions that not only failed to end Israeli occupation but deepened it. After Hamas defeated PA military contingents in June 2007 and established a rival political authority in Gaza, the siege of the Strip tightened. Hamas, despite its espoused enmity toward Israel, has indicated its willingness to negotiate. It has voiced support for the 2002 Arab League's declaration offering Israel permanent peace in exchange for returning to its internationally recognized pre-1967 borders. Hamas chief Khaled Meshal and PA Prime Minister Ismail Haniya similarly confirmed Hamas' willingness to accept 1967 borders and a two-state solution should Israel withdraw from the occupied territories.

A ceasefire is likely to be in place when Barack Obama is inaugurated on January 20, but we expect that the outcome of the Gaza fighting is likely to underline the self-delusion that has framed the US-Israeli perspective on major groups like Hamas for years, namely that Israel may choose its Palestinian interlocutors, and marginalize and criminalize those who are unwilling to negotiate on Israel's terms. While Hamas by no means speaks for all Palestinians, it is fatuous to assume that Hamas may be ignored politically or diplomatically.

In 2006, the Olmert government went to war to defeat Hezbollah and failed. A quarter-century prior, Israel launched a major invasion of Lebanon to defeat the PLO and quash Palestinian nationalism. That attempt also failed. We expect that when the Gaza war ends a battered Hamas is likely to emerge stronger politically than it was when the fighting began. Yet, the already decrepit Gaza infrastructure will be in rubble, and the reestablishment of public order will be a formidable challenge for Hamas, even if the group remains in nominal control of Gaza. There is also the very real possibility that more extreme Islamist groups will strengthen, vying with Hamas for control (as they already do in Palestinian refugee camps in Lebanon).

The Gaza war will change the political landscape of the Middle East. As such it presents an enormous if not unwelcome challenge for President-elect Obama. The new president will have to address renewed Muslim enmity toward the US, as well as an arduous challenge of peace-making between a deeply fragmented Palestinian leadership and an Israeli government even less ready or willing than its immediate predecessors to bow to the inevitable sacrifices that peace requires. History has taught that peace in this region—if in fact that is the goal—can be imposed neither with bombs nor rockets.

5

Degrees of Loss*

I recently returned to the US from a week in East Jerusalem and other parts of the West Bank. I arrived in the city on Sunday, September 26 [2010], the day the temporary freeze on Israeli settlements was set to expire. I was staying with a friend in Sheikh Jarrah, meters away from where two Palestinian families were evicted from their homes last year; more are expected to be forced out in the coming months. As the end of the settlement freeze came and went, what struck me most about it, and about the latest round of peace negotiations of which it was a part, was their utter irrelevance to the realities of Palestinian life.

Settlements now control 42 percent of the West Bank. The Arab population in Ramallah, Hebron, Bethlehem, East Jerusalem and elsewhere is being steadily boxed in, with declining access to water and other resources. Arab lands are being incorporated into Israel and consolidated into a new spatial order that aims to eliminate any physical separation between Israel and the settlements, thereby eliminating any possibility of a Palestinian state. In the West Bank, Israeli policy has clearly shifted from occupation to imposed sovereignty or de facto annexation.

One of the great achievements of Israeli policy over the last decade, with the support of a cooperative Palestinian Authority security structure, has been to make everyday life so difficult for the Palestinians that they have no energy left to oppose the occupation. People are now simply (and understandably) grateful for the absence of pain. A friend of mine from Bethlehem, a city severed by the separation wall, told me how "calm" it is now because "we rarely see Israeli soldiers inside the city anymore." Under such confinement, any small breakthrough is a success of sorts: one morning I found myself elated by the lack of traffic at the Kalandia checkpoint, which meant I got where I was going in half the time it usually took me.

---

* Originally published in the *London Review of Books Blog*, October 8, 2010.

Given the steady contraction of Palestinian life, the most recent round of US-led negotiations was not about the resolution of conflict but about the degree of loss that can be inflicted on the Palestinians by the US and Israel. The Palestinian "state" is now—and will remain for the foreseeable future—a US-Israeli initiative not a Palestinian one.

6

Gaza After the Revolution*

For the US government and media, the Israeli–Palestinian conflict has been treated as a stepchild of sorts to the revolutionary events sweeping the Middle East. This was clarified to me recently by a prominent American journalist who confided he was unable to report on Israel/Palestine because "they're just too far from the news right now."

Gaza certainly continues to be ignored. Yet on the evening of March 14 [2011]—one day earlier than planned—2,000 Palestinian youth and numerous civil society organizations gathered in a square in the middle of Gaza City calling on Hamas and Fatah to end their divisions and restore democracy in Palestine. Yesterday, March 15, thousands of people protested on the streets of Gaza, including young Hamas supporters, small groups loyal to Fatah and other small Palestinian factions, as well as Facebook activists. In Ramallah, some 8,000 demonstrators, the majority of whom were university students and young people, marched through Al Manara Square demanding national unity. Gazans are seeing their protests move to cities in the West Bank, creating a coordinated and strengthened movement.

More importantly, given the changing political landscape in neighboring Egypt, Gaza's strategic importance may become even more vital for regional security. There are emerging indications in policy circles that the Egypt-Gaza relationship and how it may evolve are far more worrisome to the US and Israel than is publicly acknowledged.

Gaza's importance was already strikingly demonstrated in a December 2007 Wikileaks cable written and classified by then US Ambassador to Egypt, Francis J. Ricciardone. Entitled "Repairing Egyptian-Israeli Communications," it reveals: "[T]he Egyptians continue to offer excuses for the problem they face: the need to 'squeeze' Hamas, while avoiding being seen as complicit in Israel's

---

* Originally published in *ForeignPolicy.com*, March 16, 2011 (slightly edited).

'siege' of Gaza. Egyptian General Intelligence Chief Omar Soliman told us Egypt wants Gaza to go 'hungry' but not 'starve.'"

Indeed, most Gazans have been impoverished and too many have known hunger, a reality (in the form of a strangulating economic siege) deliberately and principally imposed for years by Israel, the US, the EU and Egypt on a defenseless and overwhelmingly young civilian population. Perhaps most alarming, recent indicators strongly suggest that the ability of people to feed themselves and their children has diminished even further.

In a recent report on food and water insecurity in the Gaza Strip, Physicians for Human Rights-Israel (PHRI) revealed some striking statistics regarding the damage incurred. For example, levels of food insecurity—defined by the World Food Programme as a "lack of access to sufficient, safe, and nutritious food, which meets dietary needs … for an active and healthy life"—rose from 40 percent in 2003 to 61 percent towards the end of 2010. This means that over 900,000 people out of a total population of 1.5 million "do not have the self-sufficient means to grow or purchase the bare minimum amount of food for themselves and their families" (while another 200,000-plus remain vulnerable to food insecurity).

Currently, at least 75 percent of Gazan families are dependent for their basic needs on some form of humanitarian assistance—dubbed the "humanitarian minimum"—provided by international donors, all of whom (including several Arab states) are complicit in Gaza's devastation. PHRI further argues that according to an Israeli Army document, "Food Consumption in the Gaza Strip-Red Lines," "Israel's obligation to Palestinians in Gaza only extends to ensuring bare necessities required for survival. According to this principle, personal and economic development above this [humanitarian] minimum should be actively prevented."[1] And it has. The diminished level of personal well-being is revealed by the fact that without high levels of international humanitarian aid Gaza would undoubtedly suffer a widespread nutritional crisis.

Economic development was precluded long ago but Gaza's current reality is crushingly adverse, characterized by the virtual collapse of an economy that was once considered lower middle income (together with the West Bank) and an unemployment rate that reached 45 percent in 2011, among the highest in the world.

According to the UN, in August 2000, 10,614 truckloads of food and materials entered Gaza. By January 2011, this plummeted to 4,123 truckloads (as desperately needed construction materials remain banned) and exports fell from 2,460 to 107 truckloads.

Although Arabs waging revolutions may not now be protesting Palestinian conditions, their subjugation shall remain at the center of the discourse despite the preferences of US policymakers and journalists. Israel's occupation may seem exceptional to current events, but this will not last because the struggle for democracy in the Arab world will not stop at Gaza's (or Israel's) border.

There is no doubt that the same Arab people who are fighting for freedom in their own countries will challenge the immoral situation in Palestine, especially in Gaza, and ask: how can a predominantly young population, desperately willing and able to work, be made dependent on handouts? And there is equally no doubt that Palestinians will no longer accept their continued impoverishment and decline.

Although popular demands for reconciliation, democracy and ultimately an end to occupation will depend for their success on support from the Hamas and Fayyad governments, the role of the international community is absolutely crucial: it must facilitate an end to the crippling siege of Gaza—citizens from all around the world will again attempt this May to break the blockade with the next Gaza freedom flotilla—and meaningfully work toward the creation of a Palestinian unity government.

The power balance in the region is slowly but inexorably shifting in a manner that does not favor US-Israel dominance (with its acceptance and legitimizing of Israeli occupation and Palestinian dispossession). It is the Arab people—not their regimes—who have always supported Palestinian rights, and they may soon be in a position to insist on them. So, too, will Palestinians.

7

It's Worth Putting Hamas to the Test*

The first Israeli-Palestinian face-to-face meeting in over a year just took place in Amman and another meeting is scheduled for next week. Given the painfully low expectations on all sides, particularly against Israel's announcement—just hours before this week's talks were to begin—of plans to construct 300 housing units beyond the Green Line in Jerusalem, one might ask why the exercise is even being attempted?

This month also marks the third anniversary of Israel's devastating three-week war on Gaza and it appears that another attack may be brewing. Recently, the IDF Chief of Staff, Lt. General Benny Gantz, said that another strike on Gaza is not a matter of choice for Israel. The past few weeks have shown a clear statistical relationship between Israeli missile strikes against Gaza—one of which exploded on Gaza City's main commercial street last month—and an increase in homemade rockets and mortar shells fired from Gaza into Israel. Israel's attack was reportedly the first on Gaza City since its 2008–09 war on the Strip. Why would Israel attack Gaza City in December and engage in peace talks with Ramallah in January?

There may be many reasons, but one is absolutely key: to isolate Hamas and sabotage Palestinian reconciliation efforts. Perhaps this is why Israel recently warned both Fatah and Hamas that it would cut water and electricity to Gaza should a unity government be formed. Palestinian unity is something both Israel and the US especially have worked long and hard to preclude. In fact, the Oslo peace process was directly positioned against reconciliation. The resulting severing of the two territories, which was a policy goal of Oslo, undermined the Palestinian national movement and eliminated the geographical basis of a Palestinian economy. The West Bank essentially dissolved into a frag-

---

* Originally published in *The Hill*, January 6, 2012 (slightly edited). Despite every effort to contact *The Hill* to clear permissions, the author was unsuccessful.

mented, incoherent entity and the Gaza Strip was converted into an imprisoned and impoverished enclave now home to over 1.5 million people.

In 2007, Shlomo Ben-Ami, a former Israeli foreign minister, wrote: "To believe that we ended the occupation in Gaza [after Israel's 2005 disengagement] while still occupying the West Bank is to assume that Gaza is not part of a Palestinian entity."[1]

It is precisely this assumption that has long informed Israeli policy toward Gaza, particularly after Hamas's 2006 electoral victory and 2007 takeover. In this regard, Israel has successfully recast its asymmetrical relationship with Gaza from one of occupation to one of two (equal) actors at war, a recasting the international community has largely embraced. Consequently, Israel reshaped its conflict with the Palestinians to center on Gaza and on Israel's hostile relationship with Hamas, restricting the Palestinian "state" to a dismembered and increasingly annexed West Bank.

The separation of the West Bank and Gaza has another critical, unseen dimension: excising Gaza—as the principal source of resistance to Israeli occupation—from the dominant political paradigm. Gaza is the political heart and strategic core of Palestine and Palestinian nationalism, the center of resistance in the past and present. As such Gaza represents a political threat that goes well beyond—and long precedes—Hamas. Israel well understood this, which is why Gaza was cut off—marginalized, demonized and punished with a crippling siege now in its sixth year. It is also why Gaza continues to be attacked.

Hence a key feature of the Fatah-Hamas unity agreement signed last May is the return of Gaza to the Palestinian cause after years of isolation. Despite the difficult challenges that remain, the political reengagement of Gaza and its repositioning back into the center of the struggle is key to reconstructing a national movement, which is why Palestinian unity will continue to be opposed by Israel, the US and certain Arab states. Promoting negotiations that reject Hamas's participation is one way of keeping Palestinians internally divided and vulnerable. Although national unification will not come from a Fatah-Hamas agreement alone, it is an essential prerequisite.

Hamas, furthermore, has come under enormous pressure from its population in Gaza for its political and economic failures including:

the futility of firing rockets into Israel and its inability to defend Gaza against Israeli military attacks and end the debilitating siege. Gaza's economic devastation is a key constraint on the Islamist government. Conservatively, unemployment hovers around 30 percent and could easily return to the much higher levels of the past. Nearly 40 percent of Gazans live in poverty, a percentage that would be far greater without donor aid. In fact, 70–80 percent of the population remains dependent on some form of humanitarian assistance. Ten percent of all children are stunted, "so undernourished before the age of two," writes the former British Foreign Secretary, David Miliband, "that they never grow to their full potential."[2]

These problems have weakened Hamas' legitimacy, which is not lost on its leadership who also are concerned about the potential for civil unrest in Gaza, especially in light of regional changes and the unpopularity of various Hamas policies, notably the growing Islamization of society. This is not only a potentially dangerous situation for the government in Gaza but for its counterpart in the West Bank.

While there is no guarantee that engaging Hamas politically would result in diminished violence and greater moderation, its history of political pragmatism and long record of social service provision and community development (coupled with the regional ascendance of Islamist parties especially in Egypt) strongly suggest that it is worth putting Hamas to the test. Without question, Palestinian stability and future peace efforts depend upon it.

8

Before Gaza, After Gaza: Examining the New Reality in Israel/Palestine*

In the 17 years since the Oslo process began Palestinians have suffered losses not seen since the beginning of Israeli occupation and arguably since the *nakba*, the losses of 1948.[1] The scholar Joseph Massad has compellingly argued that it is wrong to think of the *nakba* as "a history of the past;" rather, it is "a history of the present," an historical epoch that remains a living, ongoing reality without end.[2] Yet, what has changed, arguably, is the conceptualization of loss itself, which has assumed altogether new dimensions. For now it is less a matter of defining losses that demand redress but of living in an altered and indistinguishable and indeterminate reality in which those losses have no place, no history, and no context, where reclamation is, in effect, meaningless, without purpose or justification.

This altered reality has been shaped and defined over the last few years by certain critical paradigmatic shifts in the way the Palestinian–Israeli conflict is conceptualized, understood, and addressed. I would like to touch upon some of them, ending with a brief reflection on the changing socioeconomic reality in Gaza.

KEY PARADIGM SHIFTS: RECONFIGURING THE DEFINING CONCEPTUAL FRAMEWORK

Since the beginning of Israeli occupation, there has always been an implicit and often explicit belief among Palestinians, many Israelis, and members of the international community that the occupation can and will end, and Israel's expansion into Palestine stopped. For

---

* Originally published in Rochelle Davis and Mimi Kirk (eds.), *Palestine and the Palestinians in the 21st Century* (Washington, DC: Center for Contemporary Arab Studies, Georgetown University and Indiana University Press, 2013) (slightly edited).

many, this was how they understood the Oslo process. The belief that occupation is reversible and *should* be reversed was largely unquestioned and uncontested and was the catalyzing force behind many social, economic and political initiatives. This belief has itself been reversed and is powerfully illustrated in the formalization, institutionalization and acceptance by Israel and the international community of Palestinian territorial and demographic fragmentation and cantonization. This represents a key paradigmatic shift in the way the conflict is understood and approached.

The changes imposed on Palestinians over the last 17 years especially have shown that the occupation cannot be stopped, at least not in the short- or medium-term. If the occupation has changed over time it is in the sheer nature of its expansion and force, not in its mitigation, contraction, or inversion. The etiology and imperative of expansion remain unchallenged, and I seriously doubt that it could be stopped even if the Israeli leadership wanted to stop it, which they do not. Perhaps the most powerful illustration of occupation's power lies in the continued expansion of Israeli settlements and their infrastructure and in the building of the separation barrier or wall.

The effect on Palestinians has been extremely damaging. Not only have lands and the use of those lands been lost—at least 38 percent of the West Bank[3] is under Israeli control and inaccessible to Palestinians—but Arab lands are being incorporated and consolidated into a new spatial and political order that aims to eliminate any physical separation between Israel and certain (and increasing) areas of the West Bank, diminishing the presence of Palestinians and precluding the emergence of any viable entity that could be called a Palestinian state (including on the eastern side of the barrier).

The denial of territorial contiguity and the reality of territorial and demographic fragmentation was facilitated by the physical isolation of the West Bank and Gaza, which was largely complete by 1998, illustrating that their separation had long been an Israeli policy goal. According to the Israeli journalist Amira Hass:

> The total separation of the Gaza Strip from the West Bank is one of the greatest achievements of Israeli politics, whose overarching objective is to prevent a solution based on international decisions and understandings and instead dictate an arrangement based

on Israel's military superiority ... Since January 1991, Israel has bureaucratically and logistically merely perfected the split and the separation: not only between Palestinians in the occupied territories and their brothers in Israel, but also between the Palestinian residents of Jerusalem and those in the rest of the territories and between Gazans and West Bankers/Jerusalemites.[4]

Indeed, the Israeli economist Shir Hever revealed that, on April 20, 2007, in a lecture delivered at the Van Leer Jerusalem Institute, Brigadier General Yair Golan, then commander of Israeli forces in the West Bank, stated that "separation and not security is the main reason for building the Wall of Separation and that security could have been achieved more effectively and more cheaply through other means."[5]

This points to another important paradigm shift. Prior to Oslo there was a belief among Israelis and within the international community that peace and occupation were incompatible. The former could not be achieved in the presence of the latter. This, too, has changed. In recent years, more and more Israelis are benefiting from the occupation. Their lives have been facilitated by the vast settlement road network built in the West Bank and by an improved economy resulting from a perceived containment of the conflict. Settlements are now regarded as natural outgrowth, a needed constituency providing protection and security, with important familial links to Israel proper. Thus, the integration of the settlement blocs and their infrastructure into Israel—that is, the argument that the West Bank is part of Israel—is no longer extraordinary or contentious; on the contrary, it is necessary and normal.

For many Israelis and several key international donors, it is no longer a question of normalizing the occupation but of removing the term altogether since it no longer applies, especially in light of a strong and expanding Israeli economy and the virtual cessation of suicide attacks inside Israel.[6] In fact, silence over the occupation has become the key condition for continued international funding of the Palestinian Authority. Hence, Palestine's effective dismemberment and the permanence of territorial fragmentation (as well as the policies of collective punishment that often accompany them) are accepted by the international community as legitimate and benign and totally manageable, especially with the virtual absence of any criticism from

Palestinian officialdom. Separating from the Palestinians and doing what is necessary politically, militarily and economically to insure and maintain that separation has also become increasingly routine.

In point of fact, many, if not most, Israelis are untouched by the everyday exigencies of the occupation, having little if any exposure to them. The occupation has been transformed from a political and legal issue with international legitimacy into a simple dispute over borders where the rules of war apply, rather than those of occupation. In this regard, Israel has successfully recast its relationship with Gaza from one of occupation to one of two actors at war, a recasting the international community has also come to accept. Indeed, some international actors now deny the existence of occupation altogether. In this regard, George Bisharat observes:

> Israeli military lawyers have pushed to re-classify military operations in the West Bank and Gaza Strip from the law enforcement model mandated by the law of occupation to one of armed conflict. Today most observers—including Amnesty International—tacitly accept Israel's framing of the conflict in Gaza as an armed conflict, as their criticism of Israel's actions in terms of the duties of distinction and the principle of proportionality betrays.[7]

This no doubt accounts, in part, for the overwhelming popular support among Israelis for the devastating war on Gaza. Hence, many Israelis and members of the international community no longer feel uncomfortable with the occupation at a time when the occupation has grown more repressive and perverse.

The inapplicability of occupation as an analytical (and legal) framework leads to another important paradigm shift regarding Israel's intentions toward the Palestinians and their territories. This shift is from one of ongoing occupation to one of annexation and imposed sovereignty (i.e., claiming that the West Bank or parts of it are de facto sovereign Israeli territory).

This shift is illustrated in part by the following policies: the building of the separation wall; massive Israeli settlement expansion; the continued confiscation of Palestinian lands; the building of the massive settlement road network from which Palestinians are effectively barred; limited access to the Jordan Valley by non-resident Palestinians; the isolation of Gaza and its physical, economic and demographic separation from the West Bank, and the subsequent reshaping of the Palestinian–Israeli conflict to center on Gaza alone and on Israel's hostile relationship with Hamas. A critical feature of this reshaping has been the transformation of Palestinians into a humanitarian problem, which I discuss below, and the identification of Gaza solely with Hamas and therefore as alien.

Hence, any resistance by Palestinians to Israel's repressive occupation, including attempts at economic empowerment, are now considered illegitimate and unlawful. Indeed, Palestinians have been severely punished for trying to defend themselves against policies that oppress them.[8] Rather, they and the governments elected to represent them are expected—indeed required—by Israel, the United States, the European Union, and some Arab states to submit to Israeli actions—in effect, to collaborate with Israeli policy—and oppose any form of popular resistance to those actions.[9] Within this new paradigm, Palestinians become aliens and intruders in their own land, living in submission and dependence. Any notion of a human community among Palestinians, let alone a national or economic one, ceases to exist. Nowhere is this more evident than in Gaza.

The paradigmatic shift from occupation to annexation also has been accepted by key members of the international community, especially after Hamas's electoral victory and seizure of Gaza. Not only have major donors participated in the draconian sanction regime imposed on Gaza, they have privileged the West Bank over Gaza in their programmatic work. Donor strategies now support and strengthen the fragmentation and isolation of the West Bank and Gaza Strip and divide Palestinians into two distinct entities, offering exclusivity to one side—economically, politically and diplomatically—and criminalizing the other. The West Bank is deserving of sustenance and Gaza, deprivation.

As Karen Abu Zayd, the Commissioner-General of UNRWA (United Nations Relief and Works Agency), warned well before the attack on Gaza, "Gaza is on the threshold of becoming the first territory to be intentionally reduced to a state of abject destitution with the knowledge, acquiescence, and—some would say—encouragement of the international community."[10] She further argues:

Humanitarian and human development work was never meant to function in an environment devoid of constructive efforts to resolve conflict or to address its underlying causes. Indeed, humanitarian work is profoundly undermined in a context where there is implicit or active complicity in creating conditions of mass suffering. This is the situation bedeviling Palestinian prospects.[11]

What emerges are, in effect, two political-economic models. The West Bank model is characterized by restricted levels of institution-building, isolated pockets of business and commercial development itself shaped by a cantonized geographical entity, and the professionalization of security forces. This model is devoid of political content and does nothing to confront the occupation; to the contrary, it advocates silence and represses criticism. The Gaza Strip model is characterized by siege, isolation, collective punishment and economic subjection, with a leadership strengthened by the occupation but unable to do anything to address it.[12] Both models have failed, and their failure underlines the fact that the Palestinian state has never been a Palestinian project.

Increasingly, economic activities are evolving as a response to decline and breakdown and to the unwillingness of the donor governments to meaningfully, i.e., politically, challenge the status quo. This unwillingness represents nothing less than collusion with maintaining Israel's occupation.

Transforming Palestinians into perpetrators, without claim, has assumed different dimensions since the election of Hamas, particularly with regard to the changing nature of physical destruction in the West Bank, which represents another critical change. The Israeli journalist Amira Hass has described to me a steady process of destroying many vestiges of Palestinian life in the West Bank as they have historically existed. Old roads long used by Palestinians traveling between major towns and surrounding villages are being eliminated, as are traditional intersections, buildings and certain commercial areas. Another illustration concerns certain road signs in the West Bank, which now have the Hebrew names of towns transliterated into Arabic and the Arabic name encased in parentheses. What is happening is no less than the erasure of a Palestinian presence in the West Bank.

Another new and related feature is the increasing bureaucratization of Israel's system of control, or what the Israeli scholar Neve Gordon calls the privatization of Zionism. Gordon argues that while the state was long responsible for urban planning and development inside Israel and the West Bank, incrementally the task has been subcontracted to the corporate sector.[13] In the West Bank, this shift (in tactics as opposed to strategy) is illustrated by the fact that some military checkpoints are no longer manned by soldiers but are administered by private Israeli security companies. This is also true for the Erez crossing point from Israel into Gaza.

Hence, in addition to the political imperatives underlying checkpoints, terminals and other physical barriers, there is now an entrenched bureaucratic imperative that has its own interests, needs and priorities. Bureaucratizing this structure depoliticizes it by making it a necessary and permanent part of everyday life. Furthermore, one must add to this Israel's intense, almost complete bureaucratic control of everyday life in the West Bank and Gaza.

KEY PARADIGM SHIFTS: SECTORAL-LEVEL CHANGES

The Economy

"We started with food aid and we have returned to food aid." This was the conclusion of a Palestinian economist in Ramallah in 2007. Her words powerfully capture what is perhaps the most dramatic paradigm shift in the way Palestinians are perceived and addressed: from a society (worthy of) pursuing developmental change to an impoverished community seeking relief, what the analyst Sami Abdel Shafi referred to as "engineering Palestinians into perpetual beggars."[14]

The resulting "humanitarianization" and immiseration of Palestinians—turning Palestinians into charity cases and paupers—has many illustrations. In 2007, for example, 30 percent of income earned by Palestinians between 1972 and 2006 was being brought into the economy as emergency aid resulting, in large part, from Israel's severing of economic and commercial ties after four decades of integration and forced dependence.[15] In 2008, external aid to the PA equaled almost 30 percent of GDP, which means that without such donor aid, there would be fiscal collapse.[16] By 2008, approximately

80 percent of families in Gaza relied on humanitarian aid to survive compared to 63 percent in 2006; currently that figure remains largely unchanged. Between 1999 and early 2008, the number of families receiving food aid from UNRWA increased from 16,174 to 182,400 or 860,000 people (although other estimates place this number at 750,000).[17] Furthermore, the World Food Programme was feeding an additional 302,000 Gazans, meaning that over 1.1 million out of 1.4 million people in Gaza were receiving food aid in 2008.

The shift from political to humanitarian priorities derives from several factors:

- the total fragmentation of the geographical base of the Palestinian economy, with the complete separation of Gaza and the West Bank and the division of the West Bank into at least 11 cantons and sub-cantons on no more than 62 percent of the land;
- the use of aid as a form of punishment inflicted by Israel (in the form of closure and then blockade) and, critically, by the international community,[18] and
- the growing ineffectiveness of international aid, particularly after 2006, as assistance—composed primarily of humanitarian relief—was being provided outside any economic framework, having little if any bearing on development or institution-building.

Hence, the steady imposition of Israeli imperatives unchallenged, and then actively supported by, the international community, coupled with the use of aid as a punitive weapon, gave rise to a clear shift in the way some foreign governments, aid agencies and other international organizations approached Israeli-Palestinian relations. This shift, acutely clear after the January 2006 elections, moved strongly away from any commitment to Palestinian self-determination toward one that emphasized relief and charity[19]—helping people survive while they are being contained and punished and their economy disabled.

Indeed, the precipitous decline of the private sector, the driver of economic growth whose impact on the sustained health of the economy is enormous, provides a powerful illustration of economic disablement and the impoverishment it produces. Prior to the horrendous attack on Gaza, for example, the private sector was on the verge of collapse due to Israeli closure and blockade preventing the import of raw materials and the export of finished products. Before Hamas's June 2007 takeover of the Strip, 54 percent of Gaza's employment was generated by the private sector. Gaza's manufacturers imported 95 percent of their inputs and exported their finished products primarily to Israel (and some to the West Bank). Between June 2005 and September 2008, the number of operating factories in Gaza had declined from 3,900 to 23.[20] Approximately 100,000 people (including 40,000 agricultural and 34,000 industrial workers), virtually the entire private sector, lost their jobs.[21]

Perhaps more ominous was the growing informalization of the economy. Prior to the December 2008 war on Gaza, the World Bank observed a redistribution of wealth from the formal private sector towards black market operators.[22] Indeed, Gaza's growing tunnel trade with Egypt has turned the once impoverished town of Rafah into a busy market where a variety of goods, including weapons, can now be purchased. Rafah's growing economy is yet another illustration of fragmentation and the distortion it produces, of creating economic islands—be they in Gaza or the West Bank—that the World Bank correctly termed "development dead-ends."[23] Furthermore, said the Bank, the "near absence of private sector activities" combined with a financial crisis deriving from the inability of people to pay for services such as water, garbage collection and sewage treatment, and the inability to import spare parts and supplies, also resulted in the collapse of the municipal sector.[24] This represented no less than the change in Gaza's already fragile economy from one driven in large part by private-sector productivity to one dependent on public-sector salaries and humanitarian assistance, a condition that obtains to varying degrees in the West Bank as well.[25]

Yet this transformation or paradigm shift that reduces Palestinians from a political to a humanitarian issue has been accompanied by another equally dangerous paradigm shift. Since the Hamas victory in January 2006, Israel's policy goal is no longer just the isolation of Gaza but its disablement, as seen in a policy shift from one that addresses the economy in some manner (whether positively or negatively) to one that dispenses with the concept of an economy altogether. That is, rather than weaken Gaza's economy through punishing closures and other restrictions as it has long done, the Israeli government has, since June 2006, imposed a form of indefinite blockade—replacing closure—that treats the economy as totally irrelevant, a disposable luxury.[26]

This was underlined by the Israeli Supreme Court's decision approving fuel cuts to Gaza in October 2007 (permissible since it would not harm "essential humanitarian needs"[27] of the population) followed in January 2008 by electricity cuts (and in May 2008 by a lowering of acceptable levels for fuel and electricity). The court stated, "We do not accept the petitioners' argument that 'market forces' should be allowed to play their role in Gaza with regard to fuel consumption."[28] Thus, according to the Supreme Court, it is permissible to harm Palestinians and create a humanitarian crisis for political reasons. Or as the analyst Darryl Li put it, "The logic of the Court's decisions on fuel and electricity suggests that once undefined 'essential humanitarian needs' are met, all other deprivation is possible."[29]

This shift also is seen symbolically in the crossing point from Karni, long the main commercial crossing point into Gaza under Israeli and Palestinian control, to Kerem Shalom, which is operated entirely by Israel. Kerem Shalom is not a commercial crossing like Karni, but more like a gate in a fence, and incapable of handling many kinds of commercial items. At Karni, there was a defined system of security procedures and distribution protocols but at Kerem Shalom, cargo is offloaded from trucks and then left on pallets in the open for Palestinians to come and pick up when they are allowed to approach—like animals in a pen. The Sufa crossing was also closed and the Coordinator for Government Activities in the Territories (COGAT) informed the UN that Sufa is no longer a crossing point between Gaza and Israel.

It is no longer—and in fact has not been for quite some time—a question of economic growth, change or reform, freedom or sovereignty, but of essential humanitarian needs, of reducing the needs and rights of 1.4 million people in Gaza to an "exercise in counting calories"[30] and truckloads of food. In this way, Israeli policy blurs and, in fact, justifies the destruction of Gaza's economic capacities, which was largely completed with the December [2008–January 2009] war. Within such a scenario aid can, at best, be no more than a palliative "slowing down socio-economic decline [rather] than a catalyst for sustainable economic development."[31] Writing about the West Bank, the World Bank similarly observed, "Large amounts of donor aid have produced insignificant growth and an increase in economic dependency despite the consistent improvement in PA governance and security performance."[32]

The Social Sector

Summarizing the approach of the donor community toward Palestinians post-Hamas, a development specialist with 30 years of experience in the West Bank and Gaza lamented: "You don't destroy a society in order to build it up again; all you wind up doing is destroying it."[33] While it is certainly premature to argue the demise of Palestinian society, it is absolutely essential to argue its decline. This decline has a long history and is marked by many factors affecting the West Bank and Gaza. Perhaps the most important concerns the family unit, which despite the continuous pressures imposed on it, has remained remarkably resilient and adaptable but now increasingly less so. The pressures resulting from territorial fragmentation and economic blockade have been onerous.

The family unit has been weakened by an expanding humanitarian crisis, resource dispossession, internal violence and disorder, and heightened insecurity. Traditional buffers in times of economic distress such as remittances, investments, loans and solidarity payments have markedly decreased due in large part to Israel's long-standing regime of economic restrictions and to the international economic and financial boycott, now entering its fifth year. The family also has suffered greatly as a result of factors tied to or resulting from two decades of political violence and economic regression. To name just a few: early marriage; the oppression of women; the traumatization of children with violence the defining feature in their lives, which has become even more extreme with the war on Gaza; the loss of childhood and growing incivility among children; the diminished authoritative role of the father resulting from his inability to provide for and protect his family; the receding of traditional forms of authority; the weakening of socializing institutions such as the school and the political faction; the decline of the community, and declining health care and educational access. These are old problems, but what is new—and long argued to me with a palpable urgency—is *their level of acuity*, another critical paradigm shift.

If there is a powerful and consistent theme among the many people interviewed in the last four years—Palestinians, Israelis and internationals (especially members of the donor community)—it is this: that the situation in Gaza and the West Bank is rapidly approaching a watershed in terms of the damage inflicted on the individual, the family and the community. The fear of unabated and irreversible decline is deep and unprecedented and directed to the fact that Palestinians are approaching a degree of damage and loss that will take billions of dollars and generations of Palestinians to reverse. This reality has many illustrations that include a population where, conservatively, 75 percent of its members now suffer from severe depression; where nearly 75 percent of all those injured between September 2000 and September 2008 were between 10 and 29 years old, and where 62 percent of those killed between September 2000 and June 2008 were between 15 and 29 years of age.[34] Economically, socially and demographically, it is impossible to outrun the reality of Gaza and the West Bank.

Against their growing deprivation, brutalization and isolation, people are, by lack of choice and force of circumstance, turning inward. Hence, the dislocating impact of territorial fragmentation and isolation on Palestinian life is seen in another important paradigmatic shift—the localization or atomization of life and the re-conceptualization of community. Since 2000, access restrictions have created an even greater sense of place, in very practical ways. The time has disappeared when a Gazan and a Nabulsi might meet at Birzeit University and eventually get married; by 2004 they were unable to even meet each other and would encounter objections from their families, who did not want their son or daughter to be unavailable to them even for visits. The same became true for business transactions; gone were the days when a foreign NGO might hire a Hebron-based construction firm to carry out a project in Nablus. The result has been a lack of intermixing. There have been fewer interactions and friendships as people enter into increasingly different political and structural situations (which, of course, the Israelis encourage as part of a divide-and-rule system of selectively applied carrot-and-stick inducements).

Israel has forced Palestinians to internalize the reality imposed on them; people choose to remain in or near their localities because it is often too difficult to move beyond them and, in Gaza, impossible to do so. Consequently, human, economic and social activities increasingly devolve to the locality, the neighborhood and even the street (as was the case in Gaza prior to Hamas's June 2007 takeover), becoming more atomized and insular. The result is clear: the emergence of particularism over universalism, the latter being far more evident as a value and a goal during the first Intifada. By 2004 (let alone at present), people were already estranged from each other, their localities separated. Because of this, the concept of community is being redefined in terms that are particular and near: *we* are worse off because *they* have one more gate, one more road, one more clinic.

In this regard there also has emerged a growing religiosity among people that is not fundamentalist in character but rather an attempt to find comfort in religion. This has been accompanied by an increasing emphasis on families and children and celebrations and festivals,[35] in an attempt, perhaps, to restore a sense of normalcy and empowerment within a political and structural situation that is decidedly abnormal and disempowering—to make, as Lisa Taraki has written, "the very pursuit of happiness a manifestation of resilience and resistance at the same time"[36]—in effect, to redefine the community within the boundaries of the enclave and solidarity as the ability to live within it. In this regard, the second Intifada represented a dramatic deterioration from the first, which aimed to create a consciousness of a people and a national collective (see Chapter 24), something that became increasingly difficult if not impossible after 2000.

The redefinition of community in this narrowed and confined sense has other consequences. By robbing people of time and space, this fragmented reality militates against positive risk-taking and change (especially in so diminished an economic environment). This is because a great deal of creative and productive human energy is being used to survive in a malformed system, one that is now made more extreme by the hostility and violence between Fatah and Hamas. The result is no less than the de-development of the human being.

The reconceptualization of community as enclave further speaks to the way in which spatial dislocation may impact political identity. For example, the word "Palestine" is used in two ways—to describe a geographical and historical region, and to describe a Palestinian state. Yet, perhaps for the first time in the history of the Palestinian national movement—itself virtually destroyed—the two have little if any connection to each other. The connection between identity—social, economic and political—and territory is being destroyed by institutionalized fragmentation and the mitigation of society. In a very real sense, Palestinians can no longer walk or traverse the land in order to claim it as they have for so long; only the Jewish people can.[37] Palestinians are less and less part of the natural landscape, which supports Amira Hass's claim with regard to the physical destruction of the Palestinian presence in the West Bank. As one Palestinian said, "I am no longer anyone's son."

AFTER THE WAR ON GAZA

After Israel's December 2008 assault, Gaza's already compromised conditions have become virtually unlivable. Livelihoods, homes and public infrastructure have been damaged or destroyed on a scale that the Israel Defense Forces itself admitted was indefensible.[38] Among the ruins lie:[39]

- 1,500 factories and workshops,
- nearly half of 122 health facilities including 15 hospitals,
- 280 schools and kindergartens and
- 6,300 homes (destroyed or partly destroyed).

These data are part of an overall picture of infrastructural damage and destruction that will cost at least $2 billion to address. Observers report destruction on a tremendous scale. In Gaza today, there is no private sector to speak of and no industry. The 2008 assault also destroyed 5,000 acres of agricultural land, including over 300,000 fruit-bearing trees and 305 agricultural wells. Most productive activity has been extinguished. One powerful expression of Gaza's economic demise— and the Gazans' indomitable will to provide for their families—is its burgeoning tunnel economy that emerged long ago in response to the siege and the absence of alternatives that it creates. Thousands of Palestinians have been employed digging tunnels into Egypt—around a thousand tunnels are reported to exist, although not all are operational. According to local economists, by 2009 between 66 and 90 percent of economic activity in Gaza was devoted to smuggling.[40]

According to the World Food Programme, the Gaza Strip requires a minimum of 400 trucks of food every day just to meet the basic nutritional needs of the population. Yet, despite a March 22, 2009 decision by the Israeli cabinet to lift all restrictions on foodstuffs entering Gaza, only 653 trucks of food and other supplies were allowed entry during the week of May 10, 2009, at best meeting 23 percent of required need.[41]

Indeed, according to Amira Hass, by May 2009 Israel allowed only 30–40 commercial items to enter Gaza, compared to 4,000 approved products prior to June 2006 when the Israeli soldier Gilad Shalit was abducted.[42] Although restrictions on the entry of food were in practice lifted during the summer of 2010 in response to international pressure after the Gaza flotilla killings, critically needed materials for rehabilitation and reconstruction are still banned as is freedom of movement. Without an immediate end to Israel's blockade and the resumption of trade and cash transfers, as well as the movement of people outside the prison that Gaza has long been, the current crisis will grow massively more acute. Unless the US administration is willing to exert real pressure on Israel for implementation—and the indications clearly suggest they are not—little will change. Not surprisingly, despite international pledges of $5.2 billion for Gaza's reconstruction, Palestinians there have been rebuilding their homes using rubble and mud.[43]

Adding to Gaza's misery is the huge rehabilitative burden of the 5,000 injured and the social burden of families left without breadwinners. Following the 2008 assault, 100,000 Gazans were left homeless, internally displaced, and temporarily residing in 58 UNRWA shelters or with private families (who themselves had lost breadwinners).[44] This, too, will strain the economy. However, the greatest problem facing Palestinians, especially children, is psychological trauma, which long preceded the December assault but which has been made more acute because of it. Children remember that the first attack on Gaza occurred while they were in school. Approximately 161 of UNRWA's 221 schools now have psychosocial support programs but many more are needed.[45]

Furthermore, the long-term impact of the enormous damage incurred by the educational system, already seriously eroded before the hostilities began, is another critical and inestimable constraint, with a majority of pupils in Gaza now failing math and science. Children returned to schools that were badly damaged or destroyed, with potentially unexploded ordnance lurking on the premises. Those that are functioning report shortages of drinking water, textbooks and other supplies such as desks, which were used as firewood during the fighting.

Given these restrictions, among many others the internal disarray of the Palestinian leadership, one wonders how the reconstruction to which President Obama has referred will be possible? There is no question that Palestinians in Gaza must be helped immediately. Programs aimed at alleviating suffering and reinstating some semblance of normalcy are ongoing but at a scale shaped entirely by the extreme limitations on the availability of goods. In this context of repressive occupation and heightened restrictions, what does it mean to reconstruct Gaza? How is it possible under such conditions to empower people and build sustainable and resilient institutions able to withstand expected external shocks? And what exactly are Palestinians being asked to sustain: an economy that the World Bank says has been "hollowed out" by Israel's security regime?[46] This, too, points to the critical need to shift the political discourse away from the notion of state building, which has proven empty, to one of ending the occupation or what Palestinians now term "liberation." Planning for long-term sustainable change, let alone development, in the presence of the stranglehold of Israeli occupation is a futile and meaningless exercise, as the last few decades have made painfully clear. The occupation must end; then one can discuss what arrangement should follow.

A few months after the war ended, I spoke with some friends in Gaza, and the conversations were profoundly disturbing. My friends spoke of the deeply felt absence of any source of protection, be it personal, communal, or institutional. There is little in society that possesses legitimacy, and there is a fading consensus on rules and an eroding understanding of what they are for. Trauma and grief overwhelm the landscape despite expressions of resilience: "We have lost all sense of the ordinary—what it is like to live an ordinary day—and perhaps more importantly we fear we will never be able to retrieve it, no matter how desperately we try." The feeling of abandonment among people appears complete, understood perhaps in their growing inability to identify with any sense of possibility. But what struck me most of all was this comment: "It is no longer the occupation or even the war that consumes us but the realization of our own irrelevance."

Toward what possible good can the infliction of such mass suffering contribute?

If Palestinians are continually denied what we all want for ourselves—an ordinary life, dignity, livelihood, safety and a piece of land where they can raise their children—then the inevitable outcome will be greater and more extreme violence across all factions, both old and increasingly new. What looms is no less than the loss of entire generations of Palestinians. If this happens—perhaps it already has—we shall all bear the cost.[47]

PART III   TOWARD PRECARITY: EXCEPTIONALIZING GAZA

- As part of the policy formulated by the Security Cabinet on September 19, 2007, Israel will limit the entry of goods into the Gaza Strip.
- In order to allow for a basic fabric of life in the Gaza Strip, the deputy defense minister approved allowing 106 trucks carrying basic humanitarian products into the Gaza Strip, mostly food (all products are specified in the appendices). In addition, food in seed form was approved for entry via the aggregate conveyor belt located near the Karni crossing.
- This research examines the main food component.
- *The goal of the analysis—to identify the point of intervention for prevention of malnutrition in the Gaza Strip.*
- The basis for the analysis is a model formulated by the Ministry of Health (at this point, according to average Israeli consumption) and a model formulated by the Palestinian Ministry of Economy.
- *The Ministry of Health is conducting work for calculating the minimal subsistence basket based on the Arab sector in Israel. The "minimum basket" allows nutrition that is sufficient for subsistence without the development of malnutrition.* [emphasis mine]

Food Consumption in the Gaza Strip—Red Lines
State of Israel
Ministry of Defense
Coordination of Government Activities in the Territories
January 1, 2008

9

Statement on Gaza before the
United Nations Security Council*

[This presentation is drawn from Sara Roy, "Afterword: The Wars on Gaza—A Reflection" in *The Gaza Strip: The Political Economy of De-development*, expanded 3rd edition (Washington, DC: Institute for Palestine Studies, 2016).]

I would like to begin by thanking the permanent missions to the UN of Malaysia and the Hashemite Kingdom of Jordan for the invitation to participate in the Arria-formula Security Council Meeting on Gaza.

In the thirty years that I have spent researching and writing about Gaza and her people, I can say without hesitation that I have never seen the kind of human, physical and psychological destruction that I see there today. Nor is there any precedent for the extraordinarily dangerous situation in which Gaza has found itself since the 2014 Operation Protective Edge (OPE).

An UNRWA official I know recently told me about a conversation he had with a senior Israel Defense Forces (IDF) officer whose responsibilities include the Gaza Strip. In that conversation, my UN colleague asked the IDF official to describe Israel's policy toward Gaza. The answer was just seven words long: "No development, no prosperity, no humanitarian crisis."

As shocking as this statement is, it fundamentally reflects Israel's near fifty-year policy in Gaza and the West Bank, which, from its beginning, aimed to prohibit any form of economic development (although a limited degree of prosperity was allowed in the early years

* Originally published in *Reflections One Year Later and Charting a New Course for Gaza*, UN Security Council Arria-formula Meeting, Israel-Palestine Non-Governmental Organization Working Group at the United Nations, New York, NY, July 20, 2015 (slightly edited).

of the occupation), thereby precluding the emergence of a Palestinian state—Israel's primary goal. There should be no doubt that these policies of preclusion—deliberate and planned—have been enormously successful, particularly over the last decade, which has been especially ruinous for Gaza given an Israeli-imposed blockade, now in its ninth year. This blockade severed almost all of the territory's ties to the outside world, ending all normal trade relations—so vital for Gaza's small economy. According to the World Bank, the blockade alone resulted in a 50 percent decrease in Gaza's GDP since 2007. When combined with the impact of OPE, the blockade was responsible for shrinking the manufacturing sector by as much as 60 percent. Consequently, the Gaza Strip has been largely disabled.

The virtual termination of Gaza's tunnel trade by Egypt—a vital albeit underground economic lifeline—dealt another economic blow. Israel's last war on Gaza one year ago—the third in six years—exacerbated an already grave situation by reducing Gaza's economy an additional $460 million, setting in motion what one local analyst called a "dynamic of disintegration," that has taken a number of forms, some of them completely unprecedented. I will focus the remaining minutes of my talk on some of these unprecedented changes.

A DRAMATIC SHIFT IN POPULAR ATTITUDES

Everyone I have spoken to in Gaza over the past year has said the same thing: that this war has profoundly changed the way people think. Perhaps most significant is the sense of collective dread and desperation that permeates the Strip, more keenly felt in OPE's aftermath than ever before.

While the classic symptoms of post-traumatic disorders are pervasive, what drives people to despair and desperation, said a Gazan friend, is less the war they endured than the inhuman conditions left unchanged after the war. "The shared experience of loss and pain during the war," he told me, "acted to bring people together toward a common goal that was meant to bring about real change. But since the end of the hostilities, a new reality has set in. Nothing has changed after this great loss and sacrifice except a vastly expanded panorama of destruction."

Psychologically, Gazans have never felt less safe and secure, knowing the fighting will at some point resume. Meanwhile, the breathing space between episodes of terror seems to get shorter and shorter. What people fear most is that the truce will end and that their lives will deteriorate even further.

A Gazan colleague summed up the situation as follows:

Gaza is more devoid of hope than it has ever been in my experience here. [Gazans] are afraid of a war with Israel; they are afraid of internecine violence; they are afraid that nothing will change. The main focus is day-to-day survival. The war has devastated conditions in Gaza, making a difficult life even more impossible. Although people expressed relief that they had survived, the relief was transient. For many, the task at hand is naked existence.

Another striking point made to me by friends and colleagues in Gaza is that they now believe Israeli officials when they say that there are "no civilians in Gaza." Gazans were truly shocked by the nature and extent of the destruction because they could see no justification for it. And if indeed Gaza's people are no longer seen as civilians, what future can Gaza hold for them? Furthermore, says a friend in Gaza:

What has also struck me is the extent to which the war has created a different picture of Israel. Before, Gazans were surprisingly nuanced in their analysis. This was especially true among the generation that had experience working inside of Israel. Now, [this is changing]. I interviewed [people who] are Fatah. They lost everything. They no longer believe in the possibility of coexistence. The scale and the indiscriminate nature of the attack; the ... calls from the Israeli public to "finish the job": this destroyed any hope.

THE ECONOMIC IMPACT OF DESTRUCTION

The disintegration of Gaza's economy has many visible manifestations including the massive destruction of civilian infrastructure resulting from OPE, which resulted in around 170,000 homes damaged or destroyed and a homeless population of up to 100,000 people. If one adds the 5,000 homes destroyed in earlier assaults and not yet rebuilt (and assumes an average of 6.1 people per family), then over 1 million Gazans—nearly 60 percent of the population—have suffered some degree of damage to, or the destruction of, their homes over the last six years.

Significantly, the assault eliminated most signs of Gaza's living economy; in other words, those economic factors that were still viable after the previous attacks were largely wiped out by this one. Thus, states the UN, an "estimated 1,000 small factories and workshops and over 4,100 establishments in the retail, wholesale, restaurant and hotel industries were destroyed or damaged." Many of these factories were critical for food and pharmaceutical production, rebuilding and other productive activities.

This points to another unprecedented feature: the virtual destruction of Gaza's middle class. The devastation of al-Shuja'iyya, an area on the eastern side of Gaza City, has been covered extensively. But al-Shuja'iyya's ruination has economic and social implications, which are not well understood but are extremely important. Many relatively well-off Gazans lived in al-Shuja'iyya. This was a center of Gaza's middle class, home to people who, through their businesses and commercial activities, provided the backbone of the Strip's local economy. They constituted not only a source of employment but also a financial resource for people in need of loans or some sort of economic assistance. Now, many if not most of these people who had been so essential to maintaining some level of economic activity in Gaza prior to OPE have themselves become needy and destitute, their homes and businesses destroyed. The loss of Gaza's middle class in this way is profoundly damaging and has contributed to the emergence of a broad new class of "poor."

The attack on Gaza's middle class can also be seen in the systematic destruction, during the final days of the 2014 fighting, of some of Gaza's most impressive high-rise buildings where many of them resided and owned commercial enterprises. These include: the 15-story Basha Tower, Gaza's oldest high-rise, which in addition to residences housed medical and dental clinics, media organizations including radio stations, and NGOs; the Italian Compound, a 13-story residential tower; the Zafir 4, a 14-story residential tower where 44 mostly middle-class families lived, and the Zurab building, a seven-story commercial center in Rafah. According to a colleague, a political analyst in Gaza:

> Stepping into this war, people were either poor or were quickly getting there. The only thing many had left for them is the ceiling on top of their heads. With [the] substantial and nearly blind destruction of entire towns and parts of large cities—particularly along the northern, eastern and southern borders of Gaza—those people now have nothing. These were people who had worked a lifetime to gradually build multiple-story buildings for themselves and for their sons and daughters. Now, they've lost it all and have no way to re-develop even if they wanted to. This is because they have aged, have no economic opportunity, are poor because they've lost their savings and have no jobs, or all of these things combined. In Gaza, it often doesn't matter what age one is; almost everyone is "retired."

My colleague's remarks point to an economic leveling of society, again without precedent. Socioeconomic divisions have disappeared to a degree not seen before: almost everyone has been impoverished, reduced to basic survival. A Gazan friend of mine calls this "the culture of the coupon." Many if not most people literally have no money other than cash and food handouts, and certain areas of Gaza have reportedly been reduced to a barter economy. Productive activity is largely at a standstill. There is little to sustain people economically except aid. Nobody has the means to rebuild homes and livelihoods. To date, not one of Gaza's destroyed homes has been rebuilt. Another colleague, a Gazan economist, commented: "The US and EU are taking us back to 1948 when Palestinians were totally dependent on aid. Why? How will Gaza's destruction ensure Israel's security?"

These losses, combined with many others I do not have the time to discuss, have resulted in extremely high (but not unprecedented) levels of unemployment and impoverishment. The unemployment rate in Gaza now stands at 43 percent (over 60 percent for Gaza's youth), the highest in the world according to the World Bank. With present unemployment so high, Gaza is nearing a point where, as economist Omar Shaban argues, it is more appropriate to speak of Gaza's level of employment, rather than of its unemployment level. Clean water is a rarity, with at least 90 percent of Gaza's supply unfit for human consumption. Electricity is sporadic, available only 4–6 hours per day, and a properly functioning sewage treatment system no longer exists.

BEYOND *SUMUD*: FLEEING GAZA

As a consequence of these and other factors, another new but relatively underreported phenomenon has emerged in Gaza: boat people. While young Gazans have for years wanted to leave for a better life, the situation after Operation Protective Edge became such that, according to a poll, 43 percent of Gazans want to emigrate. People cannot live without hope, which is why so many are now talking about leaving. It is also important to emphasize that the Gazans who are leaving by such means include children from conservative families connected to Hamas and Islamic Jihad.

Among those presumed drowned off the coast of Alexandria in September 2014 was the son of a well-known professor of shari'a law at the Islamic University of Gaza. Leaving Gaza is no longer seen as the behavior of secular or "decadent" people. Palestine was always defined by *sumud* or steadfastness, a commitment to remain on the land. This can no longer be taken for granted, at least not in Gaza.

A NOTE ON RECONSTRUCTION AND THE ROLE OF DONORS

In the present context, what does it mean to "reconstruct Gaza"? Despite the magnitude and urgency of the task at hand, efforts to "reconstruct" or "rebuild" Gaza have long been deeply problematic. Although billions of dollars have been pledged by donors, reconstruction is always planned or implemented within an unchanged (and unchallenged) political framework of continued Israeli occupation, assault and blockade.

The various reconstruction projects planned for Gaza over the years have never been part of a larger political program meant to alleviate Palestinian suffering or improve conditions. Rather, the projects have always been treated as ends in and of themselves. Meanwhile, Gaza's vulnerability to Israeli military attacks and economic sanctions is at best ignored and at worst endorsed by key forces in the West, notably the United States and the EU.

Even against such a background, however, the current plan for Gaza's reconstruction—presented to and accepted by the donors soon after OPE—represents a new low point. Never mind that Gaza's recent devastation, met largely with laissez-faire silence from Western states, is completely unprecedented; the agreed-upon plan for addressing the situation clearly prioritizes limited short-term gains at the cost of a long-term entrenchment of Israel's destructive blockade.

There are now several documents describing the reconstruction and recovery plan for Gaza. Of these, the most important and the most shocking is the Gaza Reconstruction Mechanism (GRM), which was brokered by the UN envoy Robert Serry, the Palestinian Authority, and the Government of Israel. The first priority of the GRM is to "Provide security assurances to the [Government of Israel]." Another key document concerning the plan, the Materials Monitoring Unit Project's (MMUP), Project Initiation Document, is available, but has not been widely distributed outside the donor community. The MMUP, led by UNSCO (United Nations Special Coordinator for the Middle East Peace Process), describes the mechanism for monitoring "approvals, entry, supply and use of dual use items in Gaza ... [More specifically] it essentially seeks to mobilize a multi-disciplined team located in Gaza that will monitor the supply chain of dual use items in efforts to ensure they are used for the purpose approved."

Both documents, which I have read in their entirety, do not include actual projects but detail the administrative and bureaucratic mechanisms for implementing projects. They read more like security plans, carefully laying out Israeli concerns and the ways in which the United Nations will accommodate them. They do not speak to the comprehensive recovery of the Gaza Strip.

The GRM and MMUP call for a cumbersome administrative and bureaucratic apparatus for project selection and implementation, monitoring and compliance that transfers risk to Palestinian beneficiaries and suppliers (who will be blamed and penalized for any implementation failure). Furthermore, Palestinian participants must provide a body of personal and business information—ID card numbers, address, family status, for example—that will be entered into a central IT database to which the Israeli government has access. The documents totally ignore the power asymmetries and security realities that unquestionably affect outcomes. In fact, what is being created is a permanent and complex permit and planning system, similar to the one Israel uses in Area C of the West Bank, which is under total Israeli control. Perhaps most important, Israel must approve all projects and their locations, and will be able to veto any aspect of the process on security grounds.

Furthermore, there is no mention of reviving Gaza's export trade or private-sector development (other than in relation to specific private-sector companies vetted by the Palestinian Authority and Israel for individually approved projects). Both these elements are essential for rehabilitating Gaza's moribund economy. Similarly, there is no reference to the free movement of people, another urgent need. There is no mechanism for accountability or transparency with regard to Israel. Nor will there be any mechanism for resolving disputes, which under the plan can only be decided through consensus: the occupier must agree with the occupied. In essence, the reconstruction plan as structured serves mainly to legitimize Israel's preferred security preferences.

As a colleague, an analyst in Jerusalem, succinctly put it, "Israel retains the power, the UN assumes the responsibility, and the Palestinians bear the risk."

Assuming, for the sake of argument, that the reconstruction plan is successfully implemented, its intended outcome is still completely unclear. Nothing in the documents explains what kind of economy is supposed to result, or what exactly is to be rebuilt. Is it what was lost in 2000, 2006, 2007, 2008–09, 2012, or 2014?

After all, reconstruction is not simply about buildings and public works: it's about securing a real future, and creating a sense of place, possibility and security. Life in Gaza cannot be rebuilt with cement and cash handouts. Without doubt, people desperately need assistance. But what is at issue are the terms on which that assistance will be provided, and what political ends it will serve. Gaza does not need just aid; it needs freedom and the right to interact normally with the world. Anything short of this is unsustainable.

Yet another point needs to be made here. In my decades of studying the political economy of the Occupied Territories, the international economic and development institutions involved have consistently embraced the same fundamental approach (which is repeated in the current reconstruction effort): restoring Gaza (and the West Bank) to a less compromised position of the past, rather than moving Gaza forward into the future. By this I mean returning Gaza to a relatively better—but still highly diminished—economic position it held historically, rather than catalyze a process of meaningful economic change that would propel Gaza (and the West Bank) forward to a new level of economic development. This approach, symptomatic of Gaza's—and Palestine's—marginalized status, is a repeated and dangerous failure of the donor community, which has consistently refused to challenge Israeli occupation policy, perniciously enabling the occupation and its most damaging effects.

The truth is that as long as humanitarian aid is used to address political problems, as long as it is intended to serve as a substitute for human rights, all "reconstruction" will mean for Gaza is continuing ruination.

10

Humanitarianism in Gaza:
What Not to Do*

The refugee crisis in Syria is now four years old. Gaza's is 67 years old. I was asked to speak about humanitarian action in Gaza as an example of what the international community should avoid in its approach to the Syrian humanitarian crisis. Despite the differences in the two situations, Gaza's experience with humanitarianism, broadly defined as the capacity to alleviate suffering and help those in need, may hold some vital lessons.

During my first research trip to Gaza, in 1985, and in one of my first interviews about the occupation with the late Dr. Hatem Abu Ghazaleh, he told me, "Nothing is more permanent than the temporary." The condition of Palestinians, especially in the Gaza Strip, where the majority are refugees, powerfully evokes Dr. Abu Ghazaleh's admonition.

Professor Ilana Feldman, who has written extensively on humanitarianism in Gaza, further observes, "Humanitarianism, most often pursued under UN auspices, could be said to be one of the most consistent aspects of Palestinian life since the displacement and dispossession of most of the population in the 1948 war."

A former student of mine, who worked for years in the humanitarian community in the West Bank and Gaza, similarly wrote in her exceptional master's thesis on the subject, "Despite the temporary nature of the humanitarian mandate, humanitarianism has progressed in parallel with the durability of the Israeli occupation of Gaza, creating a permanent aid infrastructure to meet the needs of the local population."

For purposes of this discussion, I argue that humanitarianism in Gaza has two principal dimensions that are vital to address, especially

---

* Originally published in "Journal Essay: The Syrian Humanitarian Crisis: What Is to Be Done?" *Middle East Policy*, Volume 22, Number 2, Summer 2015 (slightly edited).

in light of the Syrian crisis—the consistently profound and expanding need of the population, on the one hand, and the deliberate use of humanitarian aid to frustrate or achieve specific political ends, including the prolongation of conflict and suffering, on the other.

The situation in Gaza, as elsewhere in the world, speaks to a larger and extremely important debate in the field. Should humanitarian action, which can include a variety of interventions, confront the political causes of the crises it is there to address, or merely confine itself to the impact of those crises? Indeed, despite more than $25 billion of assistance given to Palestinians over the last two decades, they are no closer to their political goals than they were in 1948; arguably they are further from them. In this regard, there is no such thing as neutral aid, humanitarian or otherwise.

Now for a bit of historical context about the humanitarian imperative in Gaza. In the near three decades that I have been involved with Gaza and her people, I have never seen the kind of human, physical and economic destruction that I see in Gaza today. This has given rise to certain dynamics never before seen in that society. I am going to assume that everyone here has some knowledge of conditions in Gaza and I shall not describe them in any detail. But I will say this: at present, Gaza is characterized by unprecedented levels of unemployment and impoverishment, with a population that is largely, and according to some accounts almost entirely, aid-dependent. These are talented, resourceful and energetic people, able and desperate to work. But they are denied that right and forced instead to rely on handouts. What is happening to Gaza is catastrophic. It is also deliberate, considered and purposeful. The international community, particularly Western donor governments, has directly contributed to creating and maintaining this terrible situation.

According to a recently released report by the Association of International Development Agencies, despite pledges of $3.5 billion for Gaza's reconstruction after last summer's military assault, reconstruction has "barely begun," around 100,000 people are still homeless and not one of the 19,000 homes totally destroyed in the war has been rebuilt. The report further charges that there has been "no accountability to address violations of international law," what UNOCHA (United Nations Office for the Coordination of Humanitarian Affairs) in a separate report referred to as "a pervasive crisis of accountability,"

underscoring the total failure of the international community to challenge Israel's damaging closure on Gaza, which has long undermined
any form of economic activity, let alone economic recovery.

How did we arrive at this point? From the beginning of my work in
the territory, prior to the first Intifada, humanitarianism had a prominent place in Israeli policy. In the mid-1980s, I was there conducting
research for my doctoral dissertation. I spent a good deal of time
with Israeli government officials, all of whom made one point clear
almost immediately, some more explicitly than others: There would
be no economic development in the Palestinian territories. I was told
there were two reasons for this. The first, and relatively less important,
was the need to eliminate any source of competition with the Israeli
economy. The second and far more crucial reason was to preclude the
establishment, in any form, of a sovereign Palestinian state.

I have never forgotten what one highly placed official in the Ministry
of Defense told me almost thirty years ago. He said—I am paraphras-
ing—real economic development in the West Bank and Gaza could
produce a viable economic infrastructure that, in turn, could provide
the foundation for the establishment of a Palestinian state. This will
never be allowed to happen. Instead, I was told, Israel provides for
the social needs of the Palestinians—education, health and welfare—
and for a certain level of employment in unskilled and semi-skilled
jobs inside Israel and in their own under-developed economy. Hence,
humanitarianism was couched in the language of social services, an
improved standard of living and benign occupation, whose aim was
explicitly political and directed to extinguishing any and all Palestinian political claims.

The struggle between political claims and humanitarian needs
assumed a somewhat different form with the first Palestinian uprising,
when people struggled to end the occupation, insisting that their
problem was primarily political rather than humanitarian. Israel ultimately extinguished the uprising through massive economic pressure
and restriction, a top priority for the Israeli economy at that time,
imposing a long-term closure for the first time in 1991, a closure now
in its 24th year.

With the 1993 Oslo peace process and the expectation of a brokered
settlement to the conflict, the role of the donor community increased
dramatically, as did the level of assistance to the Palestinian popula-

tion. The Oslo process enabled Israel to claim that it was mitigating, if not ending, the occupation, when in fact it was doing the exact opposite: deepening its control of the territories through a variety of policies, including the growing isolation of Gaza from the West Bank and Israel, the territorial fragmentation of the West Bank and the large-scale expropriation of Arab land and other resources, largely for the building and expansion of Israeli settlements, all of which were meant to ensure Israel's continued presence and control.

But now Israel was pursuing its political agenda with the tacit if not explicit support of key donor countries, which in effect were, intentionally or not, providing cover for, if not actively facilitating, this agenda. To the contrary, the political and economic illusions created by Oslo and the Oslo negotiation framework and supported by a compliant Palestinian Authority and donor community, led to a range of economic programs and initiatives promoting economic peace under occupation. Economic peace argues that economic change, however defined, must precede political change, creating a context conducive to future political compromise.

In effect, this policy sees any form of economic improvement, no matter how insubstantial and meaningless, as a substitute for a just political resolution, in this case for ending occupation and the dispossession and denial that accompanies it. This approach, which still obtains, is fundamentally no different from Israeli policies in the early years of occupation, which similarly aimed to extinguish Palestinian political demands through limited economic gains, under an occupation that continued to extract resources and negate Palestinian rights.

Over the last 15 years, conditions for Palestinians have eroded dramatically and humanitarianism has assumed a dominant and defining place in Israel's relationship with Gaza. Key events include the second Palestinian uprising in 2000 and its militarization, Israel's disengagement from Gaza in 2005 and the accompanying argument that it no longer occupies Gaza, the election of Hamas in 2006 and its takeover of Gaza in 2007, and three massive assaults on Gaza in the last six years.

While a detailed analysis of the changing relationship between Israel and Gaza is beyond the scope of this talk, I would like to highlight certain points that have had a profound impact on humanitarian action in the territory. A critical feature of the last 15 years is that

Gaza's status as an occupied territory has ceased to be a matter of international concern, the focus of attention having shifted after Hamas's 2006 election and 2007 takeover to Gaza's enforced isolation, containment and punishment. Israel's recasting of its relationship with Gaza from one between occupier and occupied to one between warring parties has facilitated Israeli attacks on Gaza, rendering as illegitimate any notion of freedom or democracy for Palestinians.

A key part of this transformation has been the imposition by Israel of an intensified closure, more commonly referred to as a blockade, which has devastated Gaza's economy and produced a man-made humanitarian crisis. The Israeli government has referred to the blockade as a form of economic warfare. According to the Israeli NGO GISHA, "Damaging the enemy's economy is, in and of itself, a legitimate means in warfare and a relevant consideration, even while deciding to allow the entry of relief consignments."

Such measures are intentionally designed to undermine and deplete Gaza's economy and productive capacity as part of Israel's policy to bring down the Hamas regime and punish Gazans for supporting Hamas, and to promote the Palestinian Authority in the West Bank. In this regard, not only have major donors participated in the draconian sanction regime imposed on Gaza; they have privileged the West Bank over Gaza in their programmatic work. Consequently, donors have reinforced the division of Palestinians into two distinct and isolated entities, offering economic peace to one side and impoverishment to the other.

The recasting of Israel's relationship with Gaza from occupied territory to entity governed by the rules of war has consequences in terms of Israeli policies towards the Palestinian economy and the role of humanitarian action. Whereas prior to the first Intifada, Israel sought to control and dominate the Palestinian economy, shaping it to serve its own interests, current policy attacks Gaza's economic structure with the aim of permanently disabling it. In the process, it transforms the population from a people with national, political and economic rights into a humanitarian problem, charity cases in need of relief, which is a more extreme version of humanitarianism as it was understood during the first two decades of occupation.

A senior official at GISHA captured the essence of Israel's approach to Gaza: "In the rest of the world, we try to bring people up to the humanitarian standard. Gaza is the only place where we are trying to push them down, to keep them at the lowest possible indicators." In this way, Israel creates and uses a humanitarian problem to manage a political one. Given the policy of economic warfare against Gaza, it is but a short step from the goal of isolation and disablement to that of abstraction and deletion.

Within this construct, where Israel, with the support of the US, the EU and Egypt, especially, creates and maintains a continuous humanitarian problem, Palestinians are not only reduced to a humanitarian issue, a demographic presence in an impoverished enclave deprived of their economic and political rights and dependent on the goodwill of the international community for food, shelter and other services; they are rendered disposable and irrelevant, making no difference except as charity cases and terrorists.

Consequently, as Ilana Feldman makes clear, because Gaza's humanitarian space is restricted to military actors, recipients and humanitarian workers: "It is not only Gaza as a space, but Gazans as a people that can be further isolated by the humanitarian frame." My former student writes, "What happens when humanitarian actors who are meant to work under short-term circumstances that are immediate and life-threatening, are intentionally stripped of political agency and made to work in a highly politicized and restrictive environment that is long-term in nature and that perpetuates the conditions that create and maintain the ruin?" This is a question that aid providers must consider with regard to the Syrian humanitarian crisis.

Hence, argues my student, Gaza and the humanitarian community currently must confront a very distorted reality, whose principal features include:

- the depoliticization of Gaza and its transformation into a humanitarian problem under conditions of continued belligerent occupation;
- the derogation by the occupier of its responsibilities to the international community, where humanitarian actors are used as a political tool, and
- the implementation of policies by the occupier, notably the blockade, and restrictions on access that severely restrict the humanitarian community from fully carrying out its work, often

forcing it to do what is possible rather than what is needed. Gaza's humanitarian crisis is a result of occupation, and any discussion of humanitarian aid must confront and engage this political fact directly.

Now I would like to turn briefly to some recommendations based on the Gazan experience. A colleague and friend with thirty years of experience working as a humanitarian and development actor in different parts of the world, including a considerable amount of time in Gaza, recently wrote me the following: "In Gaza, it's difficult to escape the profound mismatch between the tools of humanitarian aid—temporary, minimalist, needs-based—and the demands of the situation, which are political, enduring, aspirational and economic. Humanitarianism is not the appropriate response to a nation in man-made limbo."

Gaza's long experience with humanitarianism holds some lessons for Syria's humanitarian crisis. Here, I draw on the work of former students and other humanitarian actors I have known. First, if the separation of the humanitarian and political realms is necessary in the short term, it is dysfunctional and harmful in the long term. Quoting a colleague:

> Gaza's chronic humanitarian need is very real, but has been artificially created and intentionally maintained. Over time, a complex humanitarian infrastructure has developed to respond to these needs and by its continued presence helps sustain them. The humanitarian community remains, while the political community is largely obstructive and complicit in maintaining these damaging conditions, opting for a policy of managing conflict through containment and impoverishment, rather than resolving conflict through political action.

Without a political resolution, this approach is as unsustainable as it is volatile.

Second, assistance, and those actors responsible for delivering it, cannot replace a political solution but must engage it. Professor Larissa Fast, a scholar of conflict resolution who has focused on aid and humanitarianism, states that in an ideal situation, humanitarian aid would not need to address root causes of conflict, since other parties would have the will and the capacities to do so, trying to address the problem politically while humanitarians address the suffering. But in Gaza, this is not the case. Hence, donor agencies need to hold Israel and their own host governments accountable for the very real and high cost of occupation. The humanitarian community should insist that donor agencies engage politically. Third, while humanitarian action cannot substitute for political intervention or compensate for the absence of a political process, it should not allow itself to become instrumentalized or weaponized by that process.

Now I would like to turn very briefly to a few recommendations that speak to more programmatic concerns of a long-term crisis that exceed the provision of immediate relief. First, in Gaza's case, the separation of the political and humanitarian spheres has produced considerable internal confusion, with little protest of the restrictions to which humanitarians are subject. As constraints on movement and service delivery increase, the humanitarian community often accedes, for fear of losing access and funding, rather than contests.

Thus, it is imperative that humanitarian actors act as a coordinated collective, with a common, clearly articulated understanding of its objectives, purpose and resources, insisting on and publicizing needed reforms without fear of retribution. In Gaza, for example, say my informants, the humanitarian community should maintain a collective position toward Israel and lobby strongly on issues like the free movement of humanitarian personnel, especially local staff wishing to enter and exit Gaza, on obtaining permits for local and international staff, on lifting access restrictions and lifting restrictions on contact with the Hamas authorities.

Second, humanitarian actors must serve as a source of information for donor agencies and donor governments concerning day-to-day conditions and the damaging impact of the policies donors are supporting. Third, Ilana Feldman has powerfully argued that "degraded expectations are part of a process and practice of isolating Gaza." Humanitarian action, therefore, must focus on empowering, not disempowering people, as has happened in Gaza, addressing and strengthening human agency before it is diminished. In this regard, it is essential to acknowledge the refugees' role in decision making, engaging people and their political representatives as agents in their own betterment and in shaping a reality where they can imagine a future for themselves and their children.

Fourth, in Gaza's highly restricted environment, humanitarian actors will seek projects for which they can obtain approval, which can include a range of contributions, from food and shelter, teacher training and mental-health rehabilitation, to certain kinds of economic activity, such as infrastructural works, water desalination and sewage-treatment projects. Whether by design or default, and despite the importance of the services provided, humanitarian action over the long term runs the risk of further weakening, if not supplanting, an already diminished local economy, effectively acting as a vital if not principal source of economic activity. It is essential, therefore, that humanitarian action, to the degree possible, becomes integrated with, not a replacement for, the local economies in which they work.

In conclusion, what is a humanitarian actor to do when donors use aid in lieu of political solutions, a looming possibility in the Syrian case? My colleague responds:

> In Gaza, we are beyond this. Now relief is the politics of choice. At present, it is very difficult to find any development funds for Gaza. Unlike the past, donors won't invest because they don't want their assets bombed. While this is understandable, the net result is that Gaza is condemned to relief, not progress. There is no investment in civil society or in imagining alternatives or futures.

Will Syria's displaced be similarly condemned to this approach, to relief instead of progress? Again, quoting my colleague, "When that happens," she says, "and when the relief is massively inadequate, as it is in Gaza today, then at some point one has to ask whether it is ethical for an actor to agree to be used to keep this tatty, threadbare lid on the place. Is it ethical to consent to implement the fairness of such scarcity?"

In the world of aid, there have been certain milestones of change. At one point, my friend says:

> We believed the recipients of humanitarian aid should be innocent. We acknowledged the distorting potential of aid in a place of scarcity and we decided that aid should do no harm, a thoroughly

different ethical standard from the one we see today. We evaluated impacts other than need. Then we began to proactively wield the power of the commodity of aid.

We came away with categories of the deserving and less-deserving displaced, and I feel as though humanitarianism has increasingly become the management of troublesome populations at the edge of perpetual conflicts. It seems to me that with Palestinians, we've reached a policy of not solving, a policy of agreeing not to envision solutions. This does not feel like an oversight; it seems like a choice. The management of inconvenient populations with no vision of anything but further management, no vision even of reconstructing the homes lost last summer.

The question I leave you with is this: will Syria's displaced be the next iteration of this truly unacceptable choice?

11

The Gaza Strip's Last Safety Net is in Danger*

The UN's refugee agency is one of the few forces standing between the people of Gaza and humanitarian catastrophe.

Not long ago, I had a conversation with an official I know from the United Nations Relief and Works Agency for Palestine Refugees in the Near East (UNRWA). The official told me about a conversation he had with a senior Israel Defense Forces officer. In that conversation, my UN colleague asked the IDF official to describe Israel's policy toward Gaza. The answer was just seven words long: "No development, no prosperity, no humanitarian crisis," by now a common refrain within Israel's military and political establishment.

This approach has been especially ruinous for Gaza over the last decade, during which Israel imposed a strangling blockade, and launched three major military assaults on Gaza since the end of 2008—the latest and largest of them last summer (Operation Protective Edge)—leveling neighborhoods, destroying infrastructure and inflicting immeasurable damage on the tiny Strip and its nearly 2 million inhabitants.

Tragically, what was once a functioning economy has become a land on the verge of economic and humanitarian collapse. According to a May 2015 World Bank report, the unemployment rate in Gaza stands at 43 percent (over 60 percent of Gaza's youth are unemployed), the highest in the world. Over 90 percent of Gaza's water supply is unfit for human consumption. Electricity is, at most, available only six hours a day, and Gaza's infrastructure has been partly destroyed. No development, no prosperity, indeed.

---

*   Originally published in *The Nation*, August 6, 2015 (slightly edited).

And now, beneath this unrelieved disaster lies another potential one, which threatens to further destabilize Gaza's already deepening instability: the decline in funding for UNRWA, the same relief agency for which my UN colleague works and one of the few forces standing between the people of Gaza and unmitigated humanitarian suffering. The situation has become so dire that, in June, the Commissioner General of UNRWA, Pierre Krähenbühl, warned that the agency might have to stop its operations within three months.

UNRWA is now in its 65th year. Established in 1949 by the UN General Assembly following the 1948 Arab–Israeli conflict, UNRWA began operations on May 1, 1950, with a mandate to provide direct relief and public works programs to Palestinians who fled or were forced from their homes. That it continues to exist more than six decades since its inception is a stark illustration of the political failure to find a just solution for the Palestinian refugees. With a staff of around 30,000 (approximately 42 percent of whom work in Gaza), UNRWA provides protection and assistance to 5.2 million Palestinian refugees throughout the Middle East—specifically, in Syria, Jordan, Lebanon, the West Bank and the Gaza Strip. Its brief includes providing healthcare, education, social services, emergency aid and infrastructure support. And it does all of this with an annual budget of $1.4 billion.

In Gaza alone, UNRWA serves 1.28 million refugees, 25 percent of the regional total. As such, and in the words of UN Secretary-General Ban Ki-moon, "At a time of turmoil in the region, UNRWA remains a vital stabilizing factor." In Gaza, it is quite fair to say that UNRWA is the *only* source of stability and constancy in an otherwise deteriorating environment. In fact, one-seventh of Gaza's economy, or approximately 14 percent of Gaza's GDP, can be traced to UNRWA, sources within the organization told me.

Yet UNRWA faces a severe financial crisis that threatens to curtail (and possibly end) its work throughout the entire region. Currently, UNRWA has a deficit of over $100 million in its General Fund, which pays for its core services such as education and health. UNRWA officials further indicated a deficit of around $230 million in its Emergency Appeal for the Occupied Palestinian Territories, 88 percent of which is for Gaza, and approximately $280 million in its Syria Appeal, both of which provide immediate cash and food aid to people in acute need. Just last week, the agency met in Jordan for an "extraordinary session" to discuss potential responses to the crisis.

In order to reduce costs, UNRWA has had to implement a number of unwelcome initiatives. It suspended its cash subsidy program, which affected 20,000 families in Gaza prior to Operation Protective Edge. In Lebanon, UNRWA will soon suspend its cash-for-rent assistance to Palestinian refugees from Syria. There are also plans to increase the size of UNRWA classrooms from 45 to 50 children and freeze the hiring of teachers and other employees. Furthermore, UNRWA may have to make the tough decision to delay the opening of its 700 schools at the start of the next academic year, which will affect around 500,000 children, half of whom are in the Gaza Strip. So at a time when Daesh and other extremist groups are recruiting, half a million children who should be in UN schools might be on the streets of the Middle East.

Furthermore, according to a senior UNRWA official, if the agency is unable to bridge its deficit by October, it will no longer be able to pay staff salaries, which will be catastrophic. In Gaza alone, where the average household size stood at 6.1 people per family in 2012, as many as 76,250 people could be left without any source of income. What then? Recently, Palestinians in Gaza and Jordan protesting UNRWA cuts threatened the agency with violence, claiming that its programmatic decisions are part of a conspiracy to eliminate the refugee issue. This is one expression of the turmoil and upheaval that will accompany further reductions in UNRWA's core services.

The problem of chronic underfunding is not new to UNRWA. At its base, it reflects larger political attitudes toward Palestinians, which view them as marginal and unwanted. But in its current incarnation, it derives from several harmful factors. First, while many major donors continue to fund UNRWA and have even increased their contributions, the needs of the agency have risen far more dramatically, given the political exigencies in the region, high population growth rates and escalating costs. Thus, the gap between the need for protection and what UNRWA can actually deliver has become extreme. The need for major donor countries to increase their contributions beyond what they have already committed is absolutely critical.

In the context of these severe restrictions on UNRWA's finances, an issue with one donor—Canada—deserves special scrutiny. Canada's decision to first reduce and then terminate funding to the agency, a decision no other major donor government has taken, has been extremely injurious to the agency.

In 2007 and 2008, Canada donated over $28 million to UNRWA each year. In both years, over half the monies were directed to the General Fund, with most of the remainder directed to the Emergency Appeal. In 2009, the Canadian government reduced its contribution by almost $10 million to just under $19 million, most of which was allocated for the Emergency Appeal with nothing for the General Fund. In fact, no monies have been allocated to the General Fund since 2009.

In 2010, Canada's contribution decreased again to around $15 million, where it remained for two more years with most, and subsequently all, of the funds for the Emergency Appeal. Beginning in 2013, Canada, apparently without any prior warning, terminated all funding to UNRWA.

The loss of $28 million from Canada constitutes the largest single loss to the agency, which it cannot replace, and has been "desperately damaging" in the words of one UNRWA official, contributing substantially to UNRWA's current deficit in the General Fund. What is most outrageous, however, is Canada's decision to terminate its $15 million contribution to the Emergency Appeal; in so doing, the Canadian government is refusing to provide food for impoverished Palestinians, the majority in Gaza.

A third factor hurting UNRWA's finances is the decline of the euro. Since most of UNRWA's contributions are donated in euros, the currency devaluation has resulted in a loss of $20–25 million over the last year. Additionally, in 2014, UNRWA spent $7.5 million just to bring materials into Gaza, a direct result of Israel's draconian packaging and import regime. These same monies could be used to build four schools for Gazan children, which is vital given that UNRWA needs to build seven schools per year in Gaza just to keep pace with the increased school-age population.

The crisis facing UNRWA also reflects a wider global problem, in which burgeoning need now exceeds existing resources. Not since World War II has the number of people exiled from their homes been so high, with nearly 60 million people who are refugees, internally displaced, or seeking asylum—one in every 122 people in the world. Yet the lack of resources is just one part of the crisis facing the humanitarian system; the inability to resolve political conflicts is the other. Furthermore, in the absence of political solutions, humanitarian aid has often become instrumentalized—that is, used to manage and manipulate political problems—as it has in Israel's relationship with Gaza.

In Gaza, dependence, debility and dread have become the occupier's politics of choice. Development, however constrained and limited, no longer has any role. The reasons are many, including the fact that donors do not want to see their projects destroyed in future conflicts. But the net result is that Gaza is condemned to relief, not progress, which is exactly what Israeli policy seeks, as stated so clearly by the IDF officer quoted at the outset.

Still, if relief is not an adequate response, it is nonetheless a necessary one, and a further reduction of UNRWA services (let alone their suspension or termination) will only deepen the sense of despair and abandonment already so powerful among Palestinian refugees wherever they reside. The political consequences of watching one's children go hungry are clear. Who among us would endure such pain in silence?

PART IV   UNDOING ATTACHMENT:
CREATING SPACES OF EXCESS

Not under foreign skies
Nor under foreign wings protected—
I shared all this with my own people
There, where misfortune had abandoned us.
[1961]

Instead of a Preface

During the frightening years of the Yezhov terror, I
spent seventeen months waiting in prison queues in
Leningrad. One day, somehow, someone "picked me out".
On that occasion there was a woman standing behind me,
her lips blue with cold, who, of course, had never in
her life heard my name. Jolted out of the torpor
characteristic of all of us, she said into my ear
(everyone whispered there)—"Could one ever describe
this?" And I answered—"I can." It was then that
something like a smile slid across what had previously
been just a face.
[The 1st of April in the year 1957. Leningrad]

VII
The Verdict

The word landed with a stony thud
Onto my still-beating breast.
Nevermind, I was prepared,
I will manage with the rest.

I have a lot of work to do today;
I need to slaughter memory,
Turn my living soul to stone
Then teach myself to live again ...

But how. The hot summer rustles
Like a carnival outside my window;
I have long had this premonition
Of a bright day and a deserted house.
[22 June 1939. Summer. Fontannyi Dom (4)]

Anna Akhmatova
Requiem

12

Yes, They Are Refugees*

The recent decision by the Trump administration to drastically cut its contribution to the United Nations Relief and Works Agency (UNRWA) has left the Palestinian refugees in a more precarious position than ever. A conference was recently held in Rome to raise money to allow UNRWA to continue its vital work providing education, health and other social services to more than 5 million Palestinian refugees in Jordan, Lebanon, Syria, the West Bank and Gaza. Given a projected budget deficit of nearly $500 million in 2018, UNRWA's funding prospects look dim.

I have examined elsewhere the importance of UNRWA's work and what might happen should its services be reduced or terminated. Here I would like briefly to address a criticism often leveled at UNRWA, that it somehow perpetuates the Palestinian refugee crisis by continuing to register as refugees descendants of the people who in 1948 were forced out of or fled what is now Israel. As Daniel Pipes, the president of the Middle East Forum, put it in January:

> I suggest that withholding funds is not the right tactic. Better would be to focus on the "Palestine refugee" status. Denying this to all but those who meet the US government's normal definition of a refugee (in this case, being at least 69 years old, stateless, and living outside the West Bank or Gaza), diminishes the irredentist dagger at Israel's throat by over 99 percent ... I propose that the president adjust US policy to ... send aid to Palestinians while making it contingent upon the overwhelmingly majority of recipients formally acknowledging that they are not now and have never been refugees.

The issue of the Palestinian refugees has plagued Israel since its establishment and was a key obstacle during the Oslo negotiations more

---

* Originally published in the *London Review of Books Blog*, March 22, 2018.

than twenty years ago. The refugees do represent a threat to Israel, though not the "irredentist dagger" that Pipes claims. Rather, the refugees stand as a living and constant reminder of the historic injustice done to Palestinians when the Jewish state was founded. Denying refugee status to future generations of Palestinians is simply a way to erase the refugee issue and, with it, the rights to which refugees are legally and morally entitled.

By what right do others—be they Israeli, American, or European— determine the status of Palestinian refugees, or how an entire national group should identify itself, especially in a world in which Palestinians' political and legal status remains largely unresolved? Would we cede our own right of self-identification to others on our behalf?

My mother and father survived Auschwitz and I grew up as a child of survivors, with the Holocaust a defining feature of my life. My children, too, are informed and shaped by their family history and the realities that inhabit that history—realities of racism, fascism, ethnocentricity and nationalism. My parents are no longer alive, yet my identity as a child of survivors remains a vital part of who I am. Would anyone claim that my children and I have no right to identify ourselves as the descendants of Holocaust survivors because those survivors have died? This would be unacceptable—in fact, unthinkable—morally, ethically and emotionally. Does anyone have a right to dictate to me my status in this regard? Without equating the losses of 1948 with the Holocaust, I would ask why Pipes and others consider it acceptable to deny Palestinians the right to self-identify as refugees because their parents, grandparents, or great-grandparents have died. This is not only a matter of politics; it is a matter of principle and basic human decency, especially in the absence of a resolution to their actual plight as refugees.

The struggle over the refugee question also speaks deafeningly to the abject failure of the international community to resolve the problem in a manner that is fair to all people, and it will remain alive until a viable answer is found. Waving a wand and pronouncing "You are no longer refugees" cannot eradicate the moral, legal and practical problems of Palestinian refugees. To believe that it can belies a fundamental misunderstanding of the lived realities of millions of disenfranchised people—and the depth of their commitment to seeing justice done. UNRWA does not perpetuate the Palestinian refugee problem. The failure of Israel and the international community to acknowledge and address the issue is what perpetuates it. The refugees and all that they stand for must also be understood as a refusal on the part of Palestinians to be silenced now and in the future.

13

Floating in an Inch of Water:
A Letter from Gaza*

Gaza has always been easy to understand and impossible to understand, painfully transparent and frustratingly opaque, full of contradictions—all of them true. This time was no different, except perhaps in one critical respect: translation seemed much more arduous. Words commonly used to describe (and reduce) Gaza, such as "impoverished," "violent" and "resilient" (the last a word I have come to dislike)—while always lacking and deficient, now felt hollow and irrelevant, even specious. This time, my encounter with Gaza demanded much more—something I felt the moment I entered the territory.

My previous visit to Gaza was in May 2014, just before Israel's brutal assault (known as Operation Protective Edge—OPE) that began a few weeks after I left. The changes I saw in the near two-and-a-half-year period between visits were dramatic. The most stunning weren't physical, as I had expected, but societal. Two things struck me: the truly damaging and frightening impact of Gaza's decade-long separation and isolation from the rest of the world, and the sense that an increasing number of people simply cannot take much more and are reaching the limit of what they can endure.

So much has been written about Gaza—her economic decline and political dysfunction and the unending predictions of another imminent war. "Why even talk about Gaza?" a friend asked rhetorically. But that, of course, is not the right question because the answer is obvious. The far more relevant and difficult question—especially now—is: "*How* is one to talk about Gaza?" What follows is my attempt at an answer.

---

* Originally published in Jamie Stern-Weiner (ed.), *Moment of Truth: Tackling Israel-Palestine's Toughest Questions,* New York: OR Books, 2018 (slightly edited).

"WE ARE PEOPLE WHO CAN FLOAT IN AN INCH OF WATER"

Gaza is in a state of humanitarian shock, due primarily to Israel's intensified closure or blockade, now entering its eleventh year, and disgracefully supported by the US, the EU and Egypt. The blockade has created severe hardship. It has ruined Gaza's economy, largely by ending the normal trade relations upon which Gaza's tiny economy depends. The impact has been devastating. Gaza, historically a place of trade and commerce, has relatively little production left, largely reduced to one common denominator: consumption. Although an easing of Israeli restrictions throughout 2016 and early 2017 led to a relatively moderate increase in largely agricultural exports to the West Bank and Israel—long Gaza's principal markets—the level of exports is minimal and not nearly enough to catalyze Gaza's weakened productive sectors, which have all but collapsed under Israeli's continuing blockade and three destructive assaults in six years.

Gaza's debility, deliberately and consciously planned and successfully executed, has left almost half the labor force without any means to earn a living. Unemployment—especially youth unemployment—is *the* defining feature of life. Everyone is consumed by finding a job or some means of earning money. "Salaries control people's minds," said one colleague.

In fact, one of the greatest sources of political tension between the Hamas government in Gaza and the Palestinian Authority (PA) in Ramallah (West Bank) concerns the continued refusal of President Abbas to pay the salaries of people working in the Hamas government. I was consistently told that if Abbas wanted to win the support of Gaza's people all he would have to do is pay the salaries of government employees (loyalty is given to the employer). Because Abbas is unwilling to do so, claiming in part that such salaries would be funneled to Hamas's military wing, he bears a great deal of responsibility for Gaza's suffering.

Abbas's refusal is all the more galling because he has been paying full salaries—ranging from an average of $500–1,000 monthly, a huge sum in Gaza today—to at least 55,000 civil servants in Gaza who worked for the PA before Hamas took control of the territory. These people are being paid *not* to work for the Hamas government (although they support over 300,000 people) because of the intense hostility between the PA and Hamas authorities. This costs the PA $45–60 million every month, monies that are largely financed by Saudi Arabia, the EU, and the US.[1] Paying people not to work has institutionalized yet another distortion within Gaza's deeply impaired economy.

However, in April 2017 Abbas cut these salaries by 30 percent overall, meaning far less money in circulation in Gaza every month. On an individual level, some people report cuts ranging from 42 to 70 percent, according to a colleague, Brian Barber, working in Gaza. He writes, "Abbas's salary cuts have come like an earthquake, leaving frightening anxiety over how [people] can manage and with a sense of deeply insulting betrayal."[2] In July 2017, furthermore, Abbas deepened Gaza's crisis by dismissing 6,145 employees working in health, education and other public sectors. This measure, like the salary cuts that preceded it, is intended to exert pressure on Hamas to relinquish control of the Strip.

Personal need is everywhere. But what is new in my long experience in Gaza is the sense of desperation, which can be felt in the different ways people behave and respond and the boundaries they are willing to cross that once were inviolate. Such behavior is not hidden but in full view, an emerging feature of daily life. In one painful example, a well-appointed woman, her face fully covered by a *niqab*, came to the Marna House Hotel where I was staying, to beg. When politely asked to leave by the hotel staff, she aggressively refused and insisted on staying, raising her voice in anger, obliging the hotel staff to forcefully escort her off the property. She clearly was not asking to stay and beg but demanding to do so. I had never seen this before in Gaza.

In another instance, also at the Marna House, I was sitting with a colleague in the hotel restaurant when a boy, a teenager, with acne on his face, came to our table quietly pleading for money for his family. By the time I reached for my wallet, the wait staff had approached and gently ushered him out of the restaurant. He did not resist. (He was so gentle and fragile in contrast to the woman in the *niqab*.) This young boy was well dressed and educated and I kept thinking he should have been home studying for an exam or out with his friends by the sea.

Instead he was begging and humiliated, asked to leave the hotel and never return.

Perhaps the most alarming indicator of people's desperation is the growth of prostitution in Gaza's traditional and conservative society. Although prostitution has always been present to varying (but very limited) degrees in Gaza, it was always considered immoral and shameful, carrying immense social consequences for the woman and her family. This appears to be changing as individual and family resources dissolve. A colleague who is a well-known and highly respected professional in Gaza told me that women, many of them well dressed, have come to his office soliciting him and "not for a lot of money." (He also told me that because of the rise of prostitution, it has become harder for girls to get married because "no one knows who is pure." Families also plead with him to provide a "safe and decent space" for their daughters by employing them in his office.)

Another friend told me how, while sitting in a restaurant, he witnessed a young woman trying to solicit a man with her parents present at a nearby table. When I asked him how he explained such incomprehensible behavior he said, "People living in a normal environment behave in normal ways; people living in an abnormal environment do not."

And Gaza's environment is abnormal by many measures. "People have no money," said a close friend. "They roll tobacco because they cannot afford a pack of cigarettes. Others do not have one shekel to give their teenage children so they wander aimlessly in the streets." At least 1.3 million out of 1.9 million people, or 70 percent of the total population (other estimates are higher), receive international humanitarian assistance, the bulk of which is food (sugar, rice, oil and milk), without which the majority could not meet their basic needs. By August 2016, 11,850 families or approximately 72,000 people remained internally displaced (from 500,000 at the height of the 2014 hostilities), of whom 7,500 families or about 46,000 people were in urgent need of temporary shelter and cash assistance.[3]

Gaza's abnormal environment is now characterized by other painful dynamics. I have written elsewhere about rising suicide rates in Gaza from hanging, immolation, jumping from heights, drug overdose, ingestion of pesticides, and firearms.[4] Gaza's divorce rate, historically low at 2 percent, now approaches 40 percent according to the UN and local healthcare professionals. "There are 2,000 domestic disputes a month in Shati camp," said one UNRWA official, "and the police cannot cope. The courts alone receive hundreds of complaints every month. The Hamas government cannot deal with the number of problems." One must also remember that almost three-quarters (72.5 percent) of Gaza's approximately 2 million people are 29 years old and younger and remain confined to Gaza, prohibited from leaving the territory; most never have.[5]

Amid such disempowerment, young people have increasingly turned toward militancy as a livelihood, joining different militant and extremist organizations simply to secure a paying job. Person after person argued that growing support for extremist factions in Gaza does not emanate from political or ideological belief as these factions might claim, but from the need to feed their families. Joining an ISIS-affiliated group is now an income-earning activity for many, perhaps most, of its recruits. (This is likely one reason why Hamas is desperate to secure enough funds to keep paying the salaries of its military wing, the al-Qassam Brigades, which is reportedly seeing an increase in its ranks as well.) It seems that young unemployed men in Gaza increasingly face two options—possible *life* if they join a military faction, or possible *death* if they do not.

One colleague, himself a religious Muslim, argued, "If the Israelis were smart, they would open two or three industrial zones, do a security check and find the most wanted among us and employ them. Al-Qassam would evaporate very quickly and everyone would be more secure. There is a difference between what is said in the mosques and what people would settle for. I tell you the mosques would be empty." I repeatedly heard about former al-Qassam fighters who left the organization when they obtained new homes in one of Gaza's housing projects, not wanting to risk the security of their home as a possible Israeli target.

In a similar vein, a local businessman told me "What we need is Israeli factories and Palestinian hands. One sack of cement employs 35 people in Gaza; with one worker in Israel you have seven people in Gaza praying for Israel's security. Imagine a 'Made in Gaza' brand. We could market regionally and it would sell like hotcakes. Gaza would benefit and so would Israel. All we want are open borders for export."

TO BE RICH IN GAZA

Amid Gaza's misery and impoverishment lies a striking contrast, an inconsistency as it were: Gaza's privileged. This sector is tiny—the number I kept hearing was 50,000—but highly visible. For some, their wealth derives from the now almost-defunct tunnel trade, which once kept Gaza's economy functioning, even thriving, albeit artificially, under Israel's damaging closure. The existence of this miniscule sector of affluence is sometimes used to argue that conditions in Gaza are much better than portrayed.

The privileged, historically vital to local production, are consumers of goods since relatively little is produced in Gaza right now. They fill Gaza's hotels, shopping malls and restaurants that have grown in response to their demand. I call it the "Gaza bubble"; others have called it "a welcome sign of normalcy."[6] One human rights worker told me that the fastest growing business in Gaza City today is restaurants because they are one of the few profitable activities left in Gaza.

The pervasive consumerism that characterizes the prosperous in Gaza is certainly not specific to Gaza, nor is the great disparity in class and scale. Of course, people should not be denied the right to consume whatever they want. Yet like the vast majority of Gazans, the affluent are also confined and beleaguered, enraged and demeaned by their inability to live freely and with any real semblance of predictability. One of Gaza's richest and most successful businessmen spent an evening with me pouring out his frustration and describing in painstaking detail the restrictions imposed on his business by Israel, which used to be an essential market: "The Israelis are destroying my business, my ability to work and why? They squeeze, squeeze, squeeze and towards what end? Where will this bring all of us?"

Others were present at this evening gathering—all of them members of Gaza's social and economic elite—and no one could see a way out. The evening alternated between exasperation and silence … always ending in irresolution. Yet my friends' disgrace, and fundamentally that is what it is, does not derive from any sense of defeat but from the knowledge that no amount of reason, law, or morality has had or will have any impact on their situation. To the contrary, appeals based on fairness, principle, or rationality have only brought them more destruction.

The moneyed may live well but they cannot buy their freedom. This is what binds them to the rest of Gaza; yet, despite their shared fate, many seem to avoid any common ground with those outside their class, something, again, not peculiar to Gaza. But while the difference between privilege and poverty is very visible in Gaza, it is also very proximate. Sometimes the distance between the two can literally be measured in yards. One evening, a Swedish friend who I happened to run into invited me to dinner at one of Gaza's best restaurants. The place was packed with families and tables of well-dressed teenagers playing with their iPads and iPhones. How many of them, if any, had ever been inside al-Shati refugee camp, literally a short walk from the restaurant? I know that some, perhaps most, never have.

Those who are considered privileged in Gaza are not necessarily people with a great deal of money. They are people with a source of income—until April 2017, those salaried employees paid not to work by the PA, people working for UNRWA, international NGOs, local public and private-sector institutions, and those (not many) who are successfully self-employed, usually merchants. There are those who do what they can to help others, but amid the despair that now permeates Gaza, charity is no longer a simple, unencumbered act of giving. It is burdened with a set of expectations and demands that can never be satisfied. A dear friend from a prominent Gaza family described his dilemma:

> After paying my taxes to Hamas, new fees springing up all the time, household expenses, food and helping friends, I am depleting my personal funds. Soon I will have to sell some assets just to pay my bills. Yes, I am much better off than most people here and I do what I can to help others but where does it stop? The tragedy of this situation is that friends look at you as a source of money. And friendships end when you can no longer provide that money. Think of what it takes to make people behave in this way. No one seems to be considering the pressure it takes to change one's core values. This is what we have been reduced to. This was never Gaza.

The question never truly considered, let alone answered, by Israel (beyond the propaganda) is, why is Gaza being punished in so heartless a manner? What does Israel truly hope to gain by its cruelty, and where is this awful, senseless policy headed? If one thinks about it crudely, Israel has exhausted all of the ways it can pressure people in Gaza. When Gazans worked in Israel, Israel had leverage; it would seal the borders and extract whatever concessions it sought.[7] Now, Israel can no longer do that in much the same way because people have adapted. They suffer but they have adapted. They even find happiness at times. All Israel can really do is menace Gaza as it long has, a policy that emanates not from any logic or examination but, as former Israeli Prime Minister Ehud Barak once explained, from "inertia." Inexplicably—or not—Israel's "security cabinet has not held a single meeting on Israeli policy concerning Gaza for at least the last four years."[8] At what point does menacing stop working as a form of coercion or as a way to achieve capitulation (to what)? What more does Israel hope to gain with its next attack on Gaza, when people there already speak about the wiping out of entire families as a normal topic of conversation?

THE END OF POLITICS AND IDEOLOGY

Survival, I learned, is also Hamas's obsession. Financial resources have contracted significantly over the last few years with government employees long being paid only a percentage of their salary and other public-sector demands consistently unmet. The Hamas government has tried to compensate for the shortfall by "gouging people for money," said one analyst, imposing a range of revenue-generating measures—new taxes, fees, penalties and price increases—that feel extortive. I was told the price of cigarettes has tripled from 8 NIS (new Israeli shekel) to 25 NIS; quarterly property taxes have doubled; a new "cleanliness tax" is now charged for street cleaning and sanitation services, and car licenses must be renewed every six months at a cost of 600 NIS—an impossible sum for most Gazans. Failure to pay can result in the confiscation of the license followed by the car. Some maintained that tunnel smuggling has been renewed (albeit at nowhere near historical levels) to generate additional tax revenue for Hamas, something I did not have the time to examine. Another well-placed source claimed: "Fifty to sixty percent of Hamas would give up Jerusalem for a Rafah [border] opening."

One trusted source argued that since most people in Gaza do not have money to pay any of these taxes and penalties, Hamas officials target those who can pay and have a sliding scale for those of somewhat lesser means. Apparently, the government is successful in collecting revenue. Said this same individual, "The pressure they [the Hamas government] are under, like all of us, is considerable but they will not break. Instead they have become more vicious. Hamas was not like this before. Extreme self-preservation is taking them far away from politics." I heard constant references to Hamas as an organization or movement rather than as a government or authority that is representative and purposeful. Nor is the PA immune from popular disdain and alienation. Some of the most poisonous criticism was reserved for Ramallah.

Hamas, one analyst pointed out, "can't exert any more control over the population than they already have. They have total control." Much like Israel, there is not much more Hamas can do to strengthen its control of Gaza. Hence, Hamas's priorities, say my sources, are now shifting from the consolidation of control—itself a diminished priority from one that earlier emphasized political ideology as the basis of Islamist rule—to "pure survival mode." This is perhaps best expressed, my colleagues say, in the unrelieved tunnel construction believed to be making its way underneath Gaza City's streets and neighborhoods. These tunnels are rumored to be 150 meters (492 feet) deep, part of a larger, murky infrastructure that would, in times of conflict, ferry the Hamas leadership underground to relative safety.

I cannot comment on the tunnel system in Gaza City other than to say that some of the people I know and trust in Gaza believe it to be a reality. Assuming they are correct, a conclusion naturally follows that is quite horrifying: in order to destroy the tunnels (if, in fact, that is possible), Israel—with Hamas's de facto consent—would have to destroy entire neighborhoods. It also follows that the Hamas leadership hopes Israel would not go to such an extreme, but it appears willing to take that risk.

The tunnel system may be understood as a powerful expression of Gaza's post-political reality, where political engagement and good governance have declined in favor of something more coarse. If in fact Hamas's power now derives less from ideological belief and political vision than from coercion and retrenchment, then what accounts for this dramatic shift in strategy, especially given Hamas's political pragmatism and past attempts at diplomatic engagement?

I was given several reasons. In the crushing aftermath of the 2014 war, the Hamas leadership was gravely disappointed with the painfully slow pace of change and the continued refusal of the international community to work with them—something my respondents say the Islamist leadership was willing to do. Another critical factor influencing Hamas's thinking was the continued and at times intensified blockade of Gaza by Israel, the West, Egypt and even Jordan. How, following the devastation inflicted, could this be justified? Adding further to the mix was the repeated failure of reconciliation efforts irrespective of who was to blame (and the weakening connection between reconciliation and peace), and last, of course, was the Hamas government's eroding finances.

Hamas's shifting focus has another dimension: the potentially larger role of its military wing in political decision making and governance (particularly given the consistent failure of the political leadership to achieve any meaningful change). This arguably was made clear with the election in early 2017 of Yahya Sinwar to head the political wing of Hamas in the Gaza Strip. Sinwar, who sat in Israeli jails for over 20 years, was the founding member of the al-Qassam Brigades. Although it is still unclear what Sinwar's election will bring to Gaza and to Israel,[9] one thing is clear, said one analyst: "Gaza is simmering."[10]

QUESTIONING HAMAS ... AND GOD

There is also in Gaza a struggle to create a normal society. There always has been. Some people, no doubt more than I realize, have not abandoned possibility and creative resistance; they see scarcity as a catalyst for change and their work assumes a variety of forms. One uses religion to reexamine social behavior and *critique* it. This is altogether new in Gaza and it is quite stunning.

Although the trend among some in Gaza is to turn to religion as a refuge, there has emerged a countertrend that also seeks refuge of another sort. This is how it was explained to me (admittedly, I did not have the time to examine this claim deeply): the misconduct and fraudulence now associated with Hamas and the inability to challenge it in any meaningful and effective manner have given rise to a social commentary on, and even critique of, Hamas's conduct that uses religion as its analytical instrument. This critique is not about conditions of life in Gaza but about the use of religion by Hamas as a coercive tool and justification for abusive behavior. By linking political behavior to religion and using religion to judge the defects in that behavior, people are "putting power on the defensive" in an altogether unprecedented way, at least in Gaza. This critique is taking place entirely on social media—Facebook, Twitter, WhatsApp—beyond the control of Hamas, which is apparently very frustrated by its inability to control or extinguish the increasingly harsh commentary. According to my sources, this social media phenomenon reaches tens of thousands of followers.

For example, I heard about the story of a cow and the brutal, unconscionable way the animal was slaughtered. The cow's cruel treatment apparently became an Internet sensation, viewed by thousands. While some people justified the slaughter in the name of Islam, others railed against it, asking, "Is this Islam? Why are we behaving like this?" A vibrant exchange apparently followed. The critique, my respondents argued, is all the more astonishing because it is not confined to a religious critique of Hamas alone but increasingly, and carefully, includes the idea of Islam and God as well. The emerging questioning of religion and God—an incendiary act by any measure in the Middle East—represents a "potential earthquake in the Islamic world," said one friend, "and it continues to grow." Given the enormous risks associated with even engaging in such a discourse, to do so is a courageous act and one, in my view, that speaks powerfully to the nonexistence of other viable and acceptable options. It certainly bears watching.

Gaza, too, is home to other forms of creative rethinking and rebuilding: a burgeoning of cultural production—art, theater, photography, music—and volunteerism among the young is apparently growing. A range of initiatives has emerged that attempt, in their own way, to address Gaza's predicament. Without a guiding (and functioning) central authority, these efforts are, by nature, self-contained and confined; still, they remain vibrant and persistent. They include the renewal of small-scale agriculture, human rights monitoring, mental health rehabilitation, environmental repair and technological innovation. The last was strongly emphasized. Gaza has a highly talented, "tech-savvy" population; if ever there were peace, an American investor stated, "Gaza's Internet sector would become another India." The number of Internet users in Gaza is reportedly equal to that of Tel Aviv, and a limited number are already subcontracting for companies in India, Bangladesh and Israel, for Google and Microsoft.

The constraining factor in Gaza has never been insufficient talent.

ASPIRING TO THE MUNDANE: SOME CONCLUDING REFLECTIONS

Perhaps the most striking feature of life in Gaza is attenuation—a narrowing of space and the certainty of that space as a place to live, and a narrowing of desire, expectation and vision. Given the immense difficulties of everyday life, the particular and the mundane—having enough food, clothing, or electricity[11]—have been elevated to an aspiration. Concerns have been pared, as have yearnings. They have become inward looking and confined, focused, understandably, on self and family. When a friend of mine asked some of his students "What is your wish?" they answered, "a new pair of trousers," "a new shirt," and "ice cream from the shop on Omar al-Mukhtar street."

The craving is not for a homeland and the fear is not its absence. The craving is for a livelihood (no matter how meager), clean water and sanctuary, and the fear is that they are unattainable. Within such incarceration, there is simply no place for dreams. Why dream when opportunities do not exist and cannot be created? Why plan when there is little if any possibility of realizing those plans? Why even resist when it is unclear who should be resisted, who will benefit and what it will achieve?

"We have no leaders with a national vision and no central authority," said an economist friend. "We need a common agenda but in Gaza today that does not exist. We are a fragmented, carved-up entity with a variety of internal and external actors each pursuing their own agenda and using Gaza as a way to promote it." I heard a common lament: we are losing our ability to think speculatively and analytically, and the capacity "to accurately judge our predicament and how to address it."

How then does one even begin to think about the greater good, of moving forward as a society—a feature that was so defining during the first Intifada, of which too many young people in Gaza know little, if anything, about. In fact, I was struck by how little the young (but well-educated) adults I met knew of the first Intifada and the Oslo years, and how acutely embedded they were in the present day. In this way, not only are they disconnected from their future, they are also disconnected from their very recent past, and the many important—and now, lost—lessons contained within it.

My friend, the respected professional I mentioned earlier, made a powerful observation: "People are afraid to enter the world or they enter it defensively with weapons. Our openness to the world is narrowing and more and more people are afraid of leaving Gaza because they do not know how to cope with the world outside, like a prisoner released from prison after years of confinement. People must be taught to think more broadly. Otherwise we are lost."

Israel's "Incomprehensible Intentions":[12] A Final Thought

"What do the Israelis want?" This question was repeatedly asked, with each questioner looking at me searchingly, sometimes imploringly, for an answer, for some insight they clearly felt they did not have.

Stated a colleague in his early fifties:

If the Israelis were [thinking], everyone could benefit. All they must do is give us a window to live a normal life and all these extremist groups would disappear. Hamas would disappear. The community must deal with … these groups, not IDF [i.e., Israeli military] tanks and planes. Our generation wants to make peace and it is foolish for Israel to refuse. The next generation may not be as willing as we are. Is that what Israel truly wants?

During the first six months of 2016, the Ministry of Interior reported that 24,138 babies were born in the Gaza Strip, averaging 132 babies born per day.[13] During the month of August 2016 alone, 4,961 babies were born in Gaza,[14] or 160 babies per day, over six babies every hour and one baby every nine minutes. The distance between Gaza City and Tel Aviv is 44 miles.

"What will Israel do when there are five million Palestinians living in Gaza?"

14

"I wish they would just disappear"*

While I have only known of Professor Stoler's work indirectly, I am truly grateful for the chance to engage with it more closely. *Duress* is a compelling work, an intellectual provocation demanding principled and heartfelt scrutiny. I am not a scholar of postcolonial studies and have not been deeply engaged with its literature, nor do I possess a familiarity with its language. Rather, I come to this reflection as someone who has studied the Israeli occupation and its impact on Palestinian society and economy for over 30 years, and as a Jew whose mother and father survived Auschwitz.

In my time living and working among Palestinians, there have been many experiences that speak to the arguments woven through *Duress*— essentially the enduring presence of colonial structures and relations whether power has left or not. Stoler's arguments that examine the duress of the colony as it is expressed and lived today have compelled certain understandings that, in a sense, exceed those arguments. I have chosen to address four.

IMPERIAL DEBRIS AND RUINATION:
ANESTHETIZING THE "OTHER"

"The symbolic power of agents, understood as the power to make things seen—*theorein*—and to make things believed, to produce and impose the legitimate or legal classification, in fact depends ... on the position occupied in space."

Pierre Bourdieu, *The Social Space and the Genesis of Groups*[1]

* Originally published in "Review Essay: Critical Dialogues." *Postcolonial Studies*, Volume 21, Number 4, December 2018, copyright © The Institute of Postcolonial Studies, reprinted by permission of Taylor & Francis Ltd, www.tandfonline.com on behalf of The Institute of Postcolonial Studies (slightly edited). [This piece was written as a response to Ann Laura Stoler's book, *Duress: Imperial Durabilities in Our Time* (Durham, NC: Duke University Press, 2016).]

The concept of "imperial debris" and the "ruination" it reflects—an important theme in *Duress*[2]—is one of the most perceptible and tangible effects of Israeli occupation as seen in Palestine's disabled economy and poisoned environment, most notably in Gaza. Another is ambiguity through which occupation is managed and enforced. And, as Stoler argues, "There is nothing 'over' about this form of ruination."[3] Yet, in the context of Israel's colonial relationship with the Palestinians, debris and ruination assume a meaning that goes beyond decimation and its physical manifestations, where "acts of ruination" arguably reflect something far more resolute and injurious than they may in other colonial contexts.

An image that has never left me was one described by Nadera Shalhoub-Kevorkian, a professor at the Hebrew University in Jerusalem. She was discussing the physical barriers and restrictions on space and movement of Palestinians living in Jerusalem and described how, in an attempt to circumvent them, Palestinian children returning home from school were forced to walk through sewer pipes.[4] What struck me about this story was the image of these children as waste flowing beneath Israeli homes, beyond sight, sound and smell. In this way, Palestinians are not only debris-making but are themselves debris, an environmental problem requiring some form of intervention and, eventually, disposal. Here, there is no "heartfelt gaze on the ruin" or even at the "lives of those living in them."[5] Here, there is no possibility of being affected or altered by the "other." Rather, there is only the "wish," as stated privately by an Israeli official, that Palestinians "would just disappear." In the context of Israel-Palestine, the act of ruination has come to be defined by something more malevolent: it is not damaged personhood that is primary (although it is created as fundamental to colonial order and control), but the denial of personhood and the psychological eradication of the person. The critic, Northrop Frye, stated it thus: "[T]he enemy become, not people to be defeated, but embodiments of an idea to be exterminated."[6]

Such ruination should be seen not as a violence *of* representation—where the colonizer acts as a surrogate or voice for the colonized—as much as it is a violence *against* representation—of any kind where no surrogate or voice is required. Violence, once an "instrument of catastrophisation,"[7] as Ophir and Azoulay correctly argue, is now better understood, in my view, as an instrument of invalidation, used to disqualify and annul, eradicating all sites of encounter with the other and replacing it with Nothingness. The aim is not the death of the "Indigenous other" but his nullification, along with the counter-memories and counter-claims that otherness naturally embodies. In this way, Israel has redefined the colonial distinction between self and other, the space that Israelis and Palestinians inhabit. In this redefined space, there can be no approach or nearing, let alone engagement (with whom?), reciprocity or redemption. Instead, there is only singularity (particularly as it concerns indigeneity) and repudiation, and the insistence on sameness and certainty. Palestinians are erased from Israel's emotional and political landscape, precluding contestation and complexity, and restoring to Jewish Israelis a knowable, unambiguous, easily interpretable clarity.

This relegation to "willful unknowing"[8] was painfully seen during Israel's 2014 assault on Gaza, known as Operation Protective Edge, when Israelis in Sderot, a town bordering Gaza (and periodically attacked by rockets fired from the Strip), gathered on a hillside, sitting on folding chairs and sofas to watch the bombing of Gaza and cheer the explosions that would, by the war's end, kill over 500 Palestinian children. (It must be said that Palestinians have also celebrated the death of Israelis.) It was known as the "Sderot Cinema," because the Israelis gathered there ate popcorn as if they were at an outdoor movie theater.

It is not the need to distinguish between the colonizer and the colonized that is primary in Israel's relationship with Palestinians but the need to secure the Jewish community by differentiating the animate—the living—from the inanimate—the nonliving, the former with claims that are humane, transcendental and resonant, the latter with none at all, where any attempt at intimacy or equation would be seen as abnormal and pathological.[9] From the earliest days of the occupation, Israel never embarked on a "civilizing" project among Palestinians; on the contrary, the mission, to borrow from Kathleen Stewart, has been the decomposition of Palestinian lives, orchestrating "their movement through decay,"[10] rendering their memory incoherent or vacant, the people incapable of recalling their own history (both recent and far), and thus disembodied, unable to locate, let alone, secure their place in the world.

THE DECISION ON JERUSALEM:
TO OUTLAW AND MAKE INVISIBLE

The decision by the United States to declare Jerusalem the capital of Israel needs to be understood as an expression of purpose more inimical than simple contested political binaries. While it is true that the Jerusalem decision, which was fundamentally Israel's, was an attempt by Israel to finally rid itself of the two-state solution—a political albatross from which Israel has long tried to free itself; it is also true—and perhaps more important for purposes of this discussion—that the decision was a response to the growing momentum, especially in the United States, for a rights-based approach to resolving the conflict that demands equal rights for Palestinians alongside Israelis.[11]

The decision on Jerusalem must therefore be understood, in part, as an attempt to maintain and enforce what Israel sees as its historical right to render Palestinians rightless. The *right to demand rights*, which a rights-based approach reifies, is more threatening than the *right* itself, because the former speaks to the agency that makes Palestinians present and irreducible, something Israel has worked so long to control and void.[12] It is the "inability to unthink rightlessness"[13] among Palestinians—the destruction of the self as Rosemary Sayigh has argued[14]—that must be maintained as a form of control: "The ascription of rightlessness to the 'other' is—and must remain—uncontestable" and beyond dispute, "a clearly established rule that is not limited by justice.[15] Declaring Jerusalem to be Israel's capital does just that; it not only purges Palestinians from the political equation and disendows them of any claims based on justice, but also insures their continued absence in Israeli eyes."[16]

The real threat, therefore, lies not in acts of Palestinian violence against Israel but in understanding that those acts are a response to injustice and dehumanization.[17] An Israeli friend explained that the threat to Israel lies "in making Palestinians intimate, in seeing the world through their eyes and in feeling the ground beneath them inside their shoes"[18]—in rejecting any endeavor that would treat them as indeterminate and notional, or consign them to abstraction. The insistence on human dignity is a theme that has run through my decades of research among Palestinians; the words that recur, meant to affirm existence: "I am a human being. I am someone's child. Why do they treat me this way?"

CRIMINALIZING THE ORDINARY:
BINDING RENEWAL TO INJUSTICE

"At the moment of vision, the eyes see nothing."

William Golding, *The Spire*

Stoler makes some critical observations regarding the nature of colonial governance in the West Bank and Gaza that I would like to engage in more detail. She speaks of "colonial intimacies" and the "reordering of the intimate," that may "ensure that no place is safe; the familiar is treacherous; and no place is home."[19] She states that intimate encounters are "predicated on humiliation, trespass, and intrusions—the sort that checkpoints, strip searches, interrogations, and midnight raids on homes foist on those subject to them."[20] Referring to the Israeli architect Eyal Weizman, Stoler further argues that the reordering of the intimate can also occur within interior spaces, as when Israeli soldiers occupy Palestinian homes and redefine the meaning of "inside," "relocat[ing] governance within half-demolished living rooms, on apartment balconies, on doorsteps, in bedrooms and hallways … Colonial occupation makes front stoops in Hebron legally off-limits and not one's own."[21]

All of this is true. Yet, the reordering of the intimate as a form of colonial control is not only a matter of producing confusion and fear between space that is public and private, but is seen more acutely in the criminalization of space in what Professor Shalhoub-Kevorkian calls "a zone of non-existence," in which Palestinians are forced to live day to day. Under Israel's colonial occupation, the intimate becomes a site of disfigurement, an obscene space, where engaging in normal, everyday acts of living and working—having dinner, going to school, shopping in a market, or planting a tree—are not only dangerous (as it was for the children in the sewer pipes), but criminal—illicit and censurable—punishable, in some instances (especially in Gaza) by death. In these obscene spaces, furthermore, innocents—most of them children—are being poisoned by the water they drink, by some of the food they eat, and by the structures in which they live, all with the knowledge if not the intent of the occupier and those who support the occupation or refuse to challenge it.[22]

The assault on the intimate really speaks to an attenuation of life: "a narrowing of space and the certainty of that space as a place to live, and a narrowing of desire, expectation and vision."[23] This is seen in the deteriorating position of women within the home: dramatic increases in divorce rates in Gaza, from 2 percent to 40 percent, and rising levels of domestic abuse. Women, whose economic responsibilities outside the home have intensified, remain primarily responsible for their families and must daily address the lack of access to clean water, nutritious food, adequate and safe housing, medical care and education, among other vital needs.[24] The intimate, so reduced, is perhaps most painfully expressed by Dr. Rajaie Batniji, a Stanford University physician, who while visiting his family in Gaza, observed: "Gaza is something of a laboratory for observing an absence of dignity." This absence means

> ... not being seen or being incompletely seen; being subsumed into a group identity; invasion of personal space (including physical violence); and humiliation ... The constant surveillance from the sky, collective punishment through blockade and isolation, the intrusion into homes and communications, and restrictions on those trying to travel, or marry, or work make it difficult to live a dignified life in Gaza.

And, Batniji continues, it is not just the Israeli occupation and blockade that tear at human dignity but also the internal power struggles among Palestinians, which have "recreated many of the most threatening aspects of the Israeli occupation [including] barriers to movement of people and goods, fear, isolation and torture." To these divisions are added the pressures of daily life, which necessitate hoarding of fuel and other necessities and an extreme dependence on foreign assistance to eat, so it is no surprise that "Many people on the street now walk with their heads down—whether it is out of fear, isolation, or a loss of dignity ... intentionally neglect[ing] the destruction that surrounds them."[25] A 17-year-old boy detained in an Israeli prison encapsulates the disfigurement of intimate space: "What it feels like to live here you ask? It's like being a shadow of your own, caught on the ground, not being able to break out and you see yourself lying there, but you cannot fill the shadow with life."[26]

PALESTINE'S MARGINALIZED CENTER: THE FALLACY OF COLONIZING GAZA—A CONCLUDING THOUGHT

On my last trip to Gaza in the fall of 2016, I was sitting with a close Palestinian friend, talking. We sat together for some time and towards the end of our conversation, he looked at me and said rather jokingly yet ruefully, "You know something, Sara, you may be the last Jew in Gaza." His words struck me, although I did not know how to respond. In the time since, I have thought about what my friend said, how he said it and what he might have meant. His words have stayed with me not as a burden but as a summons, layered with meaning and confession. If I am the last Jew in Gaza, what responsibility does this impose?

As part of this summons, I am compelled to ask this question: *how* are we to think about Gaza, about Palestinians? I ask because Palestine's deliberate ruination—seen most painfully in Gaza—now over 50 years old, has been extremely well documented and powerfully argued. Yet, it has been met, for the most part, with calm uninterest and lack of remorse, reflecting, what the historian Gabriel Kolko termed the "absence of a greater sense of abhorrence."[27]

Why are so many among us unmoved by babies frozen to death in Gaza's winter cold because their parents could not find proper shelter; by a population of 2 million people deprived of adequate amounts of water and electricity; by the devastation of a once functioning economy through closure and siege, depriving 53.7 per cent of the labor force (and around 71.1 per cent of young workers) of the right to work—forcing the overwhelming majority into want, and their daughters into prostitution? This deprivation is imposed deliberately, on a people desperate and willing to work. What purpose does Gaza's suffering serve in Israeli eyes and in ours?[28]

Gaza, like Palestine, exists in parentheses. It is where misery is seen but remains unexamined and, most crucially, unfamiliar. Redemption is therefore not possible for Gaza and compassion cannot be elicited, freeing us of any uncertainty or shame. Yet, what does it mean when resolution is found in the despair and torment of another people?

Gaza survives but is unrepentant. This lack of repentance is used, cynically, as a shield against the horrors we knowingly and willingly inflict, allowing us to remain confident and secure in the fact that Gaza will not force us to see ourselves as we truly are and have become. Gaza, to borrow from the writer Doris Lessing, is a sentimental certitude that is unchallenged and undiscussed. We are assured and vindicated, perhaps even redeemed by Gaza's struggle against the deliberate denial we impose. Therefore the struggle must be perpetuated no matter the cost. I am often asked whether there will be another war on Gaza. Assuredly, there will be.

That Gaza is small and incarcerated, removed from any viable exchange beyond its borders—with more than 13,000 men, women and children per square mile—does not weigh heavily on our collective conscience, if at all. That this area was repeatedly bombed and among those bombed were my friends and their families, people who have always welcomed me as a Jew into their homes in Gaza, matters not.[29] Living parenthetically means there are no fathers or mothers or children in Gaza, no homes or schools, no hospitals or playgrounds, no restaurants or concert halls. Children are not sweet, women are not educated, and men have no aspirations. Ordinary struggles, by which Gaza's people live and die, do not exist. Rather, Gaza is where the grass grows wild and must be "mowed" from time to time as some Israeli analysts have argued.[30]

Yet, Gaza is tenacious. It rails against the rupture enforced upon it, against our insistence to treat it as an object of inattention. Despite all attempts at displacement and invalidation, Gaza's place in the future of its people is secure: there can be no Palestine, whatever form it may assume, without Gaza.

So what is the way forward? Although, as Stoler has so cogently argued, colonialism is a continuing event, one must begin somewhere, with one humanizing action: seeing Gazans and Palestinians as we see ourselves—as parents who love their children and are desperate to protect them; as people seeking to live an ordinary life, deserving of the rights and freedoms we naturally claim for ourselves; as people who will continue to resist their oppression and subjugation, as people who demand to live outside parentheses.

In his June 2004 address to a Knesset committee meeting about Israel's planned "disengagement" from Gaza, then Prime Minister Ariel Sharon promised: "By the end of 2005 there will not be a single Jew left in the Gaza Strip."[31] I disagree, for it is in Gaza where I am truly a Jew, last or otherwise.

PART V   A JEW IN GAZA: REFLECTIONS

I could not live as a Jew among Jews alone. For me, it wasn't possible and it wasn't what I wanted. I wanted to live as a Jew in a pluralist society, where my group remained important to me but where others were important to me, too.

Taube Roy
Survivor of the Lodz Ghetto and Auschwitz

I do not try and protect Jews from ... analogies. They are there and Israel is making them. The Israeli community is forgetting what it is losing. There is no freedom if you are an occupier.

Mary Khass
Activist
Gaza, 1989

Against barbarity, poetry can resist only by cultivating an attachment to human fragility, like a blade of grass growing on a wall as armies march by.

Mahmoud Darwish

15

A Jewish Plea*

"We have nothing to lose except everything."
Albert Camus

During the summer, my husband and I had a conversion ceremony for our adopted daughter, Jess. We took her to the mikvah, a Jewish ritual bath where she was totally submerged in a pool of living water—living because it is fed in part by heavenly rain—and momentarily suspended as we are in the womb, emerging the same yet transformed. This ritual of purification, transformation and rebirth is central to Judaism and it signifies renewal and possibility.

The day of Jess's conversion was also the day that Israel began its pitiless bombing of Lebanon [in 2006] and nearly three weeks into Israel's violent assault on Gaza, a place that has been my second home for the last two decades. This painful juxtaposition of rebirth and destruction remains with me, weighing heavily, without respite. Yet, the link deeply forged in our construction of self as Jews, between my daughter's acceptance into Judaism and Israel's actions—between Judaism and Zionism—a link that I never accepted uncritically but understood as historically inevitable and understandable, is one that for me, at least, has now been broken.

For unlike past conflicts involving Israel and the Palestinian and Arab peoples, this one feels qualitatively different—a turning point—not only with regard to the nature of Israel's horrific response—its willingness to destroy and to do so utterly—but also with regard to the virtually unqualified support of organized American Jewry for Israel's brutal actions, something that is not new but now no longer tolerable to me.

---

*   Originally published in *Counterpunch*, April 7, 2007, and in Nubar Hovsepian (ed.), *The War on Lebanon: A Reader*, Northampton, MA: Olive Branch Press, 2008 (slightly edited).

I grew up in a home where Judaism was defined and practiced not so much as a religion but as a system of ethics and culture. God was present but not central. Israel and the notion of a Jewish homeland were very important to my parents, who survived Auschwitz and Chelmno. But unlike many of their friends, my parents were not uncritical of Israel. Obedience to a state was not a primary Jewish value, especially after the Holocaust. Judaism provided the context for Jewish life, for values and beliefs that were not dependent upon national or territorial boundaries, but transcended them to include the other, always the other. For my mother and father, Judaism meant bearing witness, raging against injustice and refusing silence. It meant compassion, tolerance and rescue. In the absence of these imperatives, they taught me, we cease to be Jews.

Many of the people—both Jewish and others—who write about Palestinians and Arabs fail to accept the fundamental humanity of the people they are writing about, a failing born of ignorance, fear and racism. Within the organized Jewish community especially, it has always been unacceptable to claim that Arabs, Palestinians especially, are like us, that they, too, possess an essential humanity and must be included within our moral boundaries, ceasing to be "a kind of solution," a useful, hostile "other" to borrow from Edward Said.[1] That any attempt at separation is artificial, an abstraction.

By refusing to seek proximity over distance, we calmly, even gratefully refuse to see what is right before our eyes. We are no longer compelled—if we ever were—to understand our behavior from positions outside our own, to enter, as Jacqueline Rose has written, into each other's predicaments and make what is one of the hardest journeys of the mind.[2] Hence, there is no need to maintain a living connection with the people we are oppressing, to humanize them, taking into account the experience of subordination itself, as Said would say. We are not preoccupied by our cruelty nor are we haunted by it. The task, ultimately, is to tribalize pain, narrowing the scope of human suffering to ourselves alone. Such willful blindness leads to the destruction of principle and the destruction of people, eliminating all possibility of embrace, but it gives us solace.

Why is it so difficult, even impossible, to incorporate Palestinians and other Arab peoples into the Jewish understanding of history? Why is there so little perceived need to question our own narrative (for want of a better word) and the one we have given others, preferring instead to cherish beliefs and sentiments that remain impenetrable? Why is it virtually mandatory among Jewish intellectuals to oppose racism, repression and injustice almost anywhere in the world and unacceptable—indeed, for some, an act of heresy—to oppose it when Israel is the oppressor, choosing concealment over exposure? For many among us, history and memory adhere to preclude reflection and tolerance.[3]

What happens to the other as we, a broken and weary people, continually abuse him, turning him into the enemy we now want and need, secure in a prophecy that is thankfully self-fulfilling?

What happens to a people when renewal and injustice are rapturously joined?

A NEW DISCOURSE OF THE UNCONSCIOUS

We speak without mercy, numb to the pain of others, incapable of being reached—unconscious. Our words are these:

- "... we must not forget," wrote Ze'ev Schiff, the senior political and military analyst for the Israeli newspaper *Haaretz*, "the most important aspect of this war: Hezbollah and what this terrorist organization symbolizes must be destroyed at any price ... What matters is not the future of the Shiite town of Bint Jbail or the Hezbollah positions in Maroun Ras, but the future and safety of the State of Israel." "If Israel doesn't improve its military cards in the fighting, we will feel the results in the political solution."[4]

- "We must reduce to dust the villages of the south ... " stated Haim Ramon, long known as a political dove and Israel's Minister of Justice. "I don't understand why there is still electricity there." "Everyone in southern Lebanon is a terrorist and is connected to Hezbollah ... What we should do in southern Lebanon is employ huge firepower before a ground force goes in." Israel's largest selling newspaper, *Yedioth Ahronoth* put it this way: "A village from which rockets are fired at Israel will simply be destroyed by fire. This decision should have been made and executed after the first Katyusha. But better late than never."[5]

- "... for every Katyusha barrage on Haifa, 10 Dahiya build-ings will be bombed," said the IDF Chief of Staff, Dan Halutz. Eli Yishai, Israel's Deputy Prime Minister, proposed turning south Lebanon into a "sandbox," while Knesset member Moshe Sharoni called for the obliteration of Gaza, and Yoav Limor, a Channel 1 military correspondent, suggested an exhibition of Hezbollah corpses followed by a parade of prisoners in their underwear in order "to strengthen the home front's morale."[6]

- "Remember: distorted philosophical sensitivity [*sic*] to human lives will make us pay the real price of the lives of many, and the blood of our sons," read an advertisement in *Haaretz*.[7]

- "... according to Jewish law," announced the Yesha Rabbinical Council, "during a time of battle and war, there is no such term as 'innocents of the enemy'."[8]

- "But speaking from our own Judaic faith and legal legacy," argued the Rabbinical Council of America, "we believe that Judaism would neither require nor permit a Jewish soldier to sacrifice himself in order to save deliberately endangered enemy civil-ians. This is especially true when confronting a barbaric enemy who would by such illicit, consistent, and systematic means seek to destroy not only the Jewish soldier, but defeat and destroy the Jewish homeland. New realities do indeed require new responses."[9]

- The Israeli author, Naomi Ragan, after learning that many of the war dead in Lebanon were children, wrote "Save your sympathy for the mothers and sisters and girlfriends of our young soldiers who would rather be sitting in study halls learning Torah, but have no choice but to risk their precious lives full of hope, goodness and endless potential, to wipe out the cancerous ter-rorist cells that threaten their people and all mankind. Make your choice, and save your tears."[10]

Many of us, perhaps most, have declared that all Palestinians and Lebanese are the enemy, threatening *our*—Israel and the Jewish people's—existence. Everyone we kill and every house we demolish is therefore a military target, legitimate and deserving. Terrorism is part of their culture and we must strengthen our ability to deter. Negotiation, to paraphrase the Israeli scholar Yehoshua Porat, writing during the 1982 Lebanon war, is a "veritable catastrophe for Israel." The battlefield will preserve us.

The French critic and historian, Hippolyte Taine, observed: "Imagine a man who sets out on a voyage equipped with a pair of spectacles that magnify things to an extraordinary degree. A hair on his hand, a spot on the tablecloth, the shifting fold of a coat, all will attract his attention; at this rate, he will not go far, he will spend his day taking six steps and will never get out of his room."[11]

We are content in our room and seek no exit.

In our room, compassion and conscience are dismissed as weakness, where pinpoint surgical strikes constitute restraint and civility and momentary ceasefires, acts of humanity and kindness: "Leave your home, we are going to destroy it." Several minutes later another home in Gaza, another history, is taken, crushed. The warning, though, is not for them but for us—it makes us good and clean. What better illustration of our morality: when a call to leave one's home minutes before it is bombed is considered a humane gesture.

Our warnings have another purpose: they make our actions legitimate and our desire for legitimacy is unbounded, voracious. This is perhaps the only thing Palestinians (and now the Lebanese) have withheld from us, this object of our desire. If legitimacy will not be bestowed, then it must be created. This explains Israel's obsession with laws and legalities to insure in our own eyes that we do not transgress, making evil allowable by widening the parameters of license and transgression. In this way, we insure our goodness and morality, through a piece of paper, which is enough for us.

What are Jews now capable of resisting: tyranny? Oppression? Occupation? Injustice? We resist none of these things, no more. For too many among us, they are no longer evil but necessary and good—we cannot live, survive without them. What does that make us? We look at ourselves and what do we see: a non-Jew, a child, whose pain we inflict effortlessly, whose death is demanded and unquestioned, bearing validity and purpose.

What do we see: a people who now take pleasure in hating others. Hatred is familiar to us if nothing else. We understand it and it is safe. It is what we know. We do not fear our own distortion—do we even see it?—but the loss of our power to deter, and we shake with a violent palsy at a solution that shuns the suffering of others. Our pathology is this: it lies in our struggle to embrace a morality we no longer possess and in our need for persecution of a kind we can no longer claim but can only inflict.

We are remote from the conscious world—brilliantly ignorant, blindly visionary, unable to resist from within. We live in an unchanging place, absent of season and reflection, devoid of normality and growth, and most important of all, emptied—or so we aim—of the other. A ghetto still but now, unlike before, a ghetto of our own making.

What is our narrative of victory and defeat? What does it mean to win? Bombed cars with white civilian flags still attached to their windows? More dead and dismembered bodies of old people and children littered throughout villages that have been ravaged? An entire country disabled and broken? Non-ending war? This is our victory, our achievement, something we seek and applaud. And how do we measure defeat? Losing the will to continue the devastation? Admitting to our persecution of others, something we have never done?

We can easily ignore their suffering, cut them from their food, water, electricity and medicine, confiscate their land, demolish their crops and deny them egress—suffocate them, our voices stilled. Racism does not allow us to see Arabs as we see ourselves; that is why we rage when they do not fail from weakness but instead we find ourselves failing from strength. Yet, in our view, it is we who are the only victims, vulnerable and scarred. All we have is the unnaturalness of our condition.

As an unconscious people, we have perhaps reached our nadir, with many among us now calling for a redefinition of our ethics—the core of who we are—to incorporate the need to kill women and children if Jewish security required it. "New realities do indeed require new responses," says the Rabbinical Council of America. Now, for us, violence is creation and peace, destruction.

ENDING THE PROCESS OF CREATION AND REBIRTH
AFTER THE HOLOCAUST

Can we be ordinary, an essential part of our rebirth after the Holocaust? Is it possible to be normal when we seek refuge in the margin, and remedy in the dispossession and destruction of another people? How can we create when we acquiesce so willingly to the demolition of homes, construction of barriers, denial of sustenance, and ruin of innocents? How can we be merciful when, to use Rose's words, we seek "omnipotence as the answer to historical pain"?[12] We refuse to hear their pleading, to see those chased from their homes, children incinerated in their mother's arms. Instead, we tell our children to inscribe the bombs that will burn Arab babies.

We argue that we must eliminate terrorism. What do we really know of their terrorism, and of ours? What do we care? Rather, with language that is denuded and infested—*give them more time to bomb so that Israel's borders can be natural*—we engage repeatedly in a war of desire, a war not thrust upon us but of our own choosing, ingratiating ourselves with the power to destroy others and insensate to the death of our own children. What happens to a nation, asks the Israeli writer David Grossman, that cannot save its own child, words written before his own son was killed in Lebanon?

There are among Israelis real feelings of vulnerability and fear, never resolved but used, intensified. Seeing one's child injured or killed is the most horrible vision—Israelis are vulnerable, far more than other Jews. Yet we as a people have become a force of extremism, of chaos and disorder, trying to plow an unruly sea—addicted to death and cruelty, intoxicated, with one ambition: to mock the pauper.

Judaism has always prided itself on reflection, critical examination and philosophical inquiry. The Talmudic mind examines a sentence, a word, in a multitude of ways, seeking all possible interpretations and searching constantly for the one left unsaid. Through such scrutiny, it is believed, comes the awareness needed to protect the innocent, prevent injury or harm, and be closer to God.

Now, these are abhorred, eviscerated from our ethical system. Rather the imperative is to see through eyes that are closed, unfettered by investigation. We conceal our guilt by remaining the abused, despite our power, creating situations where our victimization is assured and our innocence affirmed. We prefer this abyss to peace, which would hurl us unacceptably inward toward awareness and acknowledgment.

Jews do not feel shame over what they have created: an inventory of inhumanity. Rather we remain oddly appeased, even calmed by the desolation. Our detachment allows us to bear such excess (and commit it), to sit in Jewish cafes while Palestinian mothers are murdered in front of their children in Gaza. I can now better understand how horror occurs—how people, not evil themselves, can allow evil to happen. We salve our wounds with our incapacity for remorse, which will be our undoing.

Instead, the Jewish community demands unity and conformity: "Stand with Israel" read the banners on synagogues throughout Boston last summer. Unity around what? There is enormous pressure—indeed coercion—within organized American Jewry to present an image of "wall-to-wall unity" as a local Jewish leader put it. But this unity is an illusion—at its edges a smoldering flame rapidly engulfing its core—for mainstream Jewry does not speak for me or for many other Jews. And where such unity exists, it is hollow, built around fear not humanity, on the need to understand reality as it has long been constructed for us—with the Jew as the righteous victim, the innocent incapable of harm. It is as if our unbending support for Israel's militarism "requires putting our minds as it were into Auschwitz where being a Jew puts your existence on the line. To be Jewish means to be threatened, nothing more. Hence, the only morality we can acknowledge is saving Israel and by extension, ourselves."[13] Within this paradigm, it is dissent not conformity that will diminish and destroy us. We hoard our victimization as we hoard our identity—they are one—incapable of change, a failing that will one day result in our own eviction. Is this what Zionism has done to Judaism?

Israel's actions not only demonstrate the limits of Israeli power but our own limitations as a people: our inability to live a life without barriers, to free ourselves from an ethnic loyalty that binds and contorts, to emerge, finally, from our spectral chamber.

ENDING THE (FILIAL) LINK BETWEEN ISRAEL AND THE HOLOCAUST

How can the children of the Holocaust do such things, they ask? But are we really their rightful offspring?

As the Holocaust survivor dies, the horror of that period and its attendant lessons withdraw further into abstraction and for some Jews, many of them in Israel, alienation. The Holocaust stands not as a lesson but as an internal act of purification where tribal attachment rather than ethical responsibility is demanded and used to define collective action. Perhaps this was an inevitable outcome of Jewish nationalism, of applying holiness to politics, but whatever its source, it has weakened us terribly and cost us greatly.

Silvia Tennenbaum, a survivor and activist writes:

> No matter what great accomplishments were ours in the diaspora, no matter that we produced Maimonides and Spinoza, Moses, Mendelssohn and hundreds of others of mankind's benefactors— not a warrior among them!—we look at the world of our long exile always in the dark light of the Shoah. But this, in itself, is an obscene distortion: would the author ... Primo Levi, or the poet Paul Celan demand that we slaughter the innocents in a land far from the snow-clad forests of Poland? Is it a heroic act to murder a child, even the child of an enemy? Are my brethren glad and proud? ... And, it goes without saying, loyal Jews must talk about the Holocaust. Ignore the images of today's dead and dying and focus on the grainy black-and-white pictures showing the death of Jews in the villages of Poland, at Auschwitz and Sobibor and Bergen-Belsen. We are the first, the only true victims, the champions of helplessness for all eternity.[14]

What did my family perish for, in the ghettos and concentration camps of Poland? Is their role to be exploited and in the momentary absence of violence, to be forgotten and abandoned?

Holocaust survivors stood between the past and the present, bearing witness, sometimes silently, and even in word, often unheard. Yet, they stood as a moral challenge among us and also as living embodiments of a history, way of life and culture that long pre-dated the Holocaust and Zionism (and that Zionism has long denigrated), refusing, in their own way, to let us look past them. Yet, this generation is nearing its end and as they leave us, I wonder what is truly left to take their place, to fill the moral void created by their absence?

Is it, in the words of a friend, himself a Jew, a

> ... memory manufactory, with statues, museums and platoons of "scholars" designed to preserve, indeed ratchet up Jewish feelings of persecution and victimhood, a Hitler behind every Katyusha or border skirmish, which must be met with some of the same crude slaughterhouse tools the Nazis employed against the Jews

six decades ago: ghettos, mass arrests and the denigration of their enemy's humanity?

Do we now measure success in human bodies and in carnage, arguing that our dead bodies are worth more than theirs, our children more vulnerable and holy, more in need of protection and love, their corpses more deserving of shrouds and burial? Is meaning for us to be derived from martyrdom, or from children born with a knife in their hearts? Is this how my grandmother and grandfather are to be remembered?

Our tortured past and its images trespass upon our present not only in Israel but in Gaza and Lebanon as well. "They were temporarily buried in an empty lot with dozens of others," writes a *New York Times* reporter in Lebanon. "They were assigned numbers, his wife and daughter. Alia is No. 35 and Sally is No. 67. 'They are numbers now,' said the father. There are no names anymore."[15]

"They were shrunken figures, dehydrated and hungry," observes the *Washington Post*. "Some had lived on candy bars, others on pieces of dry bread. Some were shell-shocked, their faces blank ... One never made it. He was carried out on a stretcher, flies landing on lifeless eyes that were still open."[16]

As the rightful claimants to our past we should ask "How much damage can be done to a soul?" But we do not ask. We do not question the destruction but only our inability to complete it, to create more slaughter sites.

Can we ever emerge from our torpor, able to mourn the devastation?

OUR ULTIMATE EVICTION?

Where do Jews belong? Where is our place? Is it in the ghetto of a Jewish state whose shrinking boundaries threaten, one day, to evict us? We are powerful but not strong. Our power is our weakness, not our strength, because it is used to instill fear rather than trust, and because of that, it will one day destroy us if we do not change. More and more, we find ourselves detached from our past, suspended and abandoned, alone, without anchor, aching—if not now, eventually—for connection and succor. Grossman has written that as a dream fades it does not become a weaker force but a more potent one, desperately clung to, even as it ravages and devours.

We consume the land and the water behind walls and steel gates, forcing out all others. What kind of place are we creating? Are we fated to be an intruder in the dust, to borrow from Faulkner, whose presence shall evaporate with the shifting sands? Are these the boundaries of our rebirth after the Holocaust?

I have come to accept that Jewish power and sovereignty and Jewish ethics and spiritual integrity are, in the absence of reform, incompatible, unable to coexist or be reconciled. For if speaking out against the wanton murder of children is considered an act of disloyalty and betrayal rather than a legitimate act of dissent, and where dissent is so ineffective and reviled, a choice is ultimately forced upon us between Zionism and Judaism.

Rabbi Hillel the Elder long ago emphasized ethics as the center of Jewish life. Ethical principles or their absence will contribute to the survival or destruction of our people. Yet, today what we face is something different and possibly more perverse: it is not the disappearance of our ethical system but its rewriting into something disfigured and execrable.

What then is the source of our redemption, our salvation? It lies ultimately in our willingness to acknowledge the other—the victims we have created—Palestinian, Lebanese and also Jewish—and the injustice we have perpetrated as a grieving people. Perhaps then we can pursue a more just solution in which we seek to be ordinary rather than absolute, where we finally come to understand that our only hope is not to die peacefully in our homes as one Zionist official put it long ago, but to live peacefully in those homes.

When my daughter Jess was submerged under the waters of the mikvah for the third and final time, she told me she saw rainbows under the water. I shall take this beautiful image as a sign of her rebirth and plead desperately for ours.

16

A Response to Elie Wiesel[*]

Mr. Wiesel,

I read your statement about Palestinians, which appeared in *The New York Times* on August 4th. I cannot help feeling that your attack against Hamas and stunning accusations of child sacrifice are really an attack, carefully veiled but unmistakable, against all Palestinians, their children included. As a child of Holocaust survivors—both my parents survived Auschwitz—I am appalled by your anti-Palestinian position, one I know you have long held. I have always wanted to ask you, why? What crime have Palestinians committed in your eyes? Exposing Israel as an occupier and themselves as its nearly defenseless victims? Resisting a near half-century of oppression imposed by Jews and through such resistance forcing us as a people to confront our lost innocence (to which you so tenaciously cling)?

Unlike you, Mr. Wiesel, I have spent a great deal of time in Gaza among Palestinians. In that time, I have seen many terrible things and I must confess I try not to remember them because of the agony they continue to inflict. I have seen Israeli soldiers shoot into crowds of young children who were doing nothing more than taunting them, some with stones, some with just words. I have witnessed too many horrors, more than I want to describe. But I must tell you that the worst things I have seen, those memories that continue to haunt me, insisting never to be forgotten, are not acts of violence but acts of dehumanization.

There is a story I want to tell you, Mr. Wiesel, for I have carried it inside of me for many years and have only written about it once, a very long time ago. I was in a refugee camp in Gaza when an Israeli Army unit on foot patrol came upon a small baby perched in the sand sitting just outside the door to its home. Some soldiers approached the baby and surrounded it. Standing close together, the soldiers began shunting

---

[*]   Originally published in *Counterpunch*, September 9, 2014.

the child between them with their feet, mimicking a ball in a game of soccer. The baby began screaming hysterically and its mother rushed out shrieking, trying desperately to extricate her child from the soldiers' legs and feet. After a few more seconds of "play," the soldiers stopped and walked away, leaving the terrified child to its distraught mother.

Now, I know what you must be thinking: this was the act of a few misguided men. But I do not agree, because I have seen so many acts of dehumanization since, among which I must now include yours. Mr. Wiesel, how can you defend the slaughter of over 500 innocent children by arguing that Hamas uses them as human shields? Let us say for the sake of argument that Hamas does use children in this way; does this then justify or vindicate their murder in your eyes? How can any ethical human being make such a grotesque argument? In doing so, Mr. Wiesel, I see no difference between you and the Israeli soldiers who used the baby as a soccer ball. Your manner may differ from theirs—perhaps you could never bring yourself to treat a Palestinian child as an inanimate object—but the effect of your words is the same: to dehumanize and objectify Palestinians to the point where the death of Arab children, some murdered inside their own homes, no longer affects you. All that truly concerns you is that Jews not be blamed for the children's savage destruction.

Despite your eloquence, it is clear that you believe only Jews are capable of loving and protecting their children and possess a humanity that Palestinians do not. If this is so, Mr. Wiesel, how would you explain the very public satisfaction among many Israelis over the carnage in Gaza—some assembled as if at a party, within easy sight of the bombing, watching the destruction of innocents, entertained by the devastation? How are these Israelis different from those people who stood outside the walls of the Jewish ghettos in Poland watching the ghettos burn or listening indifferently to the gunshots and screams of other innocents within—among them members of my own family and perhaps yours—while they were being hunted and destroyed?

You see us as you want us to be and not as many of us actually are. We are not all insensate to the suffering we inflict, acceding to cruelty with ease and calm. And because of you, Mr. Wiesel, because of your words—which deny Palestinians their humanity and deprive them of their victimhood—too many can embrace our lack of mercy as if it were something noble, which it is not. Rather, it is something monstrous.

17

Hunger*

I was in the home of my beloved Aunt Frania, my mother's sister. Frania and my mother, Taube, survived the Holocaust and during seven years of horrific incarceration, including in Auschwitz, managed, miraculously, to stay together. There were many stories but the most recurrent and agonizing centered on hunger, unimaginable hunger. This hollowness translated into Frania having a powerful need to husband bread in her home at all times. We used to eat bread and butter for dessert with a cup of coffee.

On this particular day, something happened that had never happened before: Frania ran out of bread. I was standing in her kitchen while she was preparing breakfast. She opened the bin on her kitchen counter where she kept fresh bread and found only a few slices. She then opened her freezer, expecting to find at least two loaves, but found none. For a moment, she stood motionless in front of the open freezer, trying to process the want she had long ago defeated. She closed the freezer door slowly and turned to me with a look of controlled panic in her eyes. She began to tremble. Hugging her tightly, my eyes welling with tears, I promised to run out immediately and buy her bread. There was a big supermarket literally two blocks from her apartment in one of Tel Aviv's busiest shopping areas. But, of course, the abundance of food just yards from her home could not, for those few unbearable moments, mitigate her pain and her fear. Even after I ran home with a bag filled with bread, she remained apprehensive and uncertain.

It was my last day in Gaza after an intensive week of work. I was in a UN bus heading to the Erez crossing point with several UNRWA

---

* Originally published in "Fifty Years of Occupation: A Forum, Part 3," *Middle East Research and Information Project (MERIP)*, June 9, 2017.

employees. We were driving along one of Gaza City's main commercial streets. The bus stopped at a red light at a busy intersection. I was staring out the window and noticed below me, in a parallel lane, an old man in a car. He held some pita bread in his hand and was attempting to make a sandwich with some other kind of food.

Suddenly the old man looked up from his sandwich and motioned to a young boy who was about 11 or 12 years old. The boy was standing on the sidewalk, peddling packs of cigarettes he carried in a wooden tray that was clearly too big for his small frame. The young boy approached the old man and they spoke briefly. I assumed the old man was going to buy a pack of cigarettes but instead the young boy handed him two individual cigarettes, which appeared to be all he could afford. The old man paid the boy and then, in a gesture that the youngster did not expect, the man threw half of his pita sandwich into the cigarette tray. The child hurried off and I kept staring at the old man thinking about his simple act of kindness. As our bus began to move, I looked up and saw the young boy standing at the corner of the intersection ravenously eating his half of the pita bread. He ate with a hunger that startled me.

When I was asked to write this reflection on a half-century of Israeli occupation, these are the stories—one distant, one recent—that kept coming to my mind, insisting to be heard. Bread. Hunger. Deprivation. Without equating their experiences or suffering, my aunt and the little boy in Gaza are linked to each other not only by the occupation but also by what it has wrought after fifty years of denial.

Is it not policy-driven hunger and want—so far removed from settlement freezes and land swaps—more than anything else that binds Palestinians to Jews? And such deprivation is not just about hunger; it is also about place and the certainty of that place, which was never fully resolved for Frania or for the Palestinian boy.

What constitutes an acceptable response to such visceral deprivation? It must begin with what I, as a Jew, have been told I must never do: Claim a relationship between my aunt and the child in Gaza, embracing that child as part of our moral universe. Despite the variance in their lives, each of them deserves and requires the same ethical and principled response to their shared humanity, a response the occupation has, from its inception, demanded we reject.

No more.

18

Book Review, *Palestinians in Syria: Nakba Memories of Shattered Communities*, by Anaheed al-Hardan[*]

Palestinians in Syria is an exceptional and extremely timely work. Through her stunning ethnographic and sociological research, Professor Al-Hardan, herself a third-generation refugee, takes us into the once thriving—but now largely displaced (for the second time) and devastated—Palestinian community in Syria, about which little has been written. Most of her research took place before the Syrian civil war, which allowed Al-Hardan access to a community and way of life that no longer exist as it did for over sixty years. In this way, among others, *Palestinians in Syria* is invaluable as an historical and political document, and a singularly important and substantive contribution to the literature on the Israeli–Palestinian conflict, the Nakba, and refugee studies among other more general areas of study.

The author addresses a range of interconnected and powerfully articulated issues, among them: the intellectual origins of the Nakba, "a historically and politically contingent signifier" (p. 187) in Arab nationalist discourse and its political appropriation by the Palestinian national movement; the different (and sometimes divergent and contradictory) ways in which the Nakba and its narratives are understood, memorialized and mobilized by three generations of Palestinians in Syria, which al-Hardan makes clear is not without controversy and pain; the transmission of loss, the role of memory and the (re)creation of "place" among a people who, at the time of the research, had been displaced for more than six decades, and the meaning of identity, dispossession and exile among first-, second- and third-genera-

---

[*] Originally published in the *Journal of Islamic Studies*, Volume 29, Issue 3, September 2018: Anaheed al-Hardan, *Palestinians in Syria: Nakba Memories of Shattered Communities* (New York: Columbia University Press, 2016) (slightly edited).

tion Palestinians in Syria and its translation—or not—into differing expressions of political awareness and activism.

For me, the most powerful and compelling aspect of this book is the voices of ordinary Palestinians, which have rarely been heard—let alone valued. Al-Hardan allows them to speak and, when they cannot, she respects their silence. Through their memories of the Nakba and the stories and sites of memory they choose to narrate, each generation of Palestinians in Syria struggles in their own way to maintain a personal connection to a home and homeland that, while proximate, remains intangible.

Some of the most poignant Nakba memories by the first generation of Palestinians were not about the horror of the event itself but what they lost as a result of the Nakba—home, "relatives [who] were the dew and the rocks" (p. 96), community celebrations, daily chores, neighbors, trees, fields, animals, even the air. Abu Nidal, a retired schoolteacher from the Safad district who left Palestine at the age of three, recounted, "When those elderly would get together ... [p]eople would stay up until late hours at each other's houses on a daily basis ... They would talk about the homeland, how they went to other areas, this or that spring, and how they would hunt, and how they would set down traps and so forth. They would talk about the life that they had there" (p. 105).

Abu Nidal also describes how their children—his generation—would listen and drink in these stories much as I did as a young child listening to my parents' stories of their life before the Holocaust. The resonance with my own family history as a child of survivors was immediate and powerful. As I read through *Palestinians in Syria* I remembered the stories my mother and father would tell of their families and sibling relationships, a favorite sister or brother, the synagogue where they would pray and study, nasty schoolteachers and generous neighbors, the excitement of the Sabbath, and the meticulous preparation of the Sabbath meal, which was always shared with a homeless person. One man named Muhammad spoke of "relatives made of words" (p. 96) and I knew exactly what he meant: people who throughout our lives we have heard about and loved, but never knew beyond the words used to describe them.

The book ends with a reflection on the impact of Syria's civil war on the Palestinian community, expressed by an even more destructive sense of loss than that of 1948. Many of course were displaced within Syria, while others fled elsewhere including Egypt, Jordan and Lebanon. Al-Hardan was told that "the catastrophe of today is incomparable—indeed, it dwarfs—the Nakba of 1948 [p. 190] ... The Nakba is in many ways now also about the destruction of the sixty-seven-year-old Palestinian communities in Syria that were constituted anew in the aftermath of 1948 ... and is rooted in the fear ... that unlike 1948, this devastation may be final ..." (p. 188).

This excerpt from a mother displaced from her home in Khan Eshieh to a Damascus suburb powerfully captures the awful predicament facing the Palestinian community of Syria and deserves to be quoted at length:

I was thinking to myself, when our families left Palestine in 1948 and settled in Khan Eshieh, their intention was to be close to their homelands. A place from where they could immediately return once their crisis was over, a place from where every single one of them could immediately return to their own home. But unfortunately their crisis was to be prolonged, it took a long time, and they began to yearn and to miss their homeland. And unfortunately, the dream of return did not realize itself and so they decided to remain in the camp and to turn it into a little Palestine or a little homeland. They began to work on the farms and the lands and inside a little and very beautiful homeland. And they became attached to it and made us attached to it ... And now the crisis of our age has unfolded, and we are left, and people started renting apartments close to the camp ... and here we are sitting and waiting to return to our homes. And what I fear is the length of the crisis and for everyone to create his own personal homeland because we Palestinians cannot live without a homeland. But did you see how they thought it too much for us to remain in a little homeland that is three kilometers by four kilometers? This little homeland that is in fact very, very large ... [The generation of Palestine] are the ones who created this homeland for us, most of them are now gone, and this is why we may remain without a homeland for the rest of our lives. Because we are weak and our worries have broken us, while their worries made them strong. (p. 184)

"What does it mean," asks a Palestinian from Yarmouk, "when the Nakba for people has been transformed into the return to a limited geographical locality like Yarmouk Camp?" (p. 187). Under such dreadful conditions are Palestinians still able to form a "narrative that can face Israeli memory?" (p. 89).

Is this narrative, too, now lost and with it the Nakba memories that sustain it?

19

On Equating BDS with Anti-Semitism: A Letter to the Members of the German Government[*]

To the Members of the German Government:

I write to you regarding the motion recently passed by the Bundestag that equated BDS with anti-Semitism. I also write to you as Jew, a child of Holocaust survivors and as a scholar of the Israeli–Palestinian conflict.

My mother, Taube, and father, Abraham, survived Auschwitz among other horrors. My father was the only survivor in his family of six children and my mother survived with only one sister in a family that was larger than my father's. I know, without question, that if they were alive today, the motion you are being asked to endorse would terrify them, given the repression of tolerance and witness that it clearly embraces. I shall not restate what others have already written protesting your action, but I do have some thoughts I would like to share.

In September 2014, I was invited to speak on Gaza at the Heinrich Boll Stiftung after the terrible events of that summer. During the question period, a gentleman stood up who was quite agitated. He argued quite strongly that given Germany's history, it is difficult if not impossible for Germans to criticize Israel. Embedded in his statement was the belief that Germans should never engage in such criticism. He seemed to insist that I accept this. I do not. Nor would my parents.

My response to him, then, is the same as my response to you now: if your history has imposed a burden and an obligation upon you, it is to defend justice not Israel. This is what Judaism, not Zionism,

---

[*]   Originally published in *Counterpunch*, June 4, 2019.

demands. Your obligation does not lie in making Israel or the Jewish people special or selectively excusing injustice because Jews happen to be committing it; it lies in holding Israel and Jews to the same ethical and moral standards that you would demand of any people, including yourselves. If you think that by refusing to criticize Israel's brutal occupation—and punishing those who do—you are protecting and securing the State of Israel or the place of the Jewish people in the world, you are terribly misguided. Your approach achieves the exact opposite—by insisting on treating Jews as an exception, you are weakening us by again making us a kind of anomaly, an intruder, a negation of Europe. It makes us more vulnerable to and unsheltered from the racism and the true anti-Semitism now resurgent throughout the world.

Your sense of guilt, if that is the correct word, should not derive from criticizing Israel. It should reside in remaining silent in the face of injustice as so many of your forebears did before, during and after the Holocaust.

I lost a large extended family to fascism and racism. By endorsing the motion that alleges that BDS is anti-Semitic—regardless of one's position on BDS—you are criminalizing the right to free speech and dissent and those who choose to exercise it, which is exactly how fascism takes root. You also trivialize and dishonor the real meaning of anti-Semitism. How would you explain that to Taube and Abraham?

Sincerely,
Dr. Sara Roy

20

Tears of Salt: A Brief Reflection on Israel, Palestine and the Coronavirus*

On March 26, 2020, Israeli civil administration officials arrived in Khirbet Ibziq, a Palestinian community in the West Bank. They were there to prevent the construction of a field clinic (among other structures) during the Covid-19 pandemic that emerged in the West Bank just three weeks before. According to the Israeli human rights group, B'Tselem, "[The civil administration] confiscated poles and sheeting that were meant to form eight tents, two for a field clinic, and four for emergency housing for residents evacuated from their homes, and two as makeshift mosques."[1] In addition, the Israeli authorities closed a coronavirus testing clinic in East Jerusalem because the testing kits were supplied by the Palestinian Authority, which is not allowed to operate in Jerusalem.[2] On July 22, 2020, "Israeli forces demolished ... a Covid-19 testing clinic in the city of Hebron, the epicenter of the outbreak in the occupied West Bank."[3]

In the months since, the Israeli military has increased home demolitions and the destruction of infrastructure in the West Bank. On November 3, 2020, according to the UN Office for the Coordination of Humanitarian Affairs (UNOCHA), "the Israeli authorities demolished 83 structures in the Bedouin community of Humsa Al Bqai'a, in the northern Jordan Valley, displacing 73 people, including 41 children. This is the largest number of people displaced in a single incident since March 2016, and the largest number of structures demolished in a single incident since OCHA started monitoring demolitions in 2009."[4] In that same month, the authorities also destroyed a 1.5-kilometer water pipeline, severing the villages of Mughayer al-Abid and Khirbet al-Majaz in the Hebron district from their water supply.[5] In

---

* Published here for the first time.

fact, between January and October 2020, when the virus was spreading, Israel demolished 604 structures and displaced 788 people.[6]

The coronavirus has also spread to the densely populated Gaza Strip, threatening its 2 million people who are trapped under an onerous blockade now in its 14th year. According to *The Lancet*, "The Gaza Strip faces high levels of poverty, unemployment, food insecurity, and lacks sufficient water while the blockade disrupts medical supply chains, curtails the movement of patients and health workers, and severely inhibits medical capacity-building and public health development."[7] In Gaza, furthermore, physical distancing is impossible. In Jabalya refugee camp, for example, 113,990 people live on half a square mile,[8] and this is not the highest population density among Gaza's refugee camps.

Although the Israeli authorities have allowed some medical supplies (donated by international organizations) into Gaza, Israel's Defense Minister Naftali Bennett offered a deal to Gaza's Hamas authorities: ventilators and other forms of medical and humanitarian aid in exchange for the remains of two Israeli soldiers killed in the 2014 war on the Strip.[9] In making this offer, Mr. Bennett appears unconcerned that Gaza's severely diminished economy and healthcare system has been undermined by a range of Israeli-imposed measures, notably the blockade, and three wars between 2008 and 2014, which, at their peak, displaced hundreds of thousands of people, killed thousands and imposed billions of dollars of damage on Gaza's infrastructure. This has made the economy and the healthcare sector in Gaza highly dependent on donor aid, which has grown increasingly and dangerously restrictive.

Israel's action of denying first aid clinics and attaching conditions to ventilators and other forms of assistance for Palestinian communities during a healthcare emergency brings into striking relief—perhaps even more than war itself—a relentless imperative that has shaped the views of Israeli and pro-Israeli supporters toward Palestinians, Jews among them. This imperative is not about cruelty per se although it is cruel; it is about the need to protect from the risks of self-inquiry and the need to maintain the subterfuge of innocence and impunity. It is about cowardice and complicity, of intellectuals and others.

As a Jew, I am appalled by Israel's behavior but also frightened in a way that is altogether new, even after more than thirty years of sobering engagement with the conflict. I am frightened by the moral atrophy that necessarily accompanies policies that adapt so easily and willingly to the withholding, in any form, of critical life-saving measures to an unprotected people. The denial of such relief—in the absence of any struggle against it—speaks to something atrocious and deadened. It also speaks to a shameful conformism without which injustice—and worse—could not occur. I think of Camus' description in *The Plague* of a city inhabited by "people asleep on their feet," benumbed, rejecting memories that are uncomfortable and rewriting history into a kind of anti-history where too many of us now dwell, content but also anxious.

In his excellent work, *On Tyranny*, Timothy Snyder discusses the "politics of inevitability," a "sense that history could move in only one direction," which, he shows is profoundly anti-historical. For Americans, Snyder writes, that direction was toward liberal democracy particularly after the horrors of fascism, Nazism and communism.[10] For Israel (and by extension, perhaps, the larger Jewish community), the politics of inevitability is taking us toward an "unchangeable hegemony"[11] where seeing—into the past or the future—occurs only through the scope of a rifle,[12] and where our security—and humanity— are ensured by denying the same to others.

At the end of World War II, my parents returned to their shtetl in Poland hoping to find family who had survived the Holocaust; no one had, and they soon realized they could not remain because Jews were again being hunted. They went to Berlin where many Eastern European Jews fled and remained there for several years while preparing to emigrate to the United States. Shortly before their departure for the US in 1951 from Bremerhaven, my mother learned that a man was living in the area who had been a senior official in the Halbstadt concentration camp where she and her sister were sent from Auschwitz. He was a decent man, according to my mother, and tried to use his power to protect the Jewish prisoners as much as he could. My mother discovered his address—I do not know how—and went to his home. She went there to thank him.

I thought about my mother's simple but profound act as I read about Israel's disgraceful one. She allowed herself to look beyond abstraction into the soul of the German official and there she found humanity, for which she was grateful. By seeking out this man in this way, my mother could imagine a different future when, just a short time before, there was no future for her to imagine. It took courage for her to do what she did, but it also took forgiveness and faith of the kind that too many of us no longer possess. Instead, we seek a struggle that is permanent—an equilibrium created of aversion and antipathy—where compromise is betrayal and questioning profane, where negotiating the supply of breathing machines for people needing to breathe is seen as civilized, even heroic.

I suspect that many Jews and Israelis would consider my mother's act deviant, outside moral boundaries considered acceptable. But what are these boundaries and what limits of possibility do they set? This question begs another one: what is it that makes us human?

Gone is any evocation of the sacred. In its stead, we find ourselves beyond attachment in a place of self-creation (and self-destruction?) where history, reality and truth are only what we imagine them to be, where amnesia takes the place of awareness.[13]

Less than a month after crushing the first aid clinic in Khirbet Ibziq, Israelis marked Holocaust Remembrance Day, "a catastrophe brought by humans on humans," said Israel's President Reuven Rivlin.[14] While there is no equivalence between the catastrophe that befell the Jewish people and the one that potentially looms for Palestinians in Gaza, I cannot but think of the ways in which our histories and futures remain bound together despite our sustained and insistent denials.

What does it mean to live in truth, as Vaclav Havel once wrote? Tragically, for too many of us, we will never know the answer.

PART VI   THE PASSING OF A GENERATION: COMMEMORATING COURAGEOUS PALESTINIAN VOICES

When great souls die,
the air around us becomes
light, rare, sterile.
We breathe, briefly.
Our eyes, briefly,
see with
a hurtful clarity.
Our memory, suddenly sharpened,
examines,
gnaws on kind words
unsaid,
promised walks
never taken …

And when great souls die,
after a period peace blooms,
slowly and always
irregularly. Spaces fill
with a kind of
soothing electric vibration.
Our senses, restored, never
to be the same, whisper to us.
They existed. They existed.
We can be. Be and be
better. For they existed.

> Maya Angelou
> *When Great Trees Fall*

To notice is to rescue, to redeem.

> James Wood
> *Serious Noticing: Selected Essays, 1997–2019*

21

A Tribute to Eyad el-Sarraj*

Over twenty years ago, I encountered a woman in a refugee camp in Gaza whom I have never forgotten. It was a painfully brief encounter, ending as imperceptibly as it began. I was walking in the camp with some male friends when a woman unexpectedly approached me. She took my arm and pulled me toward her, and said to me, "I have nothing left to feed my children but black milk. What good am I?" Before I could respond—clearly at a loss as to how—or think to hold on to her hand, which was momentarily fastened to my arm, she disappeared into the camp, evaporating, it seemed, into an expanse of dust and air. I stood there stunned, trying to understand what had just happened, tears welling in my eyes. My friends, clearly embarrassed by the encounter, simply dismissed her as someone pitiable, even crazy.

When I was asked to write this tribute to Eyad, I immediately thought of this woman whom I shall call Nadia, and my few, searing moments with her. To this day, I wish Eyad had been with me that day in the camp; he would not have been ashamed by Nadia as my male friends apparently were but would have reached out to her and embraced her, offering the comfort she so desperately needed.

By now much has been written about Eyad—his background, his work and his many professional achievements and honors. I shall not repeat what others have said. Rather, I want to share some personal experiences with this remarkable man—one of which I have never before revealed—that powerfully express who he was.

I met Eyad in the summer of 1985 during my first visit to Gaza. I was there to do fieldwork for my doctoral dissertation on American economic assistance to the Palestinians in the Occupied Territories. I was urged to meet Dr. el-Sarraj whom, I was told, was the only psychiatrist in the Gaza Strip. He was also the director of the mental health

* Originally published in the *Journal of Palestine Studies*, Volume 43, Number 3, Spring 2014.

service in Gaza's Department of Health, which was under the control of the Israeli authorities. Our first meeting was at the Marna House, a small hotel where I was staying. Eyad walked into the parlor of the hotel and I remember a tall, handsome man whose presence filled the room. We spent a long time talking, although I do not remember for how long. What I do remember was his fierce honesty and the absence of any sense of caution or tentativeness. Where others were initially (and understandably) careful in speaking with me—a foreigner whom they did not know—Eyad was open, direct and resolute.

I did not see much of Eyad that summer but that changed when I returned to Gaza in early 1986 to do additional fieldwork for a study of conditions in the Gaza Strip for the West Bank Data Base Project, under the direction of Meron Benvenisti. One sector I was tasked to describe was health and I very much wanted to visit Shifa Hospital, then Gaza's main hospital run by the Israeli military government. However, the Israeli authorities prohibited access to Shifa by foreigners and the only way one could enter was with official permission, which was rarely granted. I called Eyad, hoping he might have some needed influence with the military administration. He listened to me and told me he would meet me at Marna House the following morning. I assumed it was to discuss how best to approach the authorities for permission. When Eyad showed up at Marna House he greeted me warmly and we had the following exchange:

"Let's go, Sara."

"Let's go where," I asked?

"Shifa."

"Shifa? You mean you got me permission?"

"No, you will never get permission and when you are inside the hospital you will understand why. I shall bring you in because you must see for yourself the conditions in the hospital."

"Eyad, you could get into serious trouble with the authorities. You might lose your job. I don't want you to take such risks for me and I am not asking you to."

"I am not worried. But you must write about what you see, about everything I show you."

At considerable risk to himself—and it was only later, from others, that I learned how great the risk actually was—Eyad surreptitiously brought me into Shifa, walking me through the entire hospital, including the operating room. He allowed me to take as much time as I needed despite the worried looks of the hospital staff. He did not say too much but he did not have to; conditions inside the hospital were appalling as the following excerpt from my published report, *The Gaza Strip Survey*, shows:

> Mice, roaches and other insects were observed scurrying through individual wards, rooms and bathrooms. Rooms were extremely dirty and in a state of decay as indicated by broken windows, peeling paint and cracked floors. Hospital beds were old and rusting and patients were observed two to a bed, lying on sheets that were torn and blood-stained. Hospital personnel indicated that the same sheets are often used for more than one patient due to a lack of supplies. Rooms are cleaned only when patients can afford to pay ... The surgical operating room [was] in a similar state of deterioration and extremely unsterile; cigarette butts were observed on the floor of the [OR].[1]

This one paragraph caught the attention of the international media and a firestorm ensued, including a four-minute segment on life inside Gaza on the [American] ABC evening news. Eyad told me that the Palestinian director of the hospital was fired and that hospital conditions soon improved but only temporarily. After Shifa was cleaned up and repaired, the military government invited various international groups and organizations into the hospital as a way of refuting my claims. The Knesset even threatened to subpoena Meron and me since they accused us of having been paid by the PLO to write the report!

* * *

I was often asked how I got access to the hospital, which I never revealed until now. I remember receiving a call in Boston from a senior official at the American embassy in Tel Aviv, who, surprised that I managed to get inside Shifa, asked me whether I had seen dogs running through the hospital as he had when he was last there. Many people thanked me for exposing the conditions in Shifa but it was Eyad who was truly responsible for doing so.

Eyad was an extremely principled man and he did not fear retribution for actions he believed in. I remember another time, years later, sitting with him in the garden of his home. It was the spring of 1996, and not long before he had been appointed the commissioner general of the Palestinian Independent Commission for Citizens' Rights. Eyad was very upset about the behavior of the Palestinian Authority in Gaza and its increasingly flagrant abuse of human rights. But what outraged him the most, it seemed to me, was the facile, almost effortless nature of the PA's abuse, the ease with which they oppressed their own people, and the total lack of remorse that defined their abuse. His anger was palpable but so were his pain and the feeling that his beloved Gaza had been betrayed once again. He told me how he was going to publicly expose the PA in an effort to initiate a process of reform. I remember feeling anxious and tense, fearing, I told him, his arrest and possible torture, which is what subsequently happened. Eyad, however, remained consistent and unwavering, telling me, "Silence is not an option."

In the near three decades of our friendship, I came to know Eyad very well. There are few people for whom I had more respect, admiration and affection. I always learned from his example. He was, as others have written, long and deeply committed to addressing trauma, especially in children, and to protecting and honoring the dignity of the individual irrespective of religion or nationality. For me, Eyad's most important legacy lies in one fundamental belief, which animated his life: while resistance to oppression can assume many forms, the most powerful form of resistance resides in maintaining one's humanity in the presence of cruelty and in seeking that humanity in others, including in one's oppressors. Such resistance, he believed, can never be extinguished.

22

Remembering Naseer Aruri*

When I was pursuing my doctoral studies in international development, I knew that I wanted to do research in the Middle East, particularly around the Israeli–Palestinian conflict. But I was unable to find a research topic that excited me, combining my disciplinary interest in development with my regional interest in the Middle East. So, I turned my attention to Africa and fell in love with Tanzania; after much thought and planning, I set my research sights on the Maasai people. One year later, however, I found myself in a totally different place, interviewing people in the refugee camps of the Gaza Strip and in factories and labor organizations inside the West Bank. I was immersed in a reality that staggered me, helped by people I barely knew—whose assistance would have been inconceivable to me just a short time before.

It was the mid-1980s and at the time, I did not fully appreciate that I was entering a field of study and academic research that was politically volatile and extremely contentious, for which there was little support and even less understanding—inside the academy and beyond. As a Jew and child of Holocaust survivors, my work was beyond comprehension to many if not most people in my own community, including certain members of my extended family, a betrayal for which some have never forgiven me.

When I think back over those thirty years there were, of course, many difficulties and painful times but more importantly, there were profound rewards and experiences that have been among the most meaningful of my life. Among those rewards are the truly remarkable human beings I came to know along the way. One cannot continue along such an arduous, albeit necessary path alone—it is simply not possible.

---

* Originally published in *Journal of Holy Land and Palestine Studies*, Volume 14, Number 2, 2015.

Naseer was preeminent among those extraordinary individuals I encountered. I read his work years before I knew him and his work showed me—as a young and inexperienced graduate student—that it is possible to challenge dominant ways of thinking and framing, that it is possible to shift, if not transform, intellectual boundaries, and exercise much-needed criticism in a society actively positioned against such criticism. Naseer showed me that it is possible and crucial to make one's work public and accessible and by doing so, resist the displacement of people's lived realities into simplistically reduced constructs. He taught me that it is essential not only to see things as they are, but how they came to be and to show that they are not inevitable but conditional, the product of human choices that can—and Naseer believed—will be changed. He embodied the role of the public intellectual and teacher in its truest sense—refusing to remain silent in the face of injustice, confronting extant orthodoxies rather than accepting them, and expanding the boundaries of legitimate debate.

Naseer was among those few courageous scholars who, at an unwelcoming and indeed, hostile time, painstakingly and with great determination, carved out the intellectual and political space that I, among myriad others, have entered and hopefully widened, legitimizing a discourse that the majority had long shunned and dismissed.

Naseer was an individual and a scholar of immense integrity and dignity, always consistent in who he was and what he believed and open to new ways of thinking and understanding. I cannot remember a time when I saw him get angry. He treated others with respect and consideration, including those with whom he disagreed.

It was my great honor and privilege to have known and learned from him. I would not be who I am without his humane and luminous example.

PART VII   THE PAST AS FUTURE:
LESSONS FORGOTTEN

We cannot be exiled and we cannot be accommodated …

We forged ourselves out of this fire and if we could do that—and we have done that—we can deal with what now lies before us …

Every white person in this country … knows one thing: they may not know … what I want but they know they would not like to be black here. If they know that, they know everything they need to know.

We are all, in any case, here.

James Baldwin
Address
University of California, Berkeley
January 15, 1979

The Israelis are creating facts on the ground.

We Palestinians are the facts.

Faisal Husseini,
responding to Daniel Seideman as told by Daniel Seidemann
Conference on *Jerusalem: From Past Divisions to a Shared Future*?
The Balfour Project
October 27, 2020

23

Gaza: Out of Sight*

No one goes to Gaza without good reason. From East Jerusalem, the journey only takes ninety minutes, but few other than Arab commuters take it. The taxis, called *services* by their clientele, leave from the Damascus Gate. They are Arabic transportation and are so identified by their license plates: blue plates, as opposed to the yellow of Israeli vehicles, and for the Gaza *service*, the letter *ayin*, for Azza, the Hebrew name for Gaza.[1]

The common route heads southward through the West Bank past Bethlehem and then the refugee camp known as the Dheisheh. The road ascends into the white and gray hills of Judea and then cuts sharply west into the carefully terraced farmland north of the Negev Desert. This final leg ends abruptly at a military checkpoint located on the border of pre-1967 Israel and the Strip. Vehicles entering and leaving Gaza must pass through this outpost, and the Arab vehicles are subject to a security inspection varying in intensity from car to car.

The countryside inside Gaza is mostly barren, dotted with Bedouin shacks and tents and small villages. The air is hot and stagnant; the sun seems to burn rather than shine.

One UN source estimates that no more than 35 foreigners are in the territory at any one time. There is no American government presence at all, unlike the West Bank, which, among other things, has the US consulate in East Jerusalem. And there are no tourists, either foreign or Israeli, as there are no tourist sights. Yet, the Israeli government has tried to lure Jewish settlers into the region by proclaiming the beach area—which, with its beautiful white sands is indeed spectacular—to be the future "Riviera of Israel." For that purpose, they point to an

---

* Originally published in French as "Gaza: hors des regards," *Revue d'études Palestiniennes*, Number 25, Autumn 1987 and co-authored with Gary Taubes. Published in English here for the first time (slightly edited).

exotic-looking beach club on the coastal road, a notable exhibit on the official tour of the territory.

Gaza City itself, with a population of 140,000, is parched and dusty. Some of the streets are no more than dirt and sand, narrow and constricting, congested with donkey-drawn carts and multi-ton trucks hauling citrus. Gaza has no height. The buildings, many of them only half-built and already decaying, are low and sprawling; the sense of flatness is oppressive.

The road into Gaza eventually leads to the *Meidan Falesteen*, Gaza's main square, and narrows again on the far side, appearing to end a quarter-mile further on in a wall of concrete and barbed wire that surrounds Israel's military headquarters in the Strip. Little of what exists behind the wall is visible from the street. An army watchtower, however, defies the seemingly one-dimensional constraints of the city and rises above it. Two soldiers sit in the head of the watchtower; one peers through binoculars at the Gazans below, the other sits behind a machine gun doing the same.

There are the outward signs of the occupation: the soldiers in Gaza, the Israeli jeeps on patrol, machine guns mounted over the two front headlights, the soldiers on the rooftops. Most conspicuous are the foot patrols. Perhaps a dozen Israeli soldiers in fatigues walking two by two down the Gazan streets. Their machine guns unslung. These are often young men, and they look frightened, nervous, sometimes arrogant, and sometimes angry. They also look, as one American volunteer worker in Gaza put it, as though they would rather be someplace else.

On Saturdays, the foot patrols are common sights. A dozen such patrols might be visible in the vicinity of the *Meidan Falesteen*. It is on Saturdays when Israeli Jews come into Gaza to shop—the prices are 15–20 per cent lower in Gaza than in Israel proper—and bomb threats and stabbings are most frequent. The soldiers' role is three-fold, according to David Greenberg, a reporter for the *Jerusalem Post* who published a diary of his month on reserve service in the territories. Primarily, they serve to guard the Jewish settlers in the territories, although many, says Greenberg, have little sympathy for these settlers. Secondly, they are there to guard against the settlers, to prevent vigilante actions against the Arab populations. And then the job that is most important, to protect themselves. Everyone, Greenberg says, "is a potential attacker."

The soldiers are instructed to talk to the locals, as the military calls them, as little as possible. And the locals avoid contact, even eye-contact, as well. Often the Arabs will pause in their activity until the soldiers have passed. A few will ignore the soldiers. Those who do watch, do it with clear animosity and some fear. The Palestinian children called the soldiers "*yehuds.*" *Yehud* means "Jew" in Arabic. The usage is most certainly derogatory. But even the children know to keep out of the soldiers' way.

This is the occupation, twenty years old. When Israeli forces took Gaza in June of 1967, the Palestinians assumed that it would be days, weeks at most, before the Egyptian Army returned. After twenty years, they still insist that the occupation is temporary, as do many Israelis. But in Gaza, even more so than in the West Bank, the occupation is the overwhelming fact of existence. Well over half of the Arab population of Gaza was born after Israel took the Strip, together with the Sinai, the Golan Heights and the West Bank in the Six Day War. After twenty years, the Palestinians of Gaza are stateless, they carry no passports, but identity cards required by the Israeli occupiers. For most Arabs and Israelis, precedents no longer exist for relationships other than that as occupied and occupier.

Gaza, as the former mayor of Gaza City, Rashad Shawwa, calls it, is in the forgotten man of the Middle East. Shawwa is a wealthy citrus farmer whom the Israelis appointed mayor in 1971, and then again in 1975, and both times deposed him when he refused to go along with the military authorities. He is the official, high official in Gaza. When the subject of Gaza comes up in the outside world, as it infrequently does, Shawwa is chosen to tell of his people's plight to the interested diplomats. For the last eight years. Shawwa has been trying to win approval to build a Polytechnic in Gaza, and although he has a promise from the American Near East Refugee Aid (ANERA) to provide a million dollars for the school, the Israelis have refused him. On the two occasions, he says, when the authorities have given him a reason, it has been that there are not enough jobs in Gaza, so why train more workers.

Shawwa is biased. And so is everybody in this corner of the world. "Gaza," says Shawwa, "is a labor camp. The Soweto of Israel." His definition of development is to "get rid of the occupation."

And Gaza, once again, is the forgotten man of the Middle East. Discussions on the resolution of the Arab–Israeli conflict naturally center on the West Bank and whether or not, or to what extent, Israel is willing to give it up. In these dialogues, Gaza sits like a geographical orphan in her out-of-the-way corner of Israel bordering the Sinai. In 1982, when Menachem Begin swore that Israel would not surrender any part of, as he put it, "Judea, Samaria, the Gaza Strip and the Golan Heights," it was only Judea and Samaria, he said, that would "belong to the Jewish people to the end of time."

Unlike the West Bank, the Gaza Strip has never been claimed by any Arab state. Although Egypt ruled Gaza from 1948 to 1967, it never offered Gazans citizenship, as Jordan has done for those Arabs in the West Bank. Gaza does not have the strategic significance of the Golan Heights, which borders on Syria and which Israel annexed in 1981. (Although in the past 3,500 years, according to a 1974 Israeli publication, the land of Israel has been invaded 85 times from the Strip; each time, control of Gaza "has been considered essential for military penetration into what is today the State of Israel.") It does not have either the geographical proximity to Jerusalem or the religious and cultural significance of the West Bank: as one UN administrator in Gaza put it "The Old Testament is mentioned in Gaza, rather than Gaza in the Old Testament." There are no Bethlehems, no Hebrons, no Shilohs, no Canaans in Gaza. This was not the homeland of the Jewish people. Jesus was not born in Gaza, nor did Judah Maccabee overcome the Syrians in Gaza.

Gaza City and its neighboring towns grew only to feed and rest the caravans traveling the principal trade route between Egypt and Syria. The territory was named, so the story goes, from "Gaza of Hashem," after Hashem ibn 'Abd al-Manaf, the great-grandfather of the prophet Mohammad, who is said to have died in the area while returning from a commercial venture in the Arabian Peninsula. When Samson went to Gaza, it was only to challenge the Philistines, and the Philistines, from whom the Palestinians derive their name, repaid him with the theft of his vision and then imprisonment.

In this region that's been debated over, prayed for, and fought over for more than four millennia, Gaza has been ignored. Now, because the poverty is so intense, the extent of the problem so unimaginable, the future so bleak, it is easiest to ignore Gaza. Within the artificial confines of the Strip is one of the worst refugee problems in the world—what has been called a demographic nightmare. The Strip itself is only 28 miles long and five miles wide, encompassing an area only one-fifteenth the size of the West Bank, and yet some 520,000 Arabs inhabit Gaza—a population density of 3,700 people per square mile, equivalent to that of Hong Kong. And that is if one does not take into account that those Arabs live on only two-thirds of the land, and the other third has been taken by Israel and is home to 2,200 Jewish settlers. The Arab population is expected to grow to over 1 million by the turn of the century. Of the total population, around 70 per cent, some 360,000, are refugees living predominantly in eight refugee camps located inside the territory.

The United Nations Relief and Works Agency (UNRWA) built the camps in 1950, expecting them to be temporary shelters for the Palestinians who fled their homes in what is now Israel in the Arab–Israeli War two years earlier. The refugees arrived in Gaza with nothing, and they have remained so through the Egyptian and Israeli occupations. The camps, which have now served as housing for over 35 years, are endless labyrinths filled with people, mostly children. They are irrigated by open sewers flowing to the Mediterranean, and crosscut by the wide Israeli roads, laid down with bulldozers in 1971 at the direction of Ariel Sharon in the successful effort to flush the Palestine Liberation Army from the camps.

Twenty years ago, those Arabs that held jobs in Gaza worked within the Strip. Today, unable to find employment in Gaza, half of the work force climb aboard buses and *services* each morning to commute to low-paying, menial jobs in Israel proper—this flow of workers includes doctors, lawyers and engineers, as well as an unknown number of children under 15. They return to Gaza each night from their jobs as street sweepers, construction workers, maids and dishwashers. For security reasons, they are barred from Israel between the hours of 1 a.m. and 4 a.m. For those Gazans who try to leave Gaza, they find it is not easy. Gazans without passports travel under a "Travel Document for Palestine Refugees" issued by Egypt, and the American embassy, for one, rarely grants Gazans visas, because of the threat of terrorism and because the Gazans may choose not to return.

With Gaza, Israel assumed a problem that seems to defy solutions as well as imagination. Israeli authorities have made few public statements about the refugees, other than that they are not their responsibility, but that of UNRWA. (Although at a 1986 conference of Tehiya—a right-wing party not necessarily representative in its thinking of the majority of Israelis—Yuval Ne'eman suggested that a "sober and realistic" solution, as the *Jerusalem Post* put it, "is to make peace conditional on the resettlement outside Greater Israel of half a million Palestinian refugees—including 300,000 in Gaza.") The refugees are simply there. They have no rootedness, no homeland other than Palestine, which no longer exists. They identify themselves not as Gazans, but as Palestinians.

They support the PLO and more and more, they admit it. To the West and to the Jewish citizens of Israel, this is a tacit statement of their threat to the Jewish homeland and the State of Israel. Israeli authorities maintain that membership in the PLO is "akin to advocating violence." To the Palestinians of Gaza and the West Bank, the PLO is their sole legal and political representative in the absence of a government, as well as their only bargaining chip in international negotiations.

Israel has attempted to resettle the refugees in government-sponsored housing projects, under what is known officially as the "Build Your Own Home" program, and which the Palestinians consider just another carrot in the Israelis' carrot-and-stick governing policy. Israel has provided the land—leased for 99 years—the mortgage and the building material, and the Arabs have to provide the labor. In some cases, the Israelis have done the building, and the Arabs have had to pay for establishment costs—roads, electricity and water networks— and the cost of construction. Before moving into the projects, however, the Arabs have also been required to demolish their camp shelter—the assessed value of which Israel puts toward the new housing—and to give up their UNRWA card, which is their meal ticket and a guarantee of clothing, medicine and schooling.

"The projects," as described in a *Jerusalem Post* editorial, "remind you of a lower middle-class neighborhood in Herzliya, a town on another former sand dune. Here are the same two-story stucco structures. neat lawns of hardy Bermuda grass, expensive TV aerials, and children in American football jerseys kicking soccer balls."

Mary Khass, a Palestinian teacher in Gaza, described the housing projects this way: "The project is surrounded by high fences, with strong flood lights all around. A 'block' consists of 24 houses ... The entrances to these blocks are very small and narrow. It is arranged in such a way that the Israelis could close the entire block within 15 minutes if necessary. The houses are so small and poorly built that it's beyond humanity."

By December 1985, after a decade of the program, one in ten Palestinian families had taken advantage of it and moved. Many simply could not raise the money required, equivalent to $25,000. The rest saw a political motive behind the housing projects and rejected it. "Getting rid of the refugee problem," as Khass put it. Normalizing it. Turning the refugees into residents of Gaza, and no longer refugees. And the refugees, as they believed when the Israelis took Gaza in 1967, refuse to accept the status quo as enough and still insist that their situation is temporary.

"We're not going anywhere," said Abdul Latif Abu Middain, a director of the Arab Citrus Marketing Board in Gaza. "Why should we go in the first place? There's absolutely no place to go. So, what's happened is we're staying here accumulating bitterness and hatred. And that has to find somewhere to go. Violence is inevitable. Life here is slow torture."

As it stands today, the occupation is indeed a hostile one. Young Palestinians have considerable contact today with their occupiers, and it has not served to bring the two groups closer together. The number of violent confrontations between Arab and Jew in the territories has risen from 400–500 per year between 1977 and 1980, to several thousand in each of the last few years. Although official Israeli sources claim that the PLO is behind all the violent acts directed at Israelis—the PLO indeed did take credit for most of them—according to Meron Benvenisti, a former deputy mayor of Jerusalem and now head of the West Bank Data Base Project, "More than 50 per cent of these acts originated in the territories with young Palestinians, with no direct orders from the PLO." These acts are carried out not by organized groups, but by youth who were born and grew up during the Israeli occupation. These young people operate in broad daylight and are apparently undeterred by the consequences of their actions.

The Israeli settlers have reacted to the violence and the tension with retaliatory raids on Palestinian towns and refugee camps, and the Israeli troops have often found themselves caught between the two groups. In the latest incidences, which rocked the Strip in January and February, over a dozen Gazans were shot, at least one fatally, during three weeks of demonstrations that were sparked by the arrest and subsequent expulsion of an Islamic University student, accused of leading a pro-Fatah youth movement.

As reported by *Al-Fajr*, a Palestinian weekly located in East Jerusalem and which is vetted by Israeli censors before publication: the military arrested at least 60 students in demonstrations, and the violence included, among other episodes, a settler shooting a Gazan student accused of stoning his car. (According to the *Jerusalem Post*, the number of guns in the settlements is estimated at roughly the number of households, and settlers have constant access to weapons, either as reservists or as civilians guarding the settlement as part of a regional defense system in coordination with the army.) A group of settlers beat refugees with gun butts and clubs in the al-Maghazi Camp, putting three in the hospital, one with multiple skull fractures, and "unidentified persons" sprayed acid on female students at a school in the Jabalya camp. Israel radio later attributed the acid episode to Arab demonstrators trying to force the students to participate in the demonstrations, an account which was publicly condemned by Gazan residents, including employees at the Islamic University and at the University of Gaza.

Israel has always found Gaza a difficult place to control, even more so than the West Bank. Historically, Gaza has been the center of PLO resistance in the Occupied Territories. And the Palestinian refugees who fled into the territory in 1948 and 1967 are more militant than elsewhere—a result, if nothing else, of their extreme poverty and their belief that they have nothing more to lose.

Israel does not make it easy to assemble information on Gaza. It officially prohibits the disclosure of information dealing with the territory. Employees of Israeli-administered offices are barred from releasing information without official permission from the appropriate government authorities, a procedure that can take months or years.

Official population statistics and demographic predictions are qualified by the fact that the last official census of the West Bank and Gaza was conducted in 1967. Palestinian sources are equally hard to come by, as the Israeli military government prohibits Palestinians from performing any research, study, or survey on Gaza. The Central Bureau of Statistics in Jerusalem publishes the most comprehensive compendium of statistics on the West Bank and Gaza, but much of the data are economic in nature and unreliable. "When you use Israeli statistics on Gaza," says one UNRWA officer, "you are approaching the fringes of statistical credibility." Some of these Israeli accounting practices, as Benvenisti put it, "border on the absurd." Benvenisti's West Bank Data Base Project is now considered perhaps the only unbiased and reliable source of economic, demographic, and social data on the territories.

Whatever the reality is in Gaza, it is a difficult one to nail down. It was the Israeli author Amos Oz who originally saw fit to label Gaza the "Soweto of the State of Israel" back in 1981. Not much seems to have changed since Oz visited Gaza, except the situation has deteriorated further.

To visit Gaza and write what appears to be reality is to be labeled pro-Palestinian by those who believe that nothing is amiss in Gaza. To point out that something seems to be very much amiss in Gaza, and that as the belligerent occupier, Israel may be very much at fault, is to be labeled naive, anti-Zionist, or even anti-Semitic. "You have fallen into the Palestinian trap," said one prominent Israeli lawyer, upon hearing a discussion of the problems in Gaza. "It's a belligerent occupation. Occupations are always tough. The alternative is annexation, which many Israelis do not want." Or as *Jerusalem Post* reporter David Krivine, put it: "Gaza is a foreign territory under military occupation. Conditions were backward there before Israel took over. They will be backward—by Western standards—when Israel leaves."

It is true that in two decades Israel has brought increased income and prosperity to the Strip, a result mainly of the money earned by Palestinians working inside Israel. In the Strip, for instance, in standard-of-living terms, the statistics are overwhelming: the percentage of households with televisions shot up from 7.5 percent in 1972 to 84.7 percent in 1985; with electric refrigerators, from 5.7 percent to 77.8 percent; with cars, from 2.3 percent to 14.1 percent, despite the one-third increase in population. It is also true, although it sounds like a rationalization, that, as Benvenisti says, "The rise in the standard of living of the subject population, sharpens its feelings of frustration and outrage."

It is true that Israel has made specific improvements in healthcare in the Strip. In the course of the occupation, Israel has established 24 new mother-child clinics in Gaza. Infant mortality rates have been lowered considerably. Vaccinations for diphtheria, pertussis, polio, TB and measles are now available inside the Strip, and most standard communicable diseases such as newborn tetanus and infantile paralysis have been completely eradicated. It is equally true, although not mentioned in the official reports of the Civil Administration of Gaza, that for the population of 520,000 in the Strip, there are only three ambulances and no anesthesiologists, or that the surgical theater at Al-Naser Hospital in Khan Younis—the hospital serves a population of 229,000 people with 243 beds and 52 doctors—was once closed by the military authorities for five months. Or that, as estimated by high-level administrators at Shifa Hospital in Gaza, Israel's per capita expenditure on health care inside Israel was $350 in 1984 compared to $30 inside the Strip.

It is true that the government-run hospitals in the Strip offer an impressive range of services, which include everything from ophthalmology to dialysis, psychiatry, urology and intensive care. However, it is also equally true that the hospitals suffer from a critical lack of basic medical equipment; blood tests at the Rimal Clinic, for instance, are done by eye as the clinic lacks testing equipment, and that which does exist is often broken. And the sanitary conditions in Shifa, at least, the main government hospital in Gaza City, are considerably less than ideal. Although the military government prohibits foreigners from visiting government-run hospitals without official clearance, an unofficial tour of Shifa revealed mice and roaches scurrying through the wards; rooms in a state of decay, with broken windows, peeling paint and cracked floors; hospital beds old and rusting, and patients lying two to a bed on sheets that were torn and blood-stained. This eyewitness account, although discredited by Israeli officials who claim to have recently invested $4 million in the hospital, was confirmed in its essentials in a recent report by the Union of Medial Relief Committees. "Many Israelis have come here to see what is going on," said a former director of psychiatric services at Shifa. "Doctors, delegations … They are generally concerned. They even cry. I invite them to stay at my house, which they do. Then they go home, and I never hear from them again."

It is true that in the 1970s, Israel built a new sewage system for Gaza City that was capable of providing services for a population projected for the year 2000. It is also true that this constituted the main improvement in the sewage system since the years of the British Mandate and that still not enough connections were made from the main system to houses in the city. Consequently, cesspits are still the plumbing of choice, and the side streets of Gaza can be seen overflowing with sewage and noxious liquids.

Whatever the truth is, one word that shows up often in knowing discussions of Gaza is "explosive." In March of last year, for instance, Avraham Katz-Oz, Israel's deputy agriculture minister under Peres, who lives on a kibbutz adjacent to the Gaza Border, wrote "The population increase staggers the imagination. If Israel doesn't open the Egyptian option to the south for this population, it will of necessity explode north and east into Israel."

But that takes into account only the frightening demographics of the Strip. Abba Eban, former foreign minister and now chairman of the Knesset's Foreign Affairs and Defense Committee, said this about life in the West Bank and Gaza:

> The Palestinians live without a right to vote or be elected, without any control over the Government that determines the conditions of their lives, exposed to restraints and punishments that could not be applied against them if they were Jews, permitted to cross into Israel to work, but without permission to sleep overnight. It is a bleak, tense, disgruntled, repressed existence, with spurts of violence always ready to explode. There is no precedent for believing that this condition can long endure without explosion.

In mid-1985 and early 1986, one of the authors [of this article], Sara Roy, a researcher and doctoral student at Harvard University, spent five months in Gaza and the West Back under the auspices of Benvenisti's West Bank Data Base Project, funded by the Ford and Rockefeller Foundations. Her report, entitled "The Gaza Strip Survey," was compiled of official and unofficial sources as well as scores of personal interviews with Gazans, and was published by the Jerusalem Post Press. The 152-page report also described the situation today as "explosive." It concluded that Israeli rule in Gaza is one of discrimination and injustice, and that Israeli policies are responsible for rendering the Gazan economy nothing more than an auxiliary of Israel's, and systematically eroding any signs of Palestinian culture and society. "Gaza is perhaps the starkest evidence of the intentional repression of a real human problem," Benvenisti said when he released the report in May 1986. "We have all been trying to evade this moral issue by treating it as a political issue. This cannot continue."

When Roy's report was released last May, not only were its findings and arguments reported in the international press and debated in the Knesset, but it unleashed a spate of reactions that ranged, as Benvenisti put it, "from expressions of dismay and shame to slanderous accusations that the study constitutes a pay-off to hostile organizations (a euphemism for the PLO), which provided the funds."

The report also sparked a revealing debate in the pages of the *Jerusalem Post*, a debate that distilled the essence of the no-win situation presented by Gaza. In it, *Post* reporter David Krivine objected to the report's "*exclusive* [Krivine's emphasis] reliance (over many points) on Arab and other derogatory sources." Benvenisti, on the other hand, claimed that Krivine objected to any references to Arab sources, because they were "ipso facto distorted and hostile. According to Krivine, absolute truth lies only with the Israeli bureaucracy."

Absolute truth in Gaza, however, is nowhere to be found. Everyone has a point of view, and everything, including the facts, of course, are biased.

There was a time at the beginning of the century, when the League of Nations assigned control of Palestine to the British, and Gaza City was the third largest port in the country, after Jaffa and Haifa. The Gaza district, which it served, was largely rural, the poorest district in the country. In 1948, when Arabs and Jews went to war, 200,000 Arabs fled into the sliver of land along the Mediterranean that was Gaza, and its society and economy buckled under the influx.

Through 19 years of Egyptian rule Egypt never considered the Strip anything more than a strategic stronghold back into Palestine. Egyptians ran Gaza harshly and the Gazans endured. The Egyptians restricted Palestinian travel, required Gazan residents to obtain a special permit to cross into Egypt, and imposed a 19-year-long nighttime curfew.

The [1948] war had isolated the Strip from its agricultural land and when Egypt closed the port at Gaza City, the Gazan economy shut down with it. Those refugees still in Gaza by the time UNRWA replaced their tents with the concrete huts of the camps (in the 1950s), were the most destitute of the society, those who couldn't afford to leave. Any Palestinians who could leave did, and settled in the West Bank or emigrated to other Arab countries. Up to half of the workforce in the Strip was unemployed; two-thirds of the population depended totally on UNRWA for food.

After the Suez War of 1956, Israel occupied Gaza for five months, prompting Egyptian President Gamel Nasser to adopt a more lenient approach afterward. He reopened the port and declared the Strip a free trade zone, and limited prosperity returned. Gaza's citrus growers began exporting to Eastern Europe and the Arab world. Egypt even allowed a limited amount of political activity. When the PLO was established in East Jerusalem in 1964, it was sponsored by the Arab League and supported by Nasser.

The Strip became Israel's by right of occupation in June 1967, and it appeared, or at least so it seemed from the policy statements of Prime Minister Levi Eshkol and Defense Minister Moshe Dayan, that Israel intended to annex the territory quickly. As a first step, the military resettled 40,000 Gazan refugees into the Northern Sinai and the West Bank. The next year, 20,000–30,000 more refugees followed. The annexation plan also provided that the indigenous residents of Gaza would become Israeli citizens. The Palestinians considered it unacceptable.

The next four years were bloody ones in Gaza. The Palestine Liberation Army (PLA), operating from within the refugee camps and with refugee support, targeted the Israeli Army and other Israeli establishments for their guerilla movement. Gazans who associated with Israelis, for whatever reasons, were targets as well. By the end of 1971, Israeli troops had rooted out the resistance from the camps. The remaining PLA fighters, as well as public demonstrators and prominent political figures, were arrested and either imprisoned or expelled to the Sinai or Jordan.

In January 1971, Israel removed Gaza's municipal council, dismissed its mayor, and placed the Strip under direct military control, and the refugee camps under 24-hour curfew. That same month, Israel deported 12,000 relatives of suspected guerrillas to detention camps in the Sinai. In August, the military destroyed 7,000 rooms in three refugee camps while laying wider roads through the camps to facilitate control. The Israeli bulldozers displaced 16,000 refugees. (That the Israeli resettlement program continued even after the defeat of the resistance until, in fact, 1976, when Israel ended the program at the request of the United States and United Nations, gave credibility to Palestinian claims that refugee resettlement had little to do with annexation and everything to do with eradicating the refugee presence in the Strip.)

Over the past 16 years, Israel has toyed time and again with the idea of limited autonomy in the Strip. In 1971, Israeli authorities appointed Shawwa as mayor of Gaza. It was Shawwa who began, with Israeli approval, the revitalization of Gaza's citrus industry. But in 1972, Shawwa alienated his constituency, backing a Hussein-proposed federation between the West Bank, Jordan and the Strip. Shawwa resigned, and the Israeli military government took over once again. In October 1975, Shawwa was again appointed mayor and once again the Palestinian nationalists took affront; this time at seeing Israeli appointments rather than free elections.

With the Camp David agreements in September 1978, the slow fuse began burning in Gaza. The Palestinian majority denounced the autonomy plan that had been crafted by Begin and accepted by Sadat. Autonomy in the Camp David Accords meant that Israel would retain control over land, water, settlements and security in the territories. The Arabs would not be allowed to establish a policymaking government, but only an administrative council. In October, the Gazans rallied to protest—the only public demonstration allowed in Gaza since 1967—and in so doing simply precipitated a series of new Israeli-imposed restrictions, particularly against the organization of future public assemblies.

At the end of 1981, Israel set up a civil administration in the Gaza Strip. It had all the civil powers of the military government but remained subject to the military commander, and both Palestinians and Israeli liberals considered it a deliberate attempt to create an irreversible legal and administrative structure, which would eventually impose the Israeli, and unwanted, version of autonomy on the territory. It was followed immediately by an Israeli-imposed excise tax on professionals. Those professionals—doctors, dentists, pharmacists, veterinarians, lawyers and engineers—struck. In response, the military welded shut the doors of 170 shops and 18 pharmacies, imposed heavy fines and arrested protestors. The strike lasted two weeks and failed to have any lasting effect. On December 2, Shawwa, once again mayor, called yet another strike protesting both the excise tax and the civil administration. The following spring, the military government ordered Shawwa to end the strike, and his refusal resulted once again in his dismissal, as well as the disbanding of Gaza's municipal council.

By April 1982, when Israel returned the Sinai Peninsula to Egypt as part of the Camp David peace process, the Gaza Strip had been deprived of most means of political expression. Five years later, Gaza still has no elected Arab mayor, no election process, no daily newspaper, and no right of public assembly.

The last election held in Gaza was in 1946. Gaza, as it was then, is still defined under international law, as an "unallocated" portion of the British Mandate of Palestine.

In the years after Camp David, Jewish settlers established 12 of the 18 settlements now inside the Strip. (Anticipating the return of Sinai to Egypt, Israel accelerated Jewish settlement in Gaza to create what it considered the necessary buffer zone with Egypt.) Nine of the settlements are located on the south coast of Gaza, along the Strip's main water aquifers. In one of the settlements, Neve Dekalim, a synagogue in the shape of an enormous Star of David rises out of the desert.

As Israel has now taken a third of the land within Gaza, the Arabs, like those in the West Bank, are left to believe, as wrote Raja She-hadeh—a West Bank attorney and author of *Occupier's Law, Israel and the West Bank*, an analysis of Israel's land acquisition tactics—that Israel hopes to eventually drive them out, to dispossess them completely of their land and therefore their livelihood. "The land without the people" is how the Gazans repeatedly describe their reading of the Israeli dream.

In the West Bank, Jews have felt what amounts to a moral obligation to settle the land they consider their biblical heritage. Gaza, as stated, has no such significance. "By what moral right," Peres asked at a 1986 meeting of the Labour Party, "do we take 50,000 dunums [a dunum is equal to one quarter of an acre] out of 350,000 in the Gaza Strip, which has the greatest population density in the country ...?"

It was three years ago, with Peres's election as prime minister of the coalition government, that the idea of annexing the territories was forcefully challenged. In 1984 and again in 1986, Israel's Labour Party unanimously resolved that permanent Israeli rule over the West Bank and Gaza contradicted the Zionist character of the state, in essence refuted its moral and democratic foundations. Yet, the settlement philosophy in the territories seems to make the annexation question moot. In two decades of occupation, the Israeli government, whether the conservative Likud or the more liberal Labour party, under which settlement of the territories began, have assured that Israeli interests in the territories, security or otherwise, would never be diluted.

Roads, electricity, water and communications systems all weave through Gaza and the West Bank, paying no attention to what is unofficially referred to as the Green Line—the artificial border of the territories—arguing for the silent and steady integration of the territories into Israel. Israeli roads in the territories avoid Arab villages and refugee camps in such a way that one can drive for miles upon miles without seeing any sign of habitation other than the barbed-wire enwrapped Jewish settlements, which are connected, grid-like, by these new roads. Official Israeli government maps distinguish not at all between the territories and Israel proper.

"As I have written on many occasions," said Amos Oz in a recent interview in the new Jewish journal *Tikkun*, "the word 'liberation' can only be applied to human beings. Lands cannot be liberated. Clearly, we have not liberated the Arabs, we have occupied them. This is an occupation, a nasty occupation and it is steadily corrupting Israeli society in many ways." Only two months after the occupation began, Oz had written a strikingly similar thought in the daily newspaper *Davar*, but he had added of the Arabs, "We have conquered them and we are going to rule over them only until our peace is secured."

Peace has yet to be secured, the rule goes on and the nature of that rule, which must assure the security of Israel, is especially severe. Because Israel does not recognize the status of Gaza and the West Bank as occupied territories—the official definition is that they are "administered territories"—it does not regard itself bound by the Fourth Geneva Convention, the body of international law which governs the responsibilities of occupying powers and which Israel itself ratified. (Although Israel does claim to apply the "humanitarian provisions" of the convention, on a de facto basis.) As early as July 1967, Israel issued Military Order 144, which annulled the supremacy of the Geneva Conventions over orders of the local military commander, and legally confirmed the legitimacy of military rule in the territories.

All management of daily affairs in Gaza rests with the area military commander, who runs Gaza with a legal system built on the remnants of Egyptian law, which was built in turn on the Emergency Codes initiated by the British Mandate in 1945 to control the Zionists. (In the West Bank, it is Jordanian law rather than Egyptian, which is the foundation.) These regulations, as David Rosenbloom, a Syracuse University professor of public administration who spent two years teaching at Tel Aviv University, says, "provide for collective and individual punishments, curfews, demolition of houses, house arrest, closing off areas, and preventive and administrative detention. They allow punishment for opinion, rather than action alone, and for refusal to provide information to the authorities."

Amended to these original Emergency Codes, however, are the 1,200 or so new military orders—many of them published only in Hebrew—instituted by area commanders of both territories, and which govern all aspects of life, including legal, civil and political rights, land and water rights, licensing, taxation, services, security, and social welfare. Since the occupation began, the military has issued orders prohibiting or restricting the planting of trees, specific crops, land reclamation, water utilization, free market trade, licensing of industrial activity, trade union activity, and access to private health-care. It has issued orders restricting freedom of travel for individual Gazans as well as the reunion of families. It has issued orders prohibiting cultural expression: including the banning of books—over 1,600 banned since 1967, constituting 100 percent of the works that encourage Palestinian and Arab nationalism—plays, films and publications. The military has issued orders prohibiting the display of Palestinian colors—this now includes any clothing that is green, red, black and white—of Palestinian maps, the singing of Palestinian songs, the writing of Palestinian poetry.

Among these orders, in particular, is Number 378, "Security Enactments," which allows for military officials to arrest and detain Palestinians without warrants for as long as six months, and for up to 18 days before the detainee must be brought before a military judge. According to Diane Orentlicher, deputy director of the Lawyers Committee for Human Rights in New York, which has compiled a report on human rights conditions in the territories, any such situation in which detainees can be held without rights of visitation for so long invites abuse.

These orders require no public review, nor does any governmental or public body inside Israel have the authority to alter or supervise the orders of the military command in Gaza or the West Bank. This includes the Supreme Court of Israel, which has only limited authority over military law in the territories. This body of military law does not, however, pertain to the Jewish settlers in the West Bank and Gaza. In 1980, Israel granted these settlers the right to create their own legal and administrative structure, composed of regional and local councils. These councils are identical to their counterparts in Israel proper, and are completely separate from the municipal system governing Arab inhabitants in the territories. These councils are listed in all official Israeli publications as though they are in Israel, and for all intents and purposes they function as such. "Anyone empowered to act in Israel according to Israeli law may so act in the territories," is the key formulation to legislation in Gaza and the West Bank.

A system of local courts also exists, a holdover from the Egyptian rule, whose domain in large part has been given over to the military courts. The jurisdiction of local courts is exclusively over the Palestinian population. Israeli citizens may not be brought to trial before these courts, rather they are tried in courts inside Israel. Local courts have no power of executing decisions so that many court judgments are never enforced.

Most cases, particularly those involving security matters, are tried in military courts. Almost all of these cases of illegal demonstrations or security violations result in prison sentences—typical for rock throwing, for instance, is nine months' imprisonment; displaying the map of Palestine, in one case, resulted in a one-year confinement to the Strip. (In security violations in which blood is drawn, one possible punishment is the demolition of the perpetrator's home, displacing the family as well. Considered a deterrent, it always occurs before legal proceedings have begun.) Although technically these cases can be appealed in Israel's High Court of Justice, they rarely are, as the Arabs rarely have the knowledge or financial resources to pursue such action. In 1984, for example, the High Court received 27 petitions from Gazan residents; in the first eight months of 1985, it received two.

These two realities—one for Jews and one for Arabs, one existing under Israeli law, one existing under military law—polarize even further the two populations. For Gazans, life itself takes on a Kafkaesque, seemingly irrational color. The Arabs are confronted daily with the contradictions, which permeate their existence, and over which they insist they have no power.

At the extremes are the acts of humiliation and harassment faced by the Arabs at the hands of Israeli troops and settlers. These have been explained away by Israeli spokesmen as the sporadic acts of "rotten apples" among the troops. But still these painful episodes are witnessed daily in the Strip and seem to be inevitably spawned by the dual existences. *Jerusalem Post* reporter, Joel Greenberg, in his diary of reserve service in Hebron, wrote, "An older member of our group says our job of policing the Arabs has an inevitably corrupting effect. The minute a youngster is given the power to tell an Arab, 'Lie down, put up your hands,' and he does it, it starts eating away at him. It's destructive."

Often the contradictions spring from competition between Israeli and Arab over the depreciating resources of the Strip, as it does with the water situation, which, in this parched semi-desert strip of land, is undeniably bad. Too many years of over-pumping by too many Arab wells have leached seawater into the aquifers, and now what is being used to irrigate the crops is saline and getting more so. In response to the water crisis, the Israeli government, through its affiliated water company, Mekorot, has restricted the digging of new wells and set limits on water usage by Palestinian farmers. Abuse of these quotas, which have been fixed now for over a decade, can result in severe fines and even lower quotas for the future.

This is understandable. But in recent years, or so say local engineers who worked on the projects, the Israeli settlers have installed over 35 new wells into the main water aquifer of Gaza, which contains freshwater, into which Arabs are forbidden to tap. Some of the settlements have freshwater swimming pools. The amount of water consumed, nevertheless, does not seem so inequitable, according to Freddy Zach, Israel's deputy coordinator of government operations in the administered area and, as cited in the *Jerusalem Post*: "The Arabs use 90 million cubic meters a year, and the Jews five to six million." The amounts seem less equitable, however, when they are adjusted to per capita numbers for the Arab and Jewish population: using Zach's figures, each Palestinian in Gaza consumes an average of 173 cubic meters per year, compared to 2326 cubic meters, 13 times as much, for each Israeli.

This feeling of mercurial injustice is exacerbated among the Palestinians by the frequency with which the military government writes and passes new orders, which then become law.

One Arab tomato farmer took Sara on a tour of his farm in order to display, among other things, his fields of rotting tomatoes. He had planted those tomatoes the year before to sell in Israel, as he had been allowed to for the past few years. This year he had been informed by the authorities that the Israel market would be closed to Gazan tomato farmers. He could sell only to the West Bank, Jordan and local markets in Gaza, none of which could absorb all of the Gazan tomato crop. Without loans or government protection, he could not compete even in Gaza with Israeli prices, and for this year, at least, his tomatoes would be dumped.

As he walked with his wife among his despoiled crop, he vacillated between anger, desperation and apathy. He had no choice. He then took Sara in his car and drove to a nearby Israeli settlement. He pointed to the settler's greenhouses, where they grew their own tomatoes. The settlers, he said, had access to finances and loans, denied to him as an Arab. He pointed to crates of tomatoes sitting in the sun, to the lush vegetation in the greenhouse, "Why should it be this way," he said. "They have all the rights. They grow tomatoes on my land; they can sell in Israel, anywhere in the world. Why can't I?"

Since 1968, the amount of land cultivated by Gazans has fallen from as high as 49,500 acres to 25,000 acres in 1985. The citrus crop, in particular, which was Gaza's cash crop prior to Israeli and Egyptian rule and the produce on which the landed gentry of Gaza amassed their wealth, has fallen off drastically. Yields have dropped from 243,700 tons in 1975 to 164,000 tons in 1984. The dwindling water resources are in part responsible. Taxes are in part responsible. Not only must Gazans pay a 15 percent excise tax, which drains their profits, they must pay a land tax, which although equal in rate to that imposed on their Israeli counterparts, is calculated on the yields of citrus achieved on those Israeli farms; yields that are substantially higher due to the government subsidies, tax breaks, loans and other financial supports available to the Israelis and withheld from Arabs. Military orders, which Israel claims are necessary to deal with the water situation, are responsible for the rest. Under military law, for example, Palestinian citrus farmers are prohibited from planting new trees or replacing old ones, or from reclaiming their own land, without official permission, in order to cultivate it. In 1984, the government issued a new order making it illegal for farmers to plant fruit trees on a commercial scale without permission from the authorities.

The quintessential example of government control in the territories was told by Raja Shehadeh in *The West Bank and The Rule of Law*: a military prohibition against picking wild thyme in the West Bank. It was speculated that the reason for such a law was to deprive the Palestinian population access to a herb that in Palestinian literature had come to symbolize the attachment of Palestinians to their land. In September 1984, the Israeli weekly supplement *Kol Ha'ir*, revealed that the order was issued to protect an Israeli family's monopoly over the production and sale of the herb in the West Bank.

The story with fishing, another traditional Gazan enterprise, is similar. For security purposes, Israel has imposed a dawn-to-dusk curfew on Gazan fishermen, and has limited their fishing to within 19 miles of the shoreline, an area that is one-quarter that of its pre-1967 size. Egypt has also imposed its own restrictions on the southern end of this area. The result is a 58 percent drop in catch between 1968 and 1985. When the Gazans struck to protest the restrictions, the military imposed fines, jailed protestors and confiscated boats.

With little work in Gaza, the Palestinians have had to look elsewhere to find it, and that has meant Israel. In 1969, Israel opened up its borders and encouraged the Palestinians of the Strip to work inside Israel, and they have in droves. More than half of Gazan laborers now commute to Israel (other estimates are higher), and Israeli authorities claim that this has reduced unemployment in Gaza from 30 percent to near zero. (Although that claim has been disputed on the grounds that it doesn't take into account the number of black-market workers.) And the money these commuters earn in Israel is brought back and spent in Gaza, leavening the local economy.

As usual in this occupation, this picture of prosperity has another side. The Gazan laborers are required to pay up to 30 percent of their wages for tax, national insurance fees and social security payments, all of which are remitted to the government employment service. But these laborers do not receive the same benefits as their Israeli counterparts. In many cases, Palestinian workers are ineligible to receive, or have little chance of claiming, the very benefits offered under the schemes for which they are charged. (Women workers, for instance, are only entitled to maternity benefits if they give birth inside Israel.)

Although wages paid to Palestinians are roughly 40 percent lower than their Israeli counterparts—$15 is considered a good day's pay— they are much higher than anything the Arabs could earn inside Gaza itself. The pull to work on Israel's side of the Green Line is powerful, and as the Strip's traditional source of employment—agriculture— grows weaker, more and more Gazans will flood the streets of Tel Aviv and Jaffa seeking work. This in turn will create a still greater dependence on Israel that may be as dangerous for Israel as it is for Gaza.

The totality of the economic occupation of Gaza is reflected clearly in the territory's balance of trade. Within a year of the occupation, over two-thirds of the imports were from Israel. Egypt was gone from the market. Jordan was in. By 1975, two-thirds of Gaza's exports were crossing the Green Line into Israel and going no further. Since 1968, Gaza has had a negative trade balance with Israel that by 1984 had amounted to $161,000,000. The Gaza Strip and the West Bank, according to the Statistical Abstract of Israel, are second only to the United States as importers of Israeli goods.

Those Palestinians who have tried to assert some control over their society or economy have found themselves impeded by, if not impaled upon, Israeli regulations. Every society in Gaza, every meeting, every cooperative is a potential threat and is controlled as such. To establish an organization of any sort, a Palestinian must first send off a letter of association to the military authorities. Individuals without any record of activism might get a permit, say the local Palestinians: those with a record won't. Once the organization is formed, it is the Israeli military that controls its activities. No meetings of three or more persons can be held without permission. No foreign funds, or for that fact, foreign donations to charitable institutions, can be received without permission from the military authority. In February, when the Gazan Carpenters' Union managed, without Israeli permission, to hold its first vote in twenty years, it was considered a major political victory in the territory.

Again, the Israeli decisions on these matters seem to an outsider to be almost maliciously arbitrary. While Israeli authorities, for instance,

allowed the Fishermen's Cooperative Society to purchase a refrigerator truck that would allow them to sell their fish within Gaza, they
refused permission for a sardine-packing plant. When Yussera Barberi,
a local community leader, wanted to buy an autobus for her pre-school
center, that, too, was denied. Indeed, since all foreign aid earmarked
for Gaza must be cleared by the Israeli authorities, many projects for
which aid is directed, arrive stillborn. Between 1977 and 1983, for
example, Israel approved only 59 percent of the proposed aid projects
involving US funds in the territories.

The case of the Red Crescent Society is worth dwelling on in this
light. Although the society is primarily a medical one, in the 1970s it
attempted to promote, as one of its members put it, "everything that is
positive in Palestinian tradition and achievement." This prompted the
military authorities to consider them radical and treat them in kind, a
consideration exacerbated by the fact that the head of the society, Dr.
Haider Abdel Shafi, has also been an outspoken critic of the occupation, and in being so has earned three years of confinement to the Strip
and one year's exile in Sinai.

In 1980, a mob of Islamic fundamentalists razed the Red Crescent
headquarters in a riot which the society's members, at least, believed
was supported by the Israeli authorities. (They point out that the
military regularly arrives at demonstrations within 15 minutes of their
onset, and yet the Red Crescent incident allowed the mob free rein for
over an hour without taking control.) Since then the military authorities have banned the cultural activities associated with the society
and strictly monitored all other activity. "We have a bank account in
Amman," says Abdel Shafi, "but since 1978, the Israelis won't allow us
to bring the money into Gaza. We had to establish a special account
to deposit our money here, and every time we want to withdraw it, we
have to apply for permission. We have continuation but not expansion,
and the continuation is very difficult."

In the early 1980s, the Red Crescent Society instituted plans to
build an Arab hospital in Gaza City. The society applied for a lease
on state land, according to Abdel Shafi, so that the authorities would
know exactly what was planned. With the lease secured, they then
proceeded with the hospital. "We hired engineers and architects to
draw up the plans," says Abdel Shafi:

By the time we got ready for the actual implementation, the building and all that we had spent came to $100,000. But we needed to get a permit to operate the hospital, which we applied for and the Israelis rejected. So, after all the time and all the work and all the money we were turned down for a hospital, and the Israelis knew right from the beginning what we were doing. They turned us down because, they said, "we already have enough hospitals, why don't you improve the hospitals you have."

After twenty years of conflict, suggested resolutions to the occupation have embodied a range of alternatives whose common denominator is that they have failed. And with each failure, the Gazans have been left further out in the cold. The reasons for these failures, not surprisingly, vary according to which side offered up the suggestion.

In the Camp David Accords of 1978, Sadat and Begin worked out an autonomy scheme for the Occupied Territories aimed at giving Palestinians limited control over specific administrative functions, the first step toward a more permanent autonomy. Palestinian objections to the Accords and, in particular, to the participation of Sadat, says Afif Safieh, a former advisor to Arafat, "were based not on the search for peace but on the approach to it."' As far as the PLO was concerned, Sadat's approach provided no role for the Palestinian people or their legal representative, the PLO, and divided Arab consensus, which, it was argued, eroded the Arab bargaining position.

The Camp David Accords, in the words of a local Gazan political leader, "brought anything but peace to Gaza." Egypt settled its territorial conflicts with Israel and, in the process, essentially disowned the Gazans, who had rejected Sadat's initiative. The government, which had previously admitted some 1,500 Gazan students a year into Egyptian universities, cut the number to less than 50 after Camp David.

In 1986, former Gaza Mayor Rashad Shawwa approached Egyptian President Hosni Mubarak with a proposal for returning Gaza to Egyptian administrative supervision, with Israeli approval, pending a final political solution to the status of the territory. "Since Egypt is the closest Arab power to us," Shawwa told *Time* magazine, "I suggested to President Mubarak that it be under Egyptian sovereignty." Mubarak rejected the proposal. Jordan's King Hussein, who sees himself as speaking for all Palestinians living under occupation, expressed little enthusiasm for the idea as well.

For a growing number of Gazans, the alternative to Egypt may indeed be Jordan, with an indigenous population more than half Palestinian. Attitudes toward the Hashemite Kingdom have varied over time and among Gaza's different social classes. The wealthy, upper class have a history of looking to Jordan and Hussein for solutions. Much of the refugee population have historically rejected the possibility of a Jordanian-led approach. Memories of Hussein's harsh crackdown on PLO forces in September 1970, remembered as "Black September," remain very much alive.

For a short time, an Hussein-Arafat agreement signed on February 11, 1985 held out some hope. But the attempted partnership between the two leaders to resolve the conflict through negotiations with Israel lasted only a year. Reasons for the break-up varied: most well-known was Arafat's refusal to unconditionally accept UN Resolution 242 (which calls for Israel's withdrawal from those territories occupied in June 1967).

Arafat insisted that acceptance of 242 be accompanied by recognition of the Palestinian right to self-determination. Hussein, who thought he had reached an agreement with Arafat on this issue, broke off relations. Less well known was Hussein's changing alliances within the Arab world: to compensate for his ineffectual relations with long-standing ally, Iraq, which was engaged in a protracted war with Iran, Hussein sought to warm previously chilled relations with the Syrian regime, an outspoken opponent of Arafat and Fatah.

The tension between Hussein and Arafat was reflected in the latest Jordanian initiative, announced by Hussein last July, a $1 billion, five-year development plan for the West Bank and Gaza Strip. The plan, unlike preceding efforts, was the first to include Gaza within its program which, many observers felt, signaled a new approach by Jordan to the Occupied Territories. Both the Israeli and American governments approved Hussein's plan, but many, if not most Palestinians in the territories, viewed it as an attempt to establish a condominium between the three powers inside the West Bank and Gaza. In essence, a plan that would normalize the occupation to a point where it would lose its political significance and undermine the influence of the PLO by establishing an alternative leadership under

Jordan. In other words, Jordan would provide the carrot while Israel continued to provide the stick.

The support that the Jordanian option received from Israel's Labour government was based on the belief that Hussein could negotiate for the Palestinians without the PLO, and through these negotiations, achieve a peace treaty with Israel. "The reality of the situation," said a prominent West Bank leader recently, "is that the Jordanian option is dying, if not altogether dead." Events have indicated to Israeli and Jordanian alike that Palestinians will not be swayed from their allegiance to the PLO and any effort to do so is most likely doomed to failure. As Mordecai Bar-On, a member of Knesset for the Citizen's Rights Party, wrote in 1986 in *Tikkun*, "The undeniable fact is that Mr. Peres leaves the Prime Minister's office with more than 90 percent of the Palestinians living under Israeli occupation still considering the PLO to be their sole political representative despite all the mistakes committed and all setbacks suffered by the PLO leadership."

In fact, a 1986 poll conducted in the Occupied Territories by *Al-Fajr*, revealed that 93 percent of the inhabitants of the West Bank and Gaza support the PLO, and consider it their sole legitimate representative. Over two-thirds of those polled expressed their personal support for Yasir Arafat, a vote of confidence particularly significant in light of the Israeli defeat of the PLO in Lebanon. Arafat, in particular, is supported vigorously by Palestinian youth inside the territories: to these youth who so believe that *they* are David, armed without even a sling, in this war against Goliath, Arafat has become the "stone we throw against the world." And just as some of the youth of Israel are recruited into the military to serve their terms in the territories, the Arab youth in Gaza turn to the PLO as the only voice of expression they have, be it violent or not.

After twenty years, it is the youth that have come to inherit the frustration, hostility and fear of the occupation, and it has served to split the Strip down the middle of each family. The older generation of Arabs still can remember a precedent for dealing with Jews in a positive way. The youth clearly cannot. Whatever foundation existed for some kind of trust between Jews and Arabs has been inexorably eroded.

Israeli author Amos Elon predicted years ago that over time Israeli Jews would become numb to the realities of the occupation, that it would become increasingly difficult to mobilize indignation over the evils committed across the Green Line. For greater evils can always be found elsewhere. Many Israelis, however, if asked, will admit that the occupation, while harsh, is only temporary. But with each passing year, this notion of the temporary becomes more and more myth, and less and less reality. And as a myth, it is dangerous, as it both nurtures an unwillingness to confront the moral and political dilemmas emerging from the occupation, as well as sanctions a system which creates those dilemmas and perpetuates them on a daily basis. In the words of a local Gazan leader, Dr. Hatem Abu Ghazaleh, "after two decades of occupation, nothing is more permanent than the temporary."

24

When a Loaf of Bread Was Not Enough:[1] Unsilencing the Past in Gaza*

> How terrible it would have been ... to have lived without even attempting to lay claim to one's portion of the earth; to have lived and died as one had been born, unnecessary and unaccommodated.
>
> V.S. Naipaul, *A House for Mr Biswas*

I last traveled to Gaza in September 2016, two years after the horrific assault on the territory known as Operation Protective Edge. The destruction of Gaza's infrastructure was still evident in some places but much of it had already been cleared away. The mountains of rubble—formerly homes, schools and hospitals—were gone but what remained was an ineliminable emptiness that echoed the destruction it had replaced.

Many things struck me on that trip but one, perhaps more than all the others, was particularly distressing.[2] In many conversations I had with young and well-educated adults, I learned that they knew little if anything about the first Palestinian uprising or Intifada, which was a formative and watershed event in Palestinian history. Their lack of knowledge was profoundly disturbing, a form of privation both tragic and self-defeating. As I observed in 2016: "I was ... struck by how little the young but well-educated adults I met knew of the first Intifada and the Oslo years, absorbed as they were by the present day. In other words, not only do they feel disconnected from a possible future, they are also cut off from their very recent past—and the many important lessons contained in it."[3] Of course, many young adults in Gaza today were toddlers or not yet born during the first Intifada.

---

* Published here for the first time.

Perhaps they never learned about the Intifada because it did not end the occupation or achieve an independent Palestinian state. Yet embedded in these defeats were certain remarkable achievements that forever changed Gaza.

This piece draws on nearly 300 pages of field notes I wrote while living and working in Gaza during the second year of the first Intifada (1988–89). It took me some time to read through my field notes, which were comprised of interviews, observations, commentary, statistics, relevant newspaper articles and excerpts from books and journals, and what I found astounded me. I found in those notes a meticulously recorded history of a truly remarkable yet deeply painful and brutal period—long since erased—that I was fortunate to experience. What leapt out from those pages were the voices of people who, through their hard work and self-sacrifice, changed how Palestinians defined themselves (and how others defined them including Israel), rejecting any notion of their inconsequence, insisting on possibility and on their rightful place in the world. Many of those Palestinians I recorded, both known and unknown, have died or have receded into history. Yet, what they were able to accomplish, both permanent and ephemeral, deserves to be acknowledged and applied but, tragically, remains lost or unknown to young Palestinians.

Rereading my notes thirty years after they were written, certain themes were dominant: the Intifada as unstoppable; the changing role of women and children; generational conflict and convergence; the empowerment of youth; the strength and limitations of strategic thinking and vision; increasing external and internal lawlessness, and, ultimately, the Intifada's breakdown. Yet, the three most unyielding and persistent aspects of my observations were these: the masterly and efficient reorganization and mobilization of Palestinian society—which was indigenous to Gaza and the West Bank—in order to achieve clear and deeply held political goals; the commitment to unified action, which widened allegiance beyond the family to the larger collective of society, and the articulation and solidification of dynamics that have since defined—or played a significant role in defining—Israel's increasingly destructive relationship with Palestinians, especially with Gaza. In what follows I revisit that time and examine some of the Intifada's most important successes (and failures) and the lessons contained within them. I conclude by reflecting on how the uprising changed the Palestinian struggle and how it was crucial for shaping where Gaza and Palestinians finds themselves today.

After more than three decades of continual involvement, my aim in revisiting this period is not to read history backwards as it were, but to better understand the present through the convulsions and achievements of the past. Looking back, it is clear that Palestinians were writing a history—a context of significance—that has long since been silenced but still insists on being heard.

RENEGOTIATING THE MEANING OF COMMUNITY

Nafta, the Arabic verb from which *intifada* (literally "shaking off") derives, expresses recovery or recuperation. The choice of this particular word goes beyond *samud* (steadfastness) ... Intifada is a more active term ... The English translation "uprising" fails to convey the sense of sloughing off passivity or of newly mobilizing elements in society's leaping to their feet to stand up for themselves.[4]

Many of my interviews and observations addressed the truly stunning changes taking place around me. The commitment to non-violent resistance was arguably the most respected. Despite constant and often cruel provocations by the Israeli Army, many of which I witnessed, the resistance remained largely non-violent—the foundation for today's civil disobedience—and found powerful expression in Gaza.[5] Related to the allegiance to non-violence was another, truly stunning change: a societal shift to the community where the individual family was no longer the primary unit of social life. Rather priority ceded to the collective and the stories that follow reflect this profound shift.

"We must take things into our own hands."

The organizational changes that were taking place and struggling to become institutionalized were perhaps the most compelling aspects of Gaza's civil resistance, particularly as they concerned the creation of alternative institutions where control was decentralized. Yet people constantly reminded me that these organizational changes were deeply tied to, and themselves reflected something far larger: (re)defining a national identity that was distinctly Palestinian and separate from that of other Arabs. "We suffer from an undefined nationality [and] the Intifada is a nation looking to implement its identity," said one local attorney. "The message of the Intifada to everyone," he said, "should be that it was shameful to keep silent during the last twenty years. Let me tell you this: I went to the area military commander and he said to me, 'Why are the Palestinians doing this? I've visited the refugee camps. Every home has a refrigerator and a TV.' I answered, 'I have a computer in my home but I have no identity.'"

An important part of the national redefinition of identity was the reassertion of control over daily life by responding to the new demands imposed by the Intifada. This was powerfully seen in the way Palestinians adjudicated their conflicts.[6] Another colleague, Adli, also a lawyer and a local activist, described some of the mediatory structures he helped implement at the grass-roots level based on traditional courts and conciliation committees (a fact that could have gotten him killed at the time): "Before the Intifada," he said, "there was a police force and they arrested criminals. Three hundred Palestinian police resigned in Gaza and were replaced by 38 Israeli police. Now there is no police force and people must take things into their own hands [and because the civil courts were weak, with no enforcement power, and for a time did not function]."

He described the process: a crime is committed. The criminal's family will then choose a mediator and will usually ask more than one person, often three, from well-respected and powerful families. The mediators act as a buffer between the two [aggrieved] families and as a shield for the criminal's family. This is because if any action is taken against the criminal's family, it is also considered an assault against the mediators who have the weight of their whole families behind him.

The family that is hurt is asked to do nothing for three days in order to calm down; this is done to allow the injured to begin healing or bury their dead. If after three days someone dies, the mediators will ask for another forty days (to allow for burial and mourning); if no one dies, the mediators will take two weeks to see how the injured individual does and then the parties begin to negotiate. Part of the negotiation usually involves asking the criminal's family for money. The mediators negotiate for the criminal's family and are usually able to reduce the amount of money paid to 1,000–3,000 JDs (Jordanian dinars).

If the mediators cannot reach a resolution, a committee will be formed to adjudicate the dispute: "These committees did not exist before the Intifada and they are more powerful than the traditional courts. They can make and enforce decisions." If the families involved are from Fatah, then committee members will be from Fatah; if the families are from both Fatah and Hamas, then the committee will be people from Fatah and Hamas, and so on. The mediators are sometimes part of the committee. Committees can be formed from three different factions and ... should always be an odd number to ensure a decision. If the people involved have no political affiliation, the matter will be referred to the popular committee of the area.

If the decision of the committee is not accepted, the family can appeal and ask for a second committee to review the judgment of the first. The decision of the second committee is binding. People must accept the principle of the committee and its power to adjudicate problems and typically do. Adli further pointed out, "If people refuse to heed the decision of the second committee, the *shebab* will go to their home and threaten them. The *shebab* have threatened to write names of people on walls as being against the Intifada. In this way, enforcement can be imposed. Usually people will accept the committee's decisions."

Adli stopped momentarily and looked at me with concern, anticipating my response to what he had just said but chose instead to continue to impress upon me the significance of the change he was describing with the following true example. A man accidentally hit and killed another man from a rival family (the families of both men were feuding). He went immediately to a mediator who, realizing the severity of the case, went directly to the local popular committee. In the meantime, the driver (who committed the accident) went to the (Israeli) military governor to turn himself in as a way to protect himself. The military governor said, "Let Yasir Arafat solve your problem." He returned to the popular committee and told them what had happened. The committee sent the driver back to the governor's office but this time with a witness. They waited four hours. As the governor was leaving his office, he recognized the man and said, "I told you, let Yasir Arafat solve your problem." Both men returned to the popular committee and the witness verified the account. The popular committee went to the bereaved family and told them the entire story. The head of that family responded, "When Yasir Arafat comes here, he will solve our problem. We will not negotiate this problem until Arafat comes." In this way an issue that could have produced considerable inter-communal violence was averted.

Mohammed the Barber: "Not only for my family"

My husband, Jay, was with me in Gaza and volunteered in a local hospital as a trauma surgeon. After a few weeks, he clearly needed a haircut and couldn't find a barber. Getting a haircut in the middle of the Intifada seemed shamefully indulgent, so Jay resigned himself to living with long hair. A young man, Mohammed, who lived in the Beach (al-Shati) refugee camp and worked at the Marna House hotel where we were living, somehow heard that Jay was trying to find a barber. He told us about his friend, also named Mohammed, who was an excellent barber in Beach camp. Mohammed insisted that Jay get his hair cut by his friend. We happily accepted and Mohammed arranged it.

The barber's home consisted of three rooms. A single, vintage barber's chair—worn but serviceable—sat in the middle of one room located in the back of the shelter. I noticed a door near this room that surprised me, which led to the adjacent alleyway. Mohammed the barber was married with nine children and they were poor. Mohammed and his wife Najla welcomed us with the warmth and grace that had become so familiar. Jay was seated and a plastic cape was wrapped around him. Mohammed asked Jay how he wanted his hair cut to which Jay replied, "short"! Mohammed began. I sat nearby watching him and his hands moved effortlessly but cautiously around Jay's head. The haircut was moving quickly, and I remember thinking to myself our visit will be over too soon. I was hoping to spend some time speaking with the family but then, again, we were there for a haircut and I did not want to impose.

Suddenly, almost abruptly, Mohammed stopped cutting. Jay and I looked at each other not understanding why. Najla then came in with a stack of large folders, which she gently placed on Jay's lap asking if he would look at them. Jay opened the top one and pulled out an X-ray. Najla explained that these were X-rays of her nine children, several of whom were deaf (clearly deafness was a congenital problem in this family). Then, all of her nine children filed into the room in a single row. One by one, each child sat dutifully on Jay's lap while Najla identified the corresponding X-ray from the pile. Jay looked at each X-ray carefully while holding each child and giving each one a big smile and a thumbs up. Each of us understood that Mohammed and Najla were not seeking a miracle cure but reassurance that they had done everything they could for their children, and that what other doctors had told them was correct. When Jay gave them that reassurance—which was the only option in that context and no harm had been done—we could see the relief on their faces.

After the ninth child had been seen, Najla brought us tea and cookies. I took advantage of the break to ask Mohammed about his work as a barber and he told me that he only does barbering part time. His other work involved transporting construction materials of some kind. Once Jay had finished his cup of tea, the haircut resumed. About ten minutes or so later, the haircut stopped again. Najla went to the door near to where we were seated and opened it. One by one, people from the camp entered the room, some with their X-rays for Jay to examine. Mohammed looked at Jay and with kindness in his voice said, "Not only for my family." As each person entered, Mohammed would introduce him or her: "Dr. Jay, this is my neighbor, X. He would like you to look at his X-ray" or "He has a problem and wants your advice." Thankfully by this time, Mohammed our friend from the hotel had returned and was able to translate, albeit crudely (which was more than I could do), the medical problems each person was describing (Mohammed's timely reappearance clearly suggested preplanning of some kind!). I went to the door where Najla was controlling the flow of traffic and looked out. I remember seeing a line of people standing along the side of the house, some holding X-rays, waiting patiently to see Jay.

I am not sure whether the line of people wanting to be seen ended or Najla decided Jay had seen enough people, but the haircut did not resume until about three hours later. I do not remember how many people Jay saw and examined, but it was not a small number. After the last person left, Najla disappeared and an unexpected stillness descended on the room. Jay returned to the barber's chair expecting the haircut to continue. Instead, Najla brought us a tray full of food, which I kept thinking this family could not afford, and insisted we partake. We gently protested but they insisted and not to eat would have been an insult. After the meal, Mohammed finished cutting Jay's hair, about four hours after we arrived. Then Mohammed took what appeared to be sewing thread, wrapped the ends around a finger (or two?) on each of his hands and used the threads to pick up the stray bits of hair that had fallen on Jay's face. I had never seen anything like it, and it was hypnotizing to watch.

Jay and I agreed before the visit that we would give the barber a good amount of money. When Jay reached for his wallet, Mohammed adamantly refused and his refusal was sincere. After a gentle tussle back and forth, Jay took the cash, folded it and placed it firmly in the pocket of Mohammed's shirt, saying "For your children."

We returned to Beach Camp a few more times for Jay's four-hour haircut and walk-in clinic. We cherished every moment of it.

WATER FOR TEA: WOMEN RESISTING BEHIND THE BARRICADES

Women's activism during the Intifada is well known and has been meticulously examined. In many respects, the role of women in Gaza, like their counterparts in the West Bank, were similar. Women had always been active in political and social life, but their work was largely service-oriented and charitable (e.g., visiting prisoners, embroidery projects, running kindergartens) and subordinate to men. Prior to the Intifada, women, particularly in the villages and refugee camps, were largely confined to traditional roles. Participation in such things as organized cottage industries was often discouraged. Democracy was not incorporated into socioeconomic or political activities. With the evolution of the Intifada, women took to the streets, often waging their own demonstrations, protecting children and physically intervening in attempted arrests. In several cases where refugee camps were placed under curfew, making it impossible for men to get to work or provide food, women were the ones who obtained food and other basic necessities and kept families intact.

In Gaza, there were many stories of women acting as couriers of information for the unified leadership and popular committees, in situations where men could not move as freely, especially when curfews were lifted temporarily. For example, women were known for grabbing small children—intentionally not their own—off the street. The child, predictably, would cry—exactly what the women couriers wanted. They would then take the crying child to their assigned destination. The soldiers, thinking that the women were going home or to a clinic, would leave them and "their" screaming child alone. Of course, once the task was completed and the information passed, the child would be rewarded and returned safely to their home. I was told—and had no reason to doubt—that the parents of these children did not object to their temporary abduction in this manner. In this way and others, a local female activist told me, "Israel helped change women's roles."

Women's committee work covered a range of political and economic actions and organizing, such as collecting clothes for prisoners, supporting families in need, visiting injured in hospital, and working with lawyers. Women's committees were located throughout the Gaza Strip and were particularly effective in monitoring the security situation in their assigned areas. In some areas of the Gaza Strip, there were only women in charge. In Beach Camp, for example, there were women in charge of certain blocks of the camp and for everything that happened in that block.

A woman activist and organizer told me:

Women are leaders in the streets and in the community. Youngsters respect the women and families take pride in their daughters and are proud if they are in prison. Men now respect women in a way they didn't before. The alertness of the population is amazing. It was not as acute before. Israelis try to find ways of oppressing us and we are constantly trying to find ways of circumventing their oppression.

She told me the story of a Bedouin family she knew:

The Bedouins are very traditional and daughters-in-law are treated as second-class citizens. In this particular family, the son was arrested due to the political activity of his wife. Before the Intifada, this would have resulted in great problems for the daughter-in-law who would have been blamed and hated. Now, the reaction of the mother-in-law was pride and acceptance of the daughter-in-law's activism. "*Ma'alesh*," said the mother-in-law, "they will not stop us. Now my son will become more political and that is good."

For a time, the Intifada changed family relations and family infrastructure, despite the fact that the traditional division of labor remained fundamentally unchallenged, which meant that women assumed both traditional and extra-domestic roles. This same activist told me, "I feel a sad happiness and a happy sadness because the people cannot stop [the Intifada]. Mothers cannot cry; they must stand firm [but] they are being robbed of something."

Despite these and other truly extraordinary changes, some of the most impressive and compelling stories about women were those less visible or vaunted, hidden inside the home where the struggle to survive was defining. I spent a great deal of time inside the refugee camps of Gaza and in people's homes where I found resistance of another kind.

I shall never forget one visit to a refugee camp in another part of the Strip. This camp had had its water supply cut off by the Israeli authorities in punishment for some offense and by the time I arrived, the camp had been without water for two, possibly three days. This was a form of collective punishment that was inflicted with some regularity at the time. My friend Abeer had arranged for me to meet with a family and their friends in the camp. When we arrived, we entered through a small, rudimentary kitchen area. We were taken to a large, spartan room where several women spanning at least three generations were already waiting. They were expecting us, and the conversation began almost before I sat down. We talked about life in the camp, the importance of the Intifada, the difficulties of their lives, their personal and political aspirations among many other topics. The discussion was animated, at times solemn and introspective, but also laced with sarcasm and humor. I was moved by their strength and sense of irony.

At some point during our discussion, the mother of the family, Um Ali, brought us a large pot of tea, which she placed in front of me. She poured a cup for me and for the others. It was a cold, raw day and I remember how good the tea tasted. Um Ali kept refilling my cup as I continued talking, making sure it was never empty. When the time came to leave, I was saddened by the thought I might never see them again. After thanking them for their wonderful hospitality, Abeer and I left and began walking through the camp. Suddenly I remembered that the water supply to the camp had been cut off. I stopped and turned to my friend: "Abeer, there is no water in the camp. How did

Um Ali get the water to make us tea?" Abeer told me that in antic-
ipation of my visit, Um Ali began collecting water from a slow drip
in her kitchen faucet to ensure that I would have enough tea to drink
while I was in her home. It took her 24 hours to collect the water for
my pot of tea.[7]

"WE ARE ONE BIG PERSON"

I spent a good amount of time in Beach Camp in part because it was
so close to where I lived and relatively easy to access although I never
went in alone. On November 21, 1988, just a few days after the PLO's
declaration of a Palestinian state and recognition of Israel, my friend
Talal and I went to the camp. What follows are descriptions of that
day drawn from my notes:

- Beach Camp has three entrances. Ironically the camp borders
  one of Gaza's most affluent areas, Rimal. Gaza is filled with
  seemingly inexplicable ironies and contradictions. Near the
  entrance of the camp, the Israeli military had confiscated a
  private, two-story home, which it uses as a base or station. It is
  critically situated so that from the second floor a considerable
  portion of the camp can be seen. Before the Intifada, soldiers
  seldom entered the camps but patrolled outside them. This has
  completely changed; now, the soldiers go inside.

- Talal and I just walked in. The borders between Rimal and the
  camp are fluid but unmistakable. I felt the moment of impact
  and sensed, most keenly, the moment of passage into the camp.
  We walked up to a group of boys whom, I thought, would have
  looked very menacing to any Israeli, but who seemed sadder
  than menacing to me. It turned out that one of them … wanted
  to know how to find Dr. Jay, the American doctor, to ask him a
  question about his leg. The connection we immediately established with the boy facilitated our further entry into the camp.
  A friend of his then escorted us to the home of a deportee. Talal
  wanted to meet the family of this man. The steel door to their
  home was locked and some neighbors sitting nearby told us that
  the family had left the camp for good.

- So, we walked just a few meters from the deportee's home and saw many women outside, hanging clothes, walking or just sitting. Women seem to outnumber men in the camps. This is probably because the men are working in Israel or [are] in jail. Talal started talking to one very old woman. He asked her age and she said she didn't know but remembered the time when the Turks were here. Within seconds of stopping to speak with her, a group of children surrounded us, followed, more tentatively, by several women. We began speaking to them and were instantly the focus of their attention and interest.

- I asked the women about the declaration of the state and everybody was happy and even optimistic but intensely aware that the road ahead would not be easy. I asked about the curfew, an event that is all too familiar and immediate. The camps in Gaza are placed under curfew quite often and for longer periods than the cities and towns. The most recent curfew was especially difficult [following the Declaration of Independence]. One woman claimed that there was a soldier stationed at every third house. No one could go outside. Opening a shutter risked physical and financial punishment, even death.[8] They said it was the tightest curfew they had ever experienced. People ran out of food especially since families are so big. There wasn't any way to go out to find food nor could families share with each other. Anyone discovered outside looking for milk incurred a fine of 500 NIS [an impossible sum for most refugee families]. Typically, during curfews, people would knock on each other's walls to see if there is an injured person, a baby needing milk, a woman in labor, etc. Somehow word is passed to doctors who have been known to sneak into the camp to help people at great risk to themselves, something that did not happen before the Intifada. "You feel that you are one big person instead of many people," one activist told me.

- One woman invited us into her home, a few feet from where we were standing. Before I could thank her and accept, she took me by the arm, and in a forceful but familiar manner I had come to love, swept me through her door. She told me that fifty people live in her shelter, which didn't seem large enough to accommodate ten. I was introduced to the patriarch of the family, a worn but proud-looking man. He told me that he has five sons, all married, and 38 grandchildren. They all live in this home as custom dictates. The house was L-shaped and had five rooms off the main corridor. Each room, and I was shown every one, housed one family and was small [and] cramped with old furniture and bed linens. The air was cold and [damp]. The walls were rotting from water leaks and were covered with strips of peeling paint. One wall in every room was decorated with pictures of fashion models that had been torn out of a magazine, and with postcards and travel posters, which managed somehow to find their way into the camp. They were the only forms of indulgence I could see. Some rooms had large photographs of young boys and men, proudly hung at the highest point on the wall just where it meets the ceiling. Some were in jail; others had died.

• The physical inadequacy of the house was riveting. Children swarmed everywhere. It was hard to move around unencumbered. The noise level was, for me, very oppressive … The grandfather said to me, "We have no money, that is why we must live like this." However, I didn't sense any shame in him. It wasn't embarrassment he felt, but dejection. His daughters-in-law were much more expressive. They showed me every corner and crevice of the place and seemed at times to push me into rooms as if to say, "See how we must live. This is the evidence. This is real. Take a good look." Amazingly, they retained their sense of humor and pride. Many jokes were made about luxurious living conditions, but through the giggles, insistent and tenacious hands kept grabbing me, gently pulling me into the same room, the same corner, the same crevice, for another look. Even the children understood the significance of my visit and designated themselves my personal ushers. I felt them all around me, urging me into the next viewing chamber.[9]

• Another woman in the group insisted we visit her home as well … We entered a space that was divided into two small rooms, which housed 13 people. I felt as if a steamroller had just gone over me. The room we entered was a cooking area—I hesitate to call it a kitchen—which consisted of one very old and worn-looking stove. The area was tiny and dank. The floors were stone, wet from the dampness and very cold. One small child sat on the floor with a piece of paper trying to write. Right next to the cooking area was the bathroom-shower area that was barely wide enough for one person ... "Imagine having a bathroom next to a kitchen!" the mother said, "What choice do we have?" It was so cold and raw inside, I began shivering but tried hard to conceal it. There are no sources of heat and many people cannot afford a space heater. I felt ashamed for shivering.

RESISTING THE DESTRUCTION OF COMMUNAL BONDS: WOMEN AS A SITE OF VIOLENCE, MEN AS A SITE OF HUMILIATION

Resistance, I learned, is fundamentally about resilience. But perhaps most of all, it is about retaining one's humanity in the face of all attempts to diminish or destroy it. In Gaza, women were the objects of such despicable attempts by the Israeli Army, and their resilience and courage has never left me. These attempts, among others, involved beating and otherwise humiliating women and children especially, in public and private spaces. And while I cannot say this was an official policy of the IDF, I can say it was a pattern of behavior that while aberrant, was purposeful, recurring throughout my time in Gaza. The most hideous, even monstrous, aspect of these beatings was a tacit understanding the soldiers had managed to impose on the population: *we will stop beating your women and children if you beat them.* I do not know how this understanding was formed. All I know is that Palestinians responded in a way that was meant to mitigate harm and eliminate the possibility of greater violence.

Teachers told stories of how soldiers would enter classrooms and begin hitting some of the children. Knowing that the only way to get rid of the soldiers was to take over, teachers would start slapping the children until the soldiers would leave. They would then comfort the children and try to distract them with play. A friend of mine at the time, a foreign diplomat who worked for UNRWA as a Refugee Affairs Officer (RAO), told me she saw soldiers dragging a 15-year old girl up some stairs before beating her. The Palestinian driver of her car went over to the girl and started to hit her, at which point the soldiers left. Once they were gone, he stopped hitting her. My friend felt she could do nothing because she feared that if she inter-vened, the soldiers would continue their assault against the child. The scene deeply upset her for many reasons, including the suggestion of sexual violence against women. "Why do you think this is happen-ing?" I asked. She answered, "To perpetuate a cycle of violence within Palestinian society," thereby breaking the bonds that hold families and society together, something Palestinians clearly understood and resisted. These beatings, of course, also were intended to humiliate and demean men—all men, not just those related to the woman or child being attacked but those witnessing the assault and powerless to defend against it. The beatings were designed to instill submission more than fear, and for a time they failed to do so (which is why they recurred).[10]

"ALL I WANT IS A FACTORY AND A FLAG"

On October 31, 1988, a leaflet of the Unified Command called on Israelis to vote for peace, for a secure Israeli state and a Palestinian state. The leaflet called on people to step up stone throwing and petrol bomb attacks, "which are not meant to kill Jews but to protest repres-sion and occupation."

Two weeks later, on November 15, 1988, Yasir Arafat declared the independent State of Palestine on the West Bank and Gaza—based on the 1947 Partition Plan and UNSCR 242 and 338—which had pre-viously and overwhelmingly been adopted by the Palestinian National Council, the PLO's legislative arm. Arafat renounced terrorism and recognized the State of Israel, calling for coexistence between an Israeli and Palestinian state. This fulfilled the American precondition for engaging with the PLO. The majority of Gazans were exultant.

A female activist put it this way: "I'm not begging for a passport, I have my roots. Look at Israel. More Jews live outside of Israel than inside. Israel is a source of identity for them. It would be the same for Palestinians."

Following Arafat's declaration, Israel immediately placed Gaza under a tight curfew (as described by the women above); anyone defying the curfew would be shot. Yet, on this particular day defy it they did, and the army for the most part did not respond. People lit-erally danced in the streets of Gaza while Israeli soldiers looked on, disbelieving the scene not far from them. In Beach Camp, people poured out of their shelters, jubilant and unafraid, puncturing the thick darkness of the camp with celebration. People embraced each other and the joy was heartfelt. I had never seen such rejoicing or felt such a sense of triumph in Gaza. A middle-aged man whom I did not know approached my friends and me and said, "I will never forget my home in Palestine; it will always be in my heart. But now, all I want is a factory and a flag."[11]

ISRAEL BEWILDERED AND ENRAGED

"We have mobile courts today. They are the soldiers."

Israel was surprised and taken aback by the Intifada. Israel did not think Palestinians were aware enough, inspired enough, or courageous enough to demand and fight for their rights. In addition to their systematic cruelty, the Israeli Army also responded in a manner that was arbitrary and gratuitous. Their response (particularly during the first two years of the first Intifada) was also disorganized and absurd, even trivial at times. As one local activist observed: "Israelis have won wars with people using arms and they cannot understand why they cannot win a war against people with no arms."[12] Some examples from my field notes reveal the army's sense of confusion and fury.

On the more disorganized and absurd end, the army would arrest people with beards and confiscate donkeys from their owners. They would order boys to kiss girls in public as a way of shaming and humiliating them, and drop leaflets calling for strikes on days different from those called by the Intifada leadership—this was meant to confuse people and possibly cause them to lose an additional day of work. On Christmas Day (1988), the military governor summoned members of Gaza's Christian community to his office so that they could wish *him* a merry Christmas.

During curfews both at night and during the day, Israeli soldiers would sometimes yell obscenities through loudspeakers. In Deir El Balah and other camps, for example, the army used loudspeakers to say, "You bastards, you gypsies, you sons of bitches, you are under curfew." One night around one in the morning, soldiers were singing at the top of their lungs: "You better behave, you sons of bitches or else." The IDF also entered a hospital and removed pictures of Abu Jihad and Arafat.

Gratuitous violence was constant and often directed at children. In what seemingly became a common practice, the IDF would, as described above, enter schools and beat pupils or throw tear gas into classrooms. In one notable incident that took place between October 4 and October 6, 1988, Israeli Army troops ordered pupils inside an UNRWA school to throw burning tires inside their school and on the roof of the school. In another case, UNRWA reported that after schoolchildren had received their food parcels, Israeli soldiers chased them and confiscated the parcels.

Another common practice of the IDF was to fill ambulances with garbage, stones and dirt and periodically prevent ambulances from bringing the injured to hospital or arrest the injured from inside the ambulance itself. The army would sometimes storm health clinics (which were clearly a target) and damage or destroy the clinic's windows, doors and lab equipment. In winter 1989 I wrote, "According to two British consultants here on a mission for UNRWA, the Israeli Army has now resorted to dropping stones and boulders on people's homes from helicopters." Around the same time, the IDF introduced a new, much harsher punishment for stone throwers. A judge in a military court sentenced a 16-year-old Gazan to five years in jail for throwing a stone at a soldier, arguing, "I do not accept the claim that a stone thrower should get a lighter punishment than someone who uses live arms."[13]

The Israeli government further announced that it was looking into a new strategy for dealing with the Intifada. It would start arresting children under the age of ten and make their parents pay heavy fines for their release. The government was also talking about what was then a relatively new deterrent: denying Palestinians the right to work in Israel.

WRESTING CONTROL: SOME REFLECTIONS

Talal came by tonight [December 12, 1988] and told me something that my students told me earlier today: The Unified Command called for five minutes of observance for the slain of the Intifada on Saturday, December 10 at 11 a.m. Precisely at that hour everyone and everything stopped. People got out of their cars in the middle of the street, shopkeepers stopped working and so on. The soldiers could do nothing about it ... Talal said it was fantastic. [author's field notes]

Thirty years later, young Palestinians protest at Gaza's border with Israel for an end to occupation and siege with no concern for their own lives. One asks: "Show me the alternative to sacrifice."[14] Others tell me that young Gazans are so desperate that they are prepared, while protesting, to incur crippling injuries such as the loss of a limb that will lead to permanent disability because such injuries will qualify for financial support and, in the case of one young man, allow his family to pay the rent for the next few months.[15]

The juxtaposition of these two events—with no intent to compare them—a generation apart is striking, and the fundamental difference between them lies in the presence of possibility, and in its absence. Yet as different as they may appear, they are integral and interconnected parts of a continuum of success and failure that continues to proceed, often without notice.

What Palestinians Achieved: Persisting Beyond Mythology

A great deal has been written about the Intifada's achievements— unifying the community around the pursuit of common goals, prioritizing the collective (where ideological purity was unimport- ant, even irrelevant) over the personal, exposing and challenging the power asymmetries between Israel and the Palestinians, defying Israeli policies, and assuming a determinative role for Palestinians not as subjects but as initiators. Palestinians were no longer quiescent and were given a voice in the West, which has not been silenced since. Their struggle was an expression of agency and dignity, and it was principally non-violent, involving both women and children. It was not their needs that Palestinians wanted addressed, but their rights— and this demand has not changed. In this regard, the Intifada shattered forever any notion of a benign occupation, a defining mythology used to preserve the morality of the Jewish state and its promise of a normal life not only for Palestinians but also for Jews. The Intifada laid bare

Israel's preference for order over justice. It also weakened Israel's image externally as a charitable benefactor of the Palestinian.

What was particularly striking about the Intifada were the confidence and awareness that Palestinians clearly possessed, which nourished and sustained their activism for an appreciable period before the uprising began to break down. They achieved a certain kind of freedom that no doubt shocked and terrified Israel. This sense of freedom found expression in the *force of truth*—confronting Israelis with the reality of a population subjugated against its will—in *non-cooperation with injustice* through civil disobedience and non-violent resistance—and in *popular organization* through decentralization and the re-appropriation of control by a people newly empowered.[16] Yet, my time in Gaza made one thing very clear: the re-appropriation of control that was so defining of the Intifada was not in itself the most worrisome aspect for Israel; after all, such control could be—and was—eradicated. What worried Israel most, then and now, was the *collective* re-assumption of control—the strengthening of individual and collective agency—for specific and clearly articulated ends: strengthening Palestinian civil society, political equality and, perhaps most of all, the need for a *political* solution to the conflict. As one local leader told me at the time, "If no Arab country could win a war with Israel, neither can we; we must use politics." The protests that distinguish the Great March of Return are fueled by the same impulse.

The Intifada changed the political reference point for Palestinians from the PLO Covenant to the Declaration of Independence, from the historical debate on Israel to UN resolutions, international law and a state of their own alongside Israel. Palestinians were not seeking the destruction of the Jewish state; they were seeking what the man in Beach Camp had aspired to: "a factory and a flag," defining a national identity of their own that was separate from that of other Arab identities within whom they had always been subsumed. As Dr. Haidar Abdel Shafi argued, "The Intifada became the identity of the Palestinian people and their inviolable right," rejecting a history that had long been imposed on them. Even an Israeli commander understood the power of identity when he said: "We are getting better and better at controlling the violence. But the essence of the Intifada is not in the actual level of activity but in the perception of the population, the sense of identity, direction and organization. These are the things that are virtually impossible for the army to control."[17]

Perhaps most critically, with the Intifada came a deepened historical understanding that the uprising was not only the product of occupation but was part of a long and protracted Palestinian struggle against Zionism to achieve independence and identity. Tragically, this connection with the past seems removed from the struggle today.

The insistence on a political solution involving compromise between Israeli and Palestinian was most threatening to Israel, for it spoke to a form of political moderation that Israel had long rejected among Palestinians. As the Israeli journalist Amira Hass put it, "If the Israeli government was really interested in a two-state solution, why have they worked so hard to prevent it?"[18]

At the 1991 Madrid conference, which emerged from the Intifada, Palestinians briefly forced diplomacy on Israel, which then had to engage with Palestinians on terms that were not Israel's alone. This insistence on the political has continued to characterize the Palestinian struggle despite the violence that now surrounds it. Although the situation in Gaza at present is far worse than anyone could have imagined thirty years ago, the animating forces behind the Intifada remain alive and defining, even if the connection to the Intifada has remained obscured for many young people. In this way, too, the Intifada showed—and Gazans continue to show—that Palestinians are capable of writing and narrating their own history and that Israel is not exempt from the burdens that history imposes.

What Israel Learned: Selling Gold for Rice

Anton Shammas once wrote, "the Israelis remember everything while learning nothing."[19] Yet, that is not entirely true, particularly as it regards the Intifada. Israel learned a great deal about Palestinians, perhaps more than the Palestinians learned about Israel. The Intifada changed how Palestinians defined themselves and it also changed how Israelis defined them.

In two lengthy interviews I did with a young man named Kassem who was imprisoned in Ansar 3,[20] an Israeli detention camp located in the Negev Desert (and considered the largest detention camp in the world at the time), I was given a detailed description of life inside the camp and the political impact it had on those detained. Re-reading those interviews, I was struck by some of Kassem's observations:

> The Israelis aren't stupid. They know Palestinians are politicized [in Ansar] but they do not care. *All they care about is stopping the Intifada.* [It] ... will not stop ... the Israelis cannot change what is inside ourselves ... No one knows where the Intifada will lead but solutions must be political ... *Now, the Israelis have woken from their dream and recognized the Palestinian problem. They recognize there is a Palestinian people in the West Bank and Gaza who want the occupation to end.* They recognize the demographic problem. Israelis understand what their borders must be. They do not know how they are going to deal with political separation because of economic reasons. It's not easy for the Israelis to give the Occupied Territories back. [emphasis mine]

Kassem's observations were correct but his conclusion was wrong.

Willy Gafni who was then the director of the International Center for Peace in the Middle East, a public policy organization located in Tel Aviv, put it this way: "The Intifada recreated the 1967 borders in Israeli minds. Israelis never thought they were dealing with a people or nation, or a problem.[21] Now they realize they are. The Intifada has succeeded in communicating that, not only to the [Israeli] people but also to the soldiers, the next generation of leaders. Now we must deal with things—symbols, people, issues—we were brought up to hate."

Hence the Intifada confronted Israel with the need to imagine—and humanize—the Palestinian, to make the Palestinian necessary[22] in ways that contradicted long-embraced understandings. This reimagining, however, did not occur. Instead, Israel learned that it must never accommodate Palestinians and must repudiate them entirely by eliminating their capacity and constricting their vision. In Gaza, Palestinians were rendered unnamable except for their biological needs, inhabiting space that is no longer "animate and resonant, or endowed with any meaning or potential."[23] Israel learned to insure for Gaza especially, a parenthetical reality, a totalizing existence apart. Gaza's state of exception, which Israel has successfully nurtured, is expressed in the unmaking of shelter and sustenance, in social space that is never insulated from violence and incoherence, where violent excess is affirmed and made intimate, in policy that regards "peace" as an instrument of oppression, where consent is rarely given and compromise rarely made; where Israel remains unquestioning and unchanged.

That the Palestinian leadership (and interfactional division and violence), whether Fatah or Hamas, has contributed to their people's undoing is indisputable—particularly with regard to human rights abuses and the crushing of dissent—but this does not absolve Israel of what it has done, and continues to do, to Gaza.[24]

A FINAL THOUGHT

Gaza is a scandal that has persisted long past its disclosure.[25] That Gaza's misery continues, with the knowledge and consent of others, speaks to the ruin in all nations. Not long ago a colleague interviewed an official in the French government who asked her: "When will it be visible that Gaza's economy is dead?" The lack of empathy and tranquil sense of cruelty evinced by this question is also part of our disgrace.

Gaza has long been characterized as a symbol of wreckage, particularly since the Intifada. Yet embedded in this characterization, which Gazans have always resisted, are certain truths rooted in the Intifada that continue to shape the Palestinian struggle, albeit silently and, for many, unknowingly. One is that the Palestinian struggle will never again recede into an unquestioned, unexamined narrative. The narrative may be disputed but it will not be muted. Similarly, although the Intifada failed to address meaningfully the gross disparity in power between Israel and the Palestinians, it succeeded in briefly challenging it, demonstrating that Palestinians would never again be the disempowered and voiceless subjects of occupation. The Intifada confronted the anonymity of Palestinian death, ensuring that the deaths—and lives—of Palestinians would no longer remain shrouded or unknown. The Intifada also succeeded in questioning the idea of Israel as a symbol or a cause, unveiling a state that occupies another people and does so brutally.

My decades of work among Palestinians, especially during the Intifada, has allowed me to bear witness to their inner life and spiritual resources, which have not been defeated. As such, I have come to understand that Israel's repression of Gaza not only represents an attack by an occupier against an occupied but also an unending attack against a society, largely composed of children and young adults, seeking freedom and dignity, and the right to live an ordinary life. By insisting that Gaza and the Palestinian struggle be understood in these terms, perhaps most of all the Intifada created a politically and morally audible testimony capable of facing Israeli memory, and that may be its greatest and most inextinguishable legacy.

PART VIII BETWEEN PRESENCE AND ABSENCE:*
PALESTINE AND THE ANTILOGIC OF DISPOSABILITY

CONCLUDING REFLECTIONS

The lover must be accepted, and not hungry.

Mahmoud Darwish
"Exile Is So Strong Within Me, I May Bring It To The Land"

Some things you forget. Other things you never do. But it's not. Places, places are still there. If a house burns down, it's gone, but the place—the picture of it—stays, and not just in my rememory, but out there, in the world. What I remember is a picture floating around out there outside my head. I mean, even if I don't think if, even if I die, the picture of what I did, or knew, or saw is still out there. Right in the place where it happened.

Toni Morrison
Beloved

Tho' much is taken, much abides; and tho'
We are not now that strength which in old days
Moved earth and heaven, that which we are, we are;
One equal temper of heroic hearts,
Made weak by time and fate, but strong in will
To strive, to seek, to find, and not to yield.

Alfred, Lord Tennyson
Ulysses

---

* "'Exile Is So Strong Within Me, I May Bring It To The Land'—A Landmark 1996 Interview With Mahmoud Darwish," *Journal of Palestine Studies*, Volume XLII, No. 1 (Autumn 2012), p. 61.

25

An Unacceptable Absence:
Countering Gaza's Exceptionalism*

Gaza remains under different forms of attack and unable to defend against them. In August 2020, for example, these attacks occurred nightly for about three weeks as Covid-19 spread. Israeli fighter jets launched missiles strikes in retaliation for incendiary balloons launched by Gazans across Gaza's border with Israel.[1] These balloons, which cause fires on the Israeli side, were meant as a distress signal, aiming to draw attention to Gaza's deteriorating economic situation, largely a result of Israel's 14-year blockade of land and sea, which has decimated the economy. In September, following mediation by Qatar, some restrictions were eased, allowing more fuel and other goods to enter the territory; electricity increased to just eight hours per day.

In October 2020, the Israeli military, replete with tanks and bulldozers, penetrated up to 300 meters into Gaza's "buffer zone" area, damaging huge areas of farmland, razing vegetation, flattening roads and destroying agricultural equipment. Israel claims it must do so for security reasons; such incursions—34 between January and August 2020—are a regular practice. In January and April 2020, Israel also carried out aerial herbicide spraying in Gaza, damaging and destroying local crops, further disfiguring the land. Said one farmer, "It looks like the Israeli military wants us to internalize that living and working in this area is impossible."[2]

The Gaza Strip and West Bank have been under Israeli occupation for 53 years—almost three-quarters of Israel's entire history.[3] The occupation extracts Palestinian resources and deprives Palestinians of their political, economic and social rights, which has been ruinous for both areas, especially Gaza, despite limited and now, largely lost

---

* A version of this chapter was originally written for a book of my work to appear in Japanese [TBA, Tokyo: Seidosha Publishers, forthcoming]. A more detailed and expanded version appears here in English for the first time.

achievements. Today, both areas face declining or negative growth, unprecedented levels of unemployment and impoverishment and an unsustainable dependence on (decreasing levels of) international assistance, which can no longer stabilize or lessen decline. The situation in Gaza is particularly grave with its economy in "free fall," according to the World Bank.[4] As I have argued throughout this book, the slow but steady demise of the Palestinian economy results largely from policies that are intentional and malign, designed to accomplish Israel's principal objective—precluding viable Palestinian economic development and with it, the possibility of a Palestinian state.

A key feature of Israeli strategy—extinguishing national rights with limited and ephemeral prosperity—what Israel and donors call "economic peace" (and "development"),[5] is as old as the occupation itself. The $50 billion Kushner Plan—which nowhere mentions the word "occupation"—is simply the most recent and strikingly unrealistic iteration of "economic peace." Like its many predecessors, the Kushner Plan will fail (particularly since it expects others to support the very programs and projects from which the US has itself divested). More recently, economic peace has assumed another, more constricted form. According to Prime Minister Netanyahu, economic peace now refers to the incentives Palestinians will receive if they agree to the Israeli government's planned annexation of their lands.

Critically, the occupation has remained unchallenged by an international order that seems willing to legitimize it as long as there is no accepted agreement to end it. A compliant and complicit donor community—notably the US and the EU—has directly and indirectly supported Israeli policy, including its most destructive expressions. Referring specifically to the Paris Economic Protocol (PEP), Tariq Dana writes that the PEP "maintained the dependency of the Palestinian economy on Israel but changed its legal status from one subject to illegal occupation policy to a regulated dependency endorsed by international agreements."[6] Although the EU has protested Israel's proposed annexation of West Bank lands and the blockade on Gaza, it remains unclear and in fact doubtful (if history provides any precedent) that the EU or the US will sanction Israel in any meaningful way going forward.[7]

Contributing to the damage imposed by external powers are internal forces. The ineptitude, domestic power struggles, and growing corruption of the West Bank and Gaza authorities—each incapable of ending the occupation—have further contributed to the immiseration of their people (see below).

Over thirty years ago (as shown in Chapter 23), the late Dr. Hatem Abu Ghazaleh, a Gaza physician and close friend, told me something that I have never forgotten: "[N]othing is more permanent than the temporary." Indeed, one of the most powerful themes that run through my decades of research in Gaza and the West Bank is the notion of the *indefinite* or the *transitional* as a state imposed on Palestinians; that is, the promise of something better and permanent that is never achieved, but where the indefinite or transitional—the "temporary" as Dr. Hatem put it—itself becomes permanent. This is not due to imperfect implementation or an error in design (as was often said in defense of the failing Oslo Accords) but rather to the design itself.

As some of the works in this collection argue, the occupation long ago became normalized, which was the intent of the now-discredited Oslo process. As such, Oslo did not represent a watershed event that many believed would lead to the end of the occupation; rather, Oslo did the opposite: transforming the occupation from a political and legal issue with international significance into a local struggle over market access and worker permits. If anything, under the Oslo process, the occupation became invisible because it became so normal.

Oslo made it possible for Israel—with almost unquestioned American support—to argue that it was working toward ending the occupation, while pursuing policies that would ensure Israel's con-tinued presence and eliminate the emergence of a viable Palestinian state and economy on land Israel wished to claim as its own.[8] The most damaging of Oslo's policies include: the near-total separation of the West Bank and Gaza, the isolation of Gaza, the internal frag-mentation of the West Bank and seizure of the majority of the land by Israel, and the provision of aid largely—and in the case of Gaza, almost exclusively—for humanitarian relief. In this way, foreign assis-tance was designed to mitigate the damaging impact on the economy rather than repair it. This is why, in part, despite having received over $38 billion in aid from 1994 to 2018 (according to the World Bank), the Palestinian economy remains debilitated.[9]

Under Oslo, the historical contest over territory was reframed by a policy of separation, isolation and containment. Within this framework, Gaza and the West Bank were separated demographically and physically. As a result, an isolated Gaza came to be seen as exceptional or marginal, existing outside a Palestinian state and a Palestinian nation. Gaza's imposed exceptionalism became a vital component of Israel's larger and more important goal of annexing parts of the West Bank.[10]

Yet, it is important to understand that the policies that have come to define Gaza as exceptional are simply extensions, albeit more extreme, of policies long used to separate and isolate Palestinians in the West Bank and in Israel. In this regard, Gaza's status is part of a long and consistent policy continuum of containment, removal and erasure. As such, Gaza became the model for the fragmentation of the West Bank into small, disconnected enclaves under constant assault. Hence, to borrow from Professor Sarah Dryden-Peterson, it is important to understand that these policies of separation and exclusion make it difficult if not impossible for Palestinians to imagine a larger sense of a collective; without that sense, exclusion becomes the defining basis for politics and policy.

THE TRANSFORMATION OF THE GAZA STRIP: IMPOSED DECLINE

The situation in Gaza is increasingly precarious, as this book has argued. The economy is sustained primarily by international assistance and, to a lesser degree, illicit funds. A more minor role is also played by local tax collection and taxes on imports. States the World Bank, "Gaza's economy has been kept afloat in recent years by large transfers including donor aid and spending through the budget of the Palestinian Authority (PA), both of which amounted to 70–80 percent of Gaza's GDP,"[11] transfers which have experienced significant declines (see below). Hence, without external aid, there would be no functioning economy able to provide any form of public or private services.

The 14-year blockade—in which Egypt is an active participant—is the principal factor underlying Gaza's economic ruination and reflects the use of economic policy as a punitive measure. Yet, it should be understood that Gaza has been under varying degrees of closure since 1991, which has increasingly restricted and, at times, completely banned the movement of people and goods. The blockade is part of Israel's closure policy, its most extreme expression, making the closure almost total.

The blockade has destroyed normal trade relations (particularly exports), upon which Gaza's small economy depends, and has paralyzed much of the economy especially private-sector activity, which the Hamas authorities have done little if anything to address. Productive activity long ago gave way to a consumption-based economy supported by relief aid. The three assaults (among others) on Gaza in 2008/09, 2012 and 2014 have been catastrophic economically. Direct economic losses resulting from the 2008/09 military operation alone (which lasted three weeks) ranged between \$1.9 and \$2.5 billion.[12] The damage incurred was equivalent to over 60 percent of the total capital stock of Gaza.[13]

The physical damage and economic losses that resulted from the 2014 hostilities amounted to \$3.1 billion. Of this, the most damage occurred to the infrastructure sector at \$2 billion, representing 64 percent of all damage and 60 percent of all losses. This was followed by the damage to Gaza's already diminished productive sector, costing \$869 million.[14] According to the UN, "The share of Gaza's productive sectors fell from 28 to 13 per cent of GDP between 1994 and 2018; the share of manufacturing halved, to 8 percent, and that of agriculture fell from 9 to 5 per cent."[15] The Palestinian Authority estimated that the cost of Gaza's reconstruction and recovery following the 2014 war was \$3.9 billion.[16]

The result has been disastrous: unprecedented levels of unemployment, food insecurity and aid dependency. In September 2018, for example, the World Bank stated that the "economy in Gaza is collapsing."[17] By the first quarter of 2020 (prior to the impact of the Covid crisis), according to the Palestinian Central Bureau of Statistics (PCBS), Gaza's unemployment rate stood at 45.5 percent.[18] By the second quarter of 2020, unemployment had reached 49.1 percent (this does not include the impact of additional Covid-imposed restrictions in August, which further lowered employment levels)—more than double the unemployment rate of 23.6 percent in 2005. By June 2020, youth (age 15–29) unemployment had increased to 69.9 percent (and 92 percent for young women).[19] This is particularly worrisome because three-quarters of the population are under 30 and prohibited by Israel from leaving Gaza.

Consequently, by 2018, around 53 percent of Gazans—or every second person (including over 400,000 children)—lived in poverty (a dramatic increase from 38.8 percent in 2011) and 68 percent were food insecure, meaning they were unable to access adequate amounts of nutritious food, a situation that has only grown worse.[20] A 2020 UN report examining economic trends between 2007 and 2018 similarly observed that Gaza's poverty rate increased from 40 percent in 2007 to 56 percent in 2017 (but in the absence of the blockade and ongoing hostilities the rate could have been far lower at 15 percent).[21] Depending upon source, current figures (which include the impact of the Covid pandemic) place poverty in Gaza between 56 and 60 percent. There is enough food in Gaza, but the primary problem is weak and worsening purchasing power.

Over 80 percent of Gaza's total population now requires humanitarian assistance, despite the fact that they are desperate to work.[22] Because of the Israeli blockade, approximately 1.6 million men, women and children have been forced into dependency on food and cash handouts.[23] Acquiring enough food on a daily basis is what presently consumes most families. Some people are now seeking food in rubbish piles,[24] and homelessness is a growing problem because people cannot afford to pay their rent. (Furthermore, the use of advanced weaponry by Israel has also resulted in heavy metal contamination of the environment and the population, in addition to the chronic water and sanitation crisis.[25]) It is no exaggeration to say that Gaza is now a humanitarian safe zone where survival depends disproportionately on (declining levels of) foreign assistance.

In fact, the 2020 UN report, which echoes the World Bank, refers to the "near collapse of the regional Gaza economy." It also found that "the estimated cumulative economic cost of the Israeli occupation in Gaza under the prolonged closure and severe economic and movement restrictions and military operations would amount to $16.7 billion ... equivalent to six times the value of [Gaza's GDP], or 107 per cent of the Palestinian GDP, in 2018."[26] Not surprisingly, Gaza's share in the Palestinian economy dropped by half, from 37 percent in 1995 to 18 percent in 2018.[27]

There are many factors that have contributed to Gaza's continued decline. As stated above, Israel's blockade and three major military assaults against the territory are the most obvious. Yet, other factors have accelerated the territory's deterioration.

Internal Hostilities

Internal conflict between the Hamas government and the Palestinian Authority has resulted in several damaging policies. Since March 2017, Mahmoud Abbas, the PA president has consistently increased pressure on the Hamas government in Gaza by removing around $45–60 million monthly from Gaza's economy. By April 2019, this resulted, for example, in the following: 3,231 PA employees had their salaries cut; 1,700 families who had relatives killed and were receiving compensation had their compensation completely eliminated; of the 11,000 people who were receiving NIS1,500 (approx. $455) per month, 112 were completely cut and the remainder received only 50 percent; pensions were reduced by 50 percent, and Abbas also retired people who were the age of his sons, raising the question of how their pensions will be paid.[28] These measures affected approximately 62,000 civil servants and their families (well over 350,000 people) and the larger economy.[29] Furthermore, these measures, while continuous, are not static. At different points, some PA employees received 75 percent of their salaries and at a later date received only 50 percent. As one colleague in Gaza told me, it is not only jobs that Palestinians urgently need, but job security. This arbitrary and unpredictable policy precludes any form of rational planning, a constant feature of life in Gaza.

The uncertainty, insecurity and social fragility that now prevail are worsened by allegations that Hamas is stealing resources, particularly fuel and medical supplies. For example, the UN asserts that there should be enough fuel for the hospitals and has concluded that Hamas is stealing at least some of the fuel entering Gaza. The same is quite possibly true of medical supplies entering through Kerem Shalom, since the amounts reported in the hospitals do not always track with the amounts that have crossed into Gaza. There is a lack of clear information about precise amounts and mechanisms by which fuel and medicines go missing and about who bears responsibility; however, it is unlikely that the Hamas authorities are unaware of the situation. The Hamas government and movement have also been accused of widespread corruption, nepotism and coercion.

Another troubling dynamic concerns the escalating violence between families in Gaza. Disputes and retaliatory attacks between families have increased, resulting in injuries and property damage.[30]

US Policy and Legislative Changes

US policy (under the Trump administration) also imposed further hardship on Palestinians and had a particularly damaging impact on the larger international assistance package for Gaza. On December 6, 2017, the Trump administration recognized Jerusalem as the capital of Israel, reversing long-standing US policy and undercutting Palestinian claims to the city. Affirming this change, the US Embassy was relocated to Jerusalem and opened on May 14, 2018, which marked the seventieth anniversary of the establishment of the State of Israel.

Furthermore, in an effort to punish the Palestinian Authority for what President Trump deemed its unwillingness to negotiate with Israel and for disagreements over the definition of who qualifies as a refugee (thereby attempting to delegitimize if not eliminate refugee status and refugee claims, particularly the right of return), the United States had, by the end of 2018, terminated all funding to the United Nations Relief and Works Agency (UNRWA), which provides greatly needed education, health and social services for Palestinian refugees throughout the Middle East. Until 2018, the US was the largest donor to UNRWA, contributing $300–$350 million annually, or around one-third of the agency's annual budget of approximately $1.1 billion.[31] These cuts were particularly devastating for Gaza where UNRWA spends approximately 40 percent of its budget supporting well in excess of 1 million refugees. For example, "in order to avoid interruptions in the provision of critical humanitarian assistance [primarily food assistance], other interventions had to be scaled back or discontinued."[32] In Gaza, these programmatic cuts included the community mental health and job creation programs and housing subsidies to those families who lost their homes in the 2014 war.[33] Furthermore, and perhaps for the first time in its history, there is the possibility that UNRWA could run out of money if donations do not increase. In 2020, UNRWA was operating on a month-to-month basis, "never more than four or five weeks away from running out of funds."[34]

On November 23, 2020, UNRWA's Commissioner-General Philippe Lazzarini announced a budget deficit of $115 million, meaning that the agency would be unable to pay the full salaries of its 28,000 employees in the last quarter of 2020. Furthermore, UNRWA predicts funding gaps in its 2020 and 2021 budgets of $248 million and $268 million respectively. These deficits have increased, due, in part, to US pressure (under the Trump administration) on Arab states to reduce and, in some cases, end their support for UNRWA.[35]

In addition, the US announced in September 2018 the withdrawal of approximately $200–$230 million in US-funded development projects in Gaza and the West Bank administered through the United States Agency for International Development (USAID) (this economic assistance was reprogrammed for "high priority projects elsewhere"[36]). The Trump administration also restricted Palestinians from participating in programs funded by USAID and the US Embassy in Israel. Although other donor countries have covered a percentage of the funds terminated by the US, the overall impact has been damaging, further weakening an already impoverished population.

The US has also defunded the Palestinian Authority through legislation. On March 23, 2018, for example, the US government enacted the Taylor Force Act, which suspended US bilateral economic assistance for the PA unless Palestinian officials stop payments "for acts of terrorism against U.S. and Israeli citizens to any individual who has been fairly tried and imprisoned for such acts, to any individual who died committing such acts, and to family members of such an individual."[37] The Anti-Terrorism Clarification Act (ATCA) followed and became law on October 3, 2018, to ensure that the Palestine Liberation Organization (PLO) and PA will be subject to jurisdiction of US courts for past acts of Palestinian terrorism against US citizens. It exposes foreign organizations that accept certain forms of US foreign assistance to the possibility of terrorism-related civil litigation in US federal courts.[38] Hence, once foreign entities such as the PA accept US funds, they must submit to the US federal court's personal jurisdiction for terrorism-related claims and run the risk of being sued.

Fearful of potential liability under the ATCA and to avoid being sued, the Palestinian Authority and PLO decided to reject the limited amounts of American foreign assistance they still received—including support for an Israeli-Palestinian security cooperation program that Israeli officials, among others, argued had substantially improved the security situation in the West Bank.[39] By February 2019—and, I believe, for the first time since the Israeli–Palestinian conflict began—there was no US aid flowing to the Palestinian government.

Hence, America's political leverage remains employed wholly on behalf of Israel, a position that was strengthened under the Trump administration. The boycott of the US by the PA/PLO has only deepened the divide. The "political distortion of U.S. engagement in this conflict," as one analyst observed, "was not related to money they gave [the Palestinians]; rather, the money they give the Israelis. That hasn't stopped, so this has only made things worse." (Similarly, in November 2019, the Trump administration overturned decades of US policy on Israeli settlements in the West Bank and East Jerusalem, declaring that they are not illegal under international law, a right the US government does not possess, according to legal scholars. This policy reversal was widely interpreted as an attempt to help Netanyahu retain power in a weakened domestic environment where he had been unable to form a government beginning in December 2018.)

New Israeli Legislation

In early 2019 the 'Law for Offsetting Funds to the PA for its Support for Terror' (*"Law for freezing funds paid by the Palestinian Authority in relation to terrorism from funds transferred to it by the Government of Israel, 5778-2018"*),[40] passed by the Israeli legislature in July 2018, came into effect. Building on the US legislation described above, the Israeli law states the government will withhold from tax monies it transfers to the PA an amount comparable to the amount the PA pays to the families of individuals "held in Israeli jails for political crimes and to families of those killed in conflict or charged and convicted by Israel of terrorism."[41] The law "stipulates that every year the defense minister will submit to the security cabinet a report summarizing the transfer of funds from the PA to prisoners and their families. This sum will be divided by 12 and the result will be withheld from the subsequent monthly transfers of taxes Israel makes to the PA."[42] Needless to say, the PA considered this illegitimate, a form of bribery, which they rejected.

The argument underlying the law is that Palestinians are motivated by money to commit acts of violence (known disparagingly as "pay to slay"). This argument, which is misleading and shown to be false, ignores several key facts: the oppressive environment created by the occupation, the collective punishment meted out to the families of those accused of terrorism, and the highly successful security coordination between the PA and Israel.[43]

On February 17, 2019, Israel withheld approximately $138.2 million or the total amount the PA paid to families of prisoners in 2018 (around $11.5 million monthly) from the total clearance revenues transferred.[44] These clearance revenues, which are taxes collected by Israel for the PA (averaging $150–$200 million per month), account for 60–70 percent of all government income. As such, they are crucial to the Palestinian Authority's fiscal stability and deeply affect Gaza (which, as shown above, has experienced (punitive) reductions in transfers from the PA since 2017). Clearance revenues accounted for an average of 42 percent of total PA expenditures between 1997 and 2017, and when coupled with foreign assistance, represented on average 72 percent of all PA expenditures over the same period.[45]

It should be noted that the overall transfer from Israel to the PA already undergoes a process of deduction for water, electricity and health. In July 2018, for example, the PA Finance Ministry said that Israel deducted NIS120 million (about US$36 million) each month to cover the costs of electricity and water supplied by Israel to the Palestinians, and of medical treatment Palestinians receive in Israeli hospitals.[46]

The PA responded to Israel's withholding of the $138 million by stating that it would not accept any of the money Israel transfers to it under the terms of the Paris Protocol and returned all of the tax money Israel collected for the PA for the month of February 2019. It is not clear whether the PA continued this policy for the remainder of 2019. However, in May 2020, responding to Israel's plan to annex parts of the West Bank, the PA suspended all civil affairs and security coordination with Israel and stated that it would no longer be bound by past agreements and understandings with the American and Israeli governments. It also "withdrew Palestinian security forces from the suburbs of occupied Jerusalem and Area C of the West Bank."[47] The suspension of ties also meant the freezing of monthly tax transfers, which resulted in a fiscal crisis for the PA and took an enormous economic toll on Palestinians in the West Bank and Gaza.

However, in November 2020, the PA resumed civil and security coordination with Israel—in effect, a return to Oslo—a decision that was controversial because the PA received little politically from Israel in return.[48] The PA's decision was due to mounting pressures both fiscal and political including: depleting bank liquidity, which meant the PA could no longer secure loans; EU donors conditioning future aid on the resumption of tax transfers from Israel; the geopolitical changes in the region resulting from Israel's normalization of relations with certain Arab countries, and the hope of better ties with the Biden administration, which "urged the Palestinians to take specific steps to show that they will not be obstructionist if the new administration engages on the Israeli–Palestinian conflict."[49] Two of these steps included "resuming security cooperation and taking the tax transfers."[50] In December, Israel transferred $1.14 billion in tax revenues owed the PA (and said it would deduct $200 million the PA gives to families of prisoners but reportedly reversed this decision).[51] Critically, the PA's pronouncement undercut unity talks between Fatah and Hamas that were being held in Cairo in November, the 2021 Palestinian legislative and presidential elections scheduled for both the West Bank and Gaza notwithstanding.

THE IMPACT OF CONTINUED ECONOMIC DECLINE ON GAZA: SOME CRITICAL CHANGES

Under current conditions—a small, blockaded economy that is heavily aid-dependent, with a local market characterized by high levels of unemployment and poor liquidity, and unable to export—the prospects for meaningful economic growth are nonexistent. In fact, the artificial economy that is now Gaza's remains in a state of perpetual decline. By the first quarter of 2018, Gaza's economy was at minus 6 percent growth, a trend that has continued since under the weight of the blockade, the PA's decision to reduce payments to Gaza, and the loss of US aid and US funding of UNRWA.[52] In another analysis, the economy's negative growth was projected to continue well into 2020 and 2021 "even if some of the clearance revenue withheld by Israel is released."[53]

Without a lifting of the blockade and an end to the movement restrictions on Gaza, *nothing* will change. In fact, although foreign aid has been vital to the local economy, it can no longer mitigate Gaza's economic deterioration, as it long has. States the World Bank: "The economic deterioration in both Gaza and the West Bank can no longer be counteracted by foreign aid … nor by the private sector which remains confined by restrictions on movement, access to primary materials and trade. Moreover, the deterioration in the fiscal situation leaves the PA with limited scope to provide relief."[54] Without question, the most destabilizing factor in Gaza at present is economic and the absence of alternatives.

One powerful expression of Gaza's economic desperation was, until early 2020, the ongoing protests at Gaza's perimeter fence with Israel, known as the "Great March of Return" (GMR). The GMR, which began in March 2018 as an unarmed protest, has resulted in massive injuries and casualties. Israel's use of live ammunition against non-violent protestors has been devastating. Between March and December 2018, for example, there were over 5,300 live ammunition injuries. (According to a local source, the absence of 140 child-size wheelchairs, which were needed for some of the injured children was the strongest indication to Gazans that the international community does not care about their non-violent protests.)

Between March 30, 2018 and September 30, 2019, 35,827 Palestinians (among them 8,340 children) were injured (as were 67 Israelis), the majority by live ammunition, rubber bullets and gas inhalation. Of these, 35,318 (99 percent) were injured as part of the GMR (as were seven Israelis).[55] Thousands of the injured will suffer permanent disabilities often made worse by the lack of proper medical treatment available in Gaza. According to Desmond Travers, co-author of the *Goldstone Report*: "The killing and wounding of Palestinian children by Israeli snipers at the Great March of Return is a direct maiming of the generation which can carry on the struggle … ."[56]

This newly injured population places enormous pressure on Gaza's already fragile and overwhelmed healthcare system, which suffers from a lack of personnel, medical supplies, essential medicines, equipment, electricity and infrastructure (due to both Israeli and PA policies and to counter-terrorism legislation).[57] Of the 324 fatalities reported between March 2018 and September 2019, 210 (65 percent), including 46 children, were GMR-related. There were also six Israeli fatalities, one of whom was GMR-related.[58] Today, according to the Palestinian Census Bureau, 2.4 percent of Gaza's population or around 48,000 people (more than one-fifth of whom are children) suffer some form of disability.[59] An incapacitated person multiplies a family's economic burden by a factor of five, a burden most families in Gaza cannot support.[60] By March 2020, however, the protests had effectively stopped. The official explanation was the Covid crisis; in reality, people stopped turning out in significant numbers.

Since the 2014 war on Gaza, the social fabric has been weakening. Drug use, trauma, prostitution, domestic violence, divorce and suicide (including among children as young as 14 years[61]) are growing and, arguably, are no longer considered exceptional. In fact, suicide and attempted suicide are growing problems among men and women and increasingly, a focus of social concern. In early July 2020, for example, two young university graduates unable to find work and a street vendor took their own lives, as did a woman who tried to hang herself but failed.[62] The number of marriages has also declined due to the simple fact that many people can no longer afford to get married. While all of these phenomena can be tied to the economic situation and financial crisis, the most alarming factor is that even with the infusion of more money into the economy, these problems will not easily disappear.[63]

For the majority of Palestinians in Gaza, it is now a question of basic survival. Gaza's extreme economic conditions have produced some other unprecedented social changes, which I have raised in this book.[64] Here I want to briefly revisit three.

Social Protest

Social protest is now a feature of the international landscape. People in Iraq, Lebanon, Algeria, Sudan, Hong Kong, Thailand, Chile, Colombia and Spain, among others, have taken to the streets to demand basic human rights and greater equity. Gazans have done and are doing the same.

In 2019, Palestinians in Gaza were protesting—across all five governorates—against rising inflation rates and cost of living, and ever-worsening conditions in Gaza. The protests were organic and apolitical and not directed against Hamas specifically. They were not aligned with any political faction. Their slogan was *"Bidna na'aish"* ("We want to live"). Depending on the source, between 3,500 and 7,000 people participated in these protests. People were protesting several (largely economic) measures, including: Gaza's acute living conditions, Hamas's tax hikes on consumer goods which were seen as excessive, the PA's economic sanctions particularly as they concerned salary cuts, intra-Palestinian political division, and the blockade.

In March 2019, at the one-year anniversary of the Great March, Hamas responded brutally to hundreds of demonstrators who were "subjected to beatings, arbitrary arrest and detention, torture and ill treatment," in clear violation of Palestinians' rights to freedom of expression and association.[65] Two months later in May 2019, Hamas police also responded harshly, arresting large numbers of people, beating them in the streets—including reported injuries to women and children—and shooting in the air. Those being arrested were mostly men and young people under 25 years. One of the young men who took his own life in early July 2020, Sleiman Alajoury, was a key organizer of the 2019 protests and had been arrested several times by Hamas security. Also arrested were Fatah supporters, right-wing Islamists, critics of Hamas and those who are not aligned or supportive of Hamas's political position. Hamas also arrested a number of journalists and human rights and civil rights activists and was strongly condemned by other factions, the Palestinian NGO Network, which includes over a hundred organizations, Amnesty International, Human Rights Watch and others.

Hamas's party line stated that the protests were controlled by Israel and PA intelligence, who wanted to bring down Palestinian armed resistance. Initially, there were some voices within Hamas who said the protestors had legitimate complaints. Those voices had soon "gotten on message," as one contact put it, and justified Hamas's harsh response by arguing that the protestors "have the wrong address for their complaints."[66] (It should also be noted that the Palestinian Authority had responded similarly to West Bank protests with restrictions on the freedom of expression and peaceful assembly, as seen, for example, in the arrests of a number of journalists.[67])

Given the many pressures and costs imposed on all forms of protest, for many in Gaza "the message is dead, but no one can say that out loud."[68]

And yet, in July 2020, Palestinian activists tried again to organize demonstrations protesting Gaza's deteriorating economic situation, using social media platforms. They were warned by Hamas that they would be arrested and accused of collaborating with Israel. But given rising suicides, dozens of people appeared in front of the offices of the Palestinian Legislative Council in Gaza City, chanting "We want to eat. We want to live." The anger directed at the Hamas government and the Palestinian Authority has not stopped, even though the demonstrations are more sporadic and have deepened Hamas's growing anxiety.[69]

The Changing Role of Hamas and its Implications for Gaza: "Hamas is no longer a resistance organization"

Popular criticism of Hamas has long existed, particularly with regard to its uneven government function and the movement's increasing and, some have argued, monopolistic commercial and business role. Hamas's role as a resistance organization was seldom challenged but over the last few years, this has begun to change and speaks to the lack of cohesion within and between different elements of Hamas, particularly with regard to future political strategies and goals. For many people, Hamas's weakening resistance role derives from many issues: the absence of resistance rhetoric from the Hamas leadership; threats and arrests by Hamas of those who do resist militarily and politically; the silencing of dissent through arrests and imprisonment or worse; and the continued participation of Hamas in negotiations with the UN and Israel when the negotiations are clearly being conducted in bad faith.

Another key factor concerns the Great March of Return, which, as stated above, had been happening on a weekly basis for almost two years before it effectively ended. The average number of participants had decreased considerably after the first year when compared with the GMR's beginning (participation on a weekly basis was considered generous if it reached 6,000 people). However, the continuation of the GMR past its one-year anniversary in March 2019 damaged Hamas's image with the population. Negative sentiment became more open on people's public social media accounts (e.g., WhatsApp, chat groups), and even among some larger families who are known and long-standing Hamas supporters.

For example, in early September 2019, two young boys, 14 and 17 years old, were killed by live fire from Israeli troops along the fence. While there was the usual condemnation of Israel, there was also significant condemnation of Hamas by prominent figures in Gaza including, I am told, from the committee organizing the Great March itself. In the words of one individual, "Why are we still dying for this if there hasn't been any real change?" Indeed, as one analyst put it: "As the GMR has become 'too strategic,' … Hamas [is] able to heat things up and cool them off based on its own needs. When they heat things up, it's disproportionately the population who suffers [with] fatalities, but also extremely high numbers of injuries, many of whom will suffer life-long effects [and] permanent disabilities" [referred to locally as "an army of amputees"].[70] This is not worth the price of more electricity. Other reasons why Gazans no longer see Hamas as a resistance organization include:

- The usurpation by Hamas of what was originally a popular initiative and making it appear to be a tool of the movement. In so doing, said one local analyst: "Hamas killed what little collective spirit there still was for popular mobilization in Gaza," and
- The view that Hamas has become a strategic asset of Israel and a tool in maintaining its own occupation of Gaza. This derives from Hamas's security coordination with Israel and Egypt. As one local informant pointed out: "Once people see it that way any fatality becomes linked to what Hamas did or did not do. [For example], did they look away when a youth went towards the fence knowing what was likely to happen but calculating they could get something out of Israel?" Or as another individual put it more bluntly: "If there's no fuel, let's sacrifice three youths and we can have some more fuel."[71]

Another distressing incident were the two suicide bombings, that occurred in Gaza on August 27, 2019, 35 minutes apart. Two individuals belonging to the Palestinian Islamic Jihad (PIJ) carried them out, though apparently not in the organization's name. They attacked Hamas traffic policemen and two were killed, as well as the attackers, while several others were injured. While there is more that could be said on this issue, many in Gaza regard this attack not so much a sign of worsening inter-Palestinian political rivalries, but rather as a way of saying to Hamas that it is no longer able to maintain even basic security for its own personnel let alone for the larger population—that Hamas is only concerned with its own survival and controlling Gaza—and perhaps that resistance should reside in other actors such as the Islamic Jihad.[72] (Interestingly, I was told the incident led to greater cooperation between Hamas and the PIJ and to a very rare occurrence where the PIJ publicly participated in arresting some of its own members.) That said, Hamas must contend with an ongoing threat, albeit limited at least for now, from different Salafist jihadist groups operating in Gaza.

The weakening of Hamas's resistance role can be analyzed in different ways, particularly with regard to future consequences for Gaza. However, for purposes of this discussion, I would ask this question: what happens when the occupation is perceived by Palestinians as not only Israeli-imposed but also Hamas-imposed? What then happens to the meaning and role of resistance and the legitimacy it confers on Hamas specifically and within the Palestinian political context more generally? Is the duality between resistance and governance, which Hamas has long had to address, giving way to something more dangerous and pernicious; if so, what are the implications for Hamas, for its ability to stand against containment, and for Palestinians in Gaza?

The Imperative of Emigration

One answer to some of the questions posed above is emigration. While young Gazans have for years wanted to leave for a better life and greater opportunity, the situation after the summer of 2014 worsened dramatically. Prior to the outbreak of the Covid crisis, growing numbers were leaving Gaza via Egypt across the Mediterranean Sea to different destinations (there are at least four known routes that Gazans take: through Hong Kong, Ecuador, Cuba and Indonesia). According to *The Economist*, "Palestinians have not produced boat people since the war that created Israel in 1948."[73]

My last trip to Gaza was in September 2016. At that time, people were consumed with finding employment and securing some source of income. Since then, the economic and political situation in Gaza has declined markedly but what is *new* are two interrelated phenomena: the acute resignation among people to the downward economic spiral, and the deepened desire to leave Gaza through whatever means possible. As one young man put it: "I don't know whether to hope for the future or not; the only dream I have left is to leave."[74]

Emigration remains a principal concern—some would say, obsession—where many people are focusing their thought and energy. They leave hoping for better jobs, access to education and safety. Stories of hardship from those who have already made it to other countries do not dissuade those wanting to leave, as they believe "out is better than in, even if it means death."[75] It is not merely the desire to leave that is so striking but more so the growing lack of attachment to Gaza and, arguably, Palestine, that appears to be fueling it.

Exact numbers are difficult if not impossible to obtain but available sources such as the Hamas government, the UN and the Rafah crossing, indicate that anywhere from 30,000 to 50,000 people emigrated from Gaza in 2016–19. The brain drain (and capital flight) is palpable. In the fall of 2019, the Ministry of Civil Affairs reported that 200 doctors left Gaza for jobs in Qatar, Turkey and elsewhere. Those who can secure cash to leave tend to be the better educated but others who are able also leave. One source recounted how there was visibly more gold in the gold market (a sign that people cannot obtain cash in other ways) and there are many stories of how some families intended to use that cash-for-gold to emigrate. Prior to the coronavirus (see below), leaving was one of the few successful and sustainable economic activities. In fact, as early as 2014, *The Economist* stated that "people-smuggling" has become one of Gaza's few growing industries.[76]

The director of a local human rights organization put it this way: "This is a new, smarter *nakba*. It's slow, but it is very much in progress … How did Palestinians get pushed to the point where its youth are willing to pay to leave? The whole point of our struggle used to be about coming back."[77] In an ironic turn, Gazans are beginning to come back. Having lost their jobs and source of income in their destination countries due to the coronavirus, some Palestinians are returning to Gaza where they at least have a familial safety net. Yet, the return of a family member to Gaza is not only costly, for it is expensive to return to Gaza; it also and more importantly means a loss to the family of an income source in the form of remittances, which increases the burden on the family. One friend in Gaza said that she believes that

Gazans who return from working abroad are also doing so because the pressure of being the one person who must provide for the family is so great that it is easier to be in Gaza.

This raises another critical issue. Given the absence of alternatives, the family unit has become a critical source of support and protection. More people are turning to fewer family members for help and this represents a key change. It is not unusual—in fact, I am told it is now quite common—for one individual with some form of income to be the sole source of support for people in both the nuclear and extended family. One colleague said that typically one salary will support five families, which means resources including food are spread more thinly. The pressures on the family unit are immense at a time when that unit has far greater burdens and far fewer resources.

THE COVID-19 CRISIS AND ITS IMPACT ON GAZA: KEY FEATURES

As in other parts of the world, the coronavirus has become another defining feature of Gaza's socioeconomic reality. However, any assessment of the impact of the coronavirus on Gaza must first account for the dire conditions in both the economy and healthcare system—notably, the almost total lack of clean water (and decaying sewage treatment and sanitation infrastructure),[78] limited and erratic supplies of fuel and electricity, and a shortage of medicines and other needed equipment—that long pre-dated the emergence of the virus.[79] A further distinction needs to be made between the immediate medical needs of Covid-19 patients and the immediate economic effect on the population, since the two are vastly different.

Beginning in March 2020, the Covid-19 response in Gaza was managed principally by a number of actors: a Covid task force consisting of the West Bank and Gaza governments (and coordination between their Ministries of Health), the Ministries of the Interior and Health in Gaza, the United Nations Office for the Coordination of Humanitarian Affairs (UNOCHA), the World Health Organization (WHO), the United Nations Children's Fund (UNICEF), UNRWA and other UN organizations. By the end of May, approximately 1,490 people had been quarantined in Gaza for three weeks in different locations (including some inside their homes and schools): a field hospital in Rafah (originally built for GMR injuries); special facilities built specifically for Covid patients in the southern and northern parts of the Strip, and beach hotels and resorts reserved for Hamas officials, members and supporters in the Gaza City area.[80] By early June, only 3,000 tests had been administered and processed locally. Although Israeli military laboratories had started to test patient samples of Covid-19 from Gaza, they stopped doing so on April 22, 2020, citing a political decision. Only 100 samples had been tested in Israel.[81] Another source indicated that patient samples are still being sent to Israel for testing. (By November 2020, between 2,000 and 3,000 tests per day were being administered, vastly insufficient to need.[82])

By May 28, 2020, there were 61 known infections (an increase from 30 six days before) with 18 fully recovered and one fatality.[83] One month later, there were 72 known cases of people who tested positive for Covid and by mid-August, the number had increased to 83 (out of 2,243 quarantined).[84] Those infected had entered Gaza from Egypt at Rafah and the border crossing was subsequently closed.

Until late August, the number of infected people had remained extremely low, due to measures taken by the Hamas authorities.[85] According to local and international sources, the most important of these measures included: coordination with UN agencies directly through local service providers such as hospitals; working through UN agencies to obtain needed medical supplies from other (Arab) countries; tight control over the two entry points into Gaza at Erez in the north and Rafah in the south, and arranging, indirectly, for doctors from Gaza to receive training in Israeli hospitals.[86] Furthermore, at the request of, and in coordination with the UN and other international organizations, Israel had reportedly been less obstructive with regard to the entry into Gaza of specific and critically needed medical supplies.

On August 24, however, the Gaza authorities announced that four people from the same family had tested positive outside quarantine facilities, raising the fear of community spread. By September 10, that fear had been realized when the Ministry of Health revealed 1,551 cumulative confirmed cases in Gaza, with the majority in the Gaza City area and North Gaza. By September 14, that number reached 1,927,[87] and by October 12 increased to 4,102 and 26 deaths. Just over two weeks later on October 30, the number of people who had contracted the virus rose by 55 percent to 6,347 and 33 had died.[88] By mid-November, over 14,000 people (cumulatively) had been infected and 65 had died.[89] By December 15, 2020, there were 29,211 cumulative confirmed cases and 210 deaths.[90]

Although the situation has worsened with the now-exponential rise in the number of infected people, the hospitalization and fatality rates have remained relatively low (at least through the fall of 2020) because Gaza's population is overwhelmingly young.[91] It is unclear whether this trend will continue[92] given the dearth of resources (drugs, blood, testing kits, masks, gowns, ventilators) in Gaza, making the Strip ill-equipped to deal with community spread and rising positivity rates (reported internal fighting between Gaza's Ministry of Health and Ministry of Interior has added to the problem). Gaza only has 100 ventilators and as of November 2020, 79 were being used.[93] In fact, by mid-December 2020, Covid-19 testing stopped temporarily due to a lack of testing materials at a time when cases were surging; however, the WHO was able to address the shortage in testing kits. (It is also safe to assume that the number of infections is underreported.) In addition, "Gaza has less than a one-month supply of nearly half of all essential medicines. It also has critical shortages of medical disposables."[94]

The economic impact of the Covid-19 crisis has been disproportionately damaging. Local authorities have closed schools, restaurants, wedding halls, businesses (formal and informal), mosques[95] and many public venues such as beaches and parks, bringing public life to a standstill. As the community spread increased, Gaza has been under varying degrees of lockdown, deepening its isolation. On December 3, 2020, for example, the Ministry of Interior and National Security issued a series of preventive measures including the imposition of a complete lockdown on Friday and Saturday of each week, and the closure of all mosques, schools, universities and kindergartens (except high schools and nurseries).[96]

The construction sector, a primary driver of the economy, came to a complete halt. As a result, thousands of people lost their source of income in the spring of 2020. According to the United Nations, industrial activity in Gaza declined dramatically with approximately 35 percent of companies closing, representing a loss of 13,000 jobs. In addition, more than 10,000 workers temporarily lost their source of income in the restaurant and tourism sector, and an estimated 50 percent of people employed in Gaza's IT sector are no longer working. To these, one must add up to 5,000 Gazans working in Israel's construction and agricultural sectors who were let go.[97] (Approximately 500–600 Gazans remain working in Israel.) According to another source, over 7,000 taxi drivers (who brought students and teachers to school), 5,000–6,000 service and food industry workers, 4,000–7,000 construction workers and 3,000 kindergarten teachers all lost their jobs.[98] The Palestinian Central Bureau of Statistics reports that 42,900 people lost their source of income between March and June 2020.[99]

A report issued by Islamic Relief Worldwide in November 2020 describes the alarming economic impact of Covid-19 resulting from the ongoing blockade and lockdown: tens of thousands have lost their jobs including 80 percent of small-scale agricultural laborers; monthly incomes of workers have dropped by nearly 90 percent from $244 to $29; almost 60 percent of the population can no longer afford basic necessities including food, medicine and other essential supplies, and 82 percent suffer from mental health issues due to their inability to support their families.[100] According to the Gaza Workers Union, the combined impact of the blockade and Covid crisis has put overall unemployment in Gaza above 70 percent.[101]

On April 7, 2020, Gaza's Ministry of Labor opened registration for those directly affected by the crisis: 130,000 people registered for assistance in three days but only 38,000 were deemed eligible. Of those, only 10,000 people—teachers in private schools, workers in the transportation, hotel and restaurant sectors—received just $100 (from Qatari funds). The remaining 28,000 eligible people received nothing because funds were depleted and the Qatari government, which was paying for the coronavirus response, reportedly did not want to pay any more.[102]

The economic and societal impact of the coronavirus on Gaza has been devastating. It is important to keep in mind that when the virus has passed (or has been brought under control), Gaza's economy and healthcare system will be weaker than they were before the onset of Covid-19. Therefore, containing the virus should not be equated with a mitigation, let alone resolution, of Gaza's long-standing economic and healthcare exigencies. The only way to address those exigencies sustainably is by ending the blockade and the occupation.[103]

WHAT COMES NEXT: POPULAR PERCEPTIONS
AND A NOTE ON THE BIDEN ADMINISTRATION

Within Gaza and the West Bank, there is a strong, pervasive feeling that the national project has ended. In its place are factional politics and the absence of a unifying project at the national and local levels. As one friend in Gaza told me: "People have lost hope and our demands have declined. Our past demands have become meaningless. No one speaks of Jerusalem or the right-of-return. We just want food security and open crossings."[104] Hence, what comes next is painfully unclear, creating a deep sense of uncertainty, instability and fear. The Covid-19 pandemic has merely deepened the sense of insecurity, as have a series of retaliatory Israeli airstrikes on Gaza during the summer and fall of 2020.[105] Gaza's rising suicide rate, particularly over the summer of 2020, attests to the vulnerability and hopelessness especially among youth.[106]

For Palestinians, there is very little trust in, if not outright disdain for, both authorities including the Palestinian Authority and President Abbas. Few believe in the possibility of political reconciliation. Instead, people see disunity and the absence of any meaningful strategy that would propel them forward (rather, there are multiple strategies that contradict each other). No organ is seen to possess any political responsibility or accountability. This includes the judiciary and the Palestinian Legislative Council, which are considered either moribund or co-opted, and an *active* PLO, which, one analyst observed, is now outside the living memory of over half the Palestinian population. No faith is placed in the international community's willingness or ability to address Palestinians' most urgent issues. The resulting political and economic vacuum is "unprecedented in the last 60 years."[107] The feeling of exclusion and abandonment in Gaza is real and intensifying.

The two-state solution is laughable, particularly among young Palestinians. Instead, they call for a "life of dignity" and all relevant political parties, not just Israel, are being held to account for their failures in this regard. As one informant stated, "The international community has to shift away from 'there is no Plan B' when no one—not even them—thinks Plan A is practically doable."[108]

Yet the Biden administration believes that Plan A is in fact doable, albeit rhetorically; indeed, for them, the two-state solution is the only acceptable (and maximum) negotiating position, which doesn't bode well for Gaza, for Palestinians, or for a workable resolution to the conflict. Although Biden does not agree with the settlements or even with the occupation, he (and Kamala Harris) remains an unwavering supporter of Israel and Israel's "right to defend itself," including during the 2014 war on Gaza.[109] As I argued in Chapter 8, there was a time decades ago when people believed peace and occupation were incompatible and that ending the occupation was an essential prerequisite to peace. This is no longer true, as seen in the fact that Biden specifically removed the word "occupation" from the Democratic National Committee platform.

It is likely that the Biden administration will reassume the largely symbolic position of opposing settlement expansion (but doing little if anything to stop it) and reestablishing working relations with the PA/PLO leadership if for no other reason than to distinguish its approach from the decidedly one-sided approach of the Trump administration. However, the objective of a renewed relationship with the Palestinian leadership will be less about advancing a meaningful political process and more about facilitating the distribution of humanitarian assistance, ease general hardship and strengthen security coordination with Israel. Funding for USAID projects in specific sectors will likely return. Similarly, funding for the PA security force is expected to continue and may increase. Funding for UNRWA—if it does restart, which is not at all certain—is unlikely to be at pre-Trump levels.[110]

Insofar as Gaza is concerned, a European Middle East analyst predicted the following with regard to the Biden administration:

> The Biden Administration can and likely will bring assistance back … but they will need to figure out how. There are two initial constraints—the Taylor Force Act and the ATCA—will dampen the answer, as will the likely set of characters' perspectives on Gaza (and Hamas). There are already concerns that they are susceptible to accusations about being too "pro-Palestinian," so anything to do with Gaza that is not purely humanitarian (e.g., emergency health, shelter, WASH [water, sanitation and hygiene]) will be an incredibly heavy lift. As for contact with Hamas … [t]here will likely not be multiple channels to unofficial representatives or conflict parties. They will still be interested in information about factions' positions,

interests, and alliances, though will be more likely to collect that through "traditional" diplomatic channels.

Now, poised to regain some relevance and standing with the US, the PA sees no urgency for reconciliation with Hamas. The view is that Hamas is a movement whose pro-resistance rhetoric will soon look irrelevant, if not embarrassing, when and if Biden revives the façade of the peace process. Though the actual likelihood of a serious push for a MEPP [Middle East peace process] is next-to-zero, Ramallah has yet to be convinced of that. Peace process or no, as one contact put it, "why would [Abbas] now feel the need to fast-track Hamas's ability to undermine his party's rule in the West Bank?" There is no benefit for [Abbas] in going for elections, much less reconciliation; in short, there is more to be gained from an improved relationship with the US than there is to be gained from Hamas.[111]

A CONCLUDING THOUGHT

In 1946, Chaim Weizmann, the first president of Israel, argued for the economic viability of the Zionist project, stating:

> The economic absorptive capacity of a country is what its population makes it. Natural conditions, area, fertility, climate, will exercise their influence ... but by themselves they can give no indication of the number of inhabitants which the country can ultimately sustain. Ultimate results will depend on whether a people is educated and intelligent ... whether its social system does or does not encourage the widest expansion of economic effort; whether intelligent use is made of natural resources; and finally—and in very high degree— on whether the government exerts itself to increase the country's absorptive capacity or is indifferent to it.[112]

I would argue that it is these very factors—an educated populace, a healthy and empowered social system capable of supporting economic and societal development, access to and productive use of natural resources, and indigenous control over Palestine's absorptive capacity—that Israel has attempted to undermine and preclude over more than a half-century of occupation. Nowhere is this more visible than in Gaza.

The pressures on the population must be removed. People need clean water, a reliable energy supply, housing, improved health and education services, medicines, pharmaceuticals, etc. Job creation is crucial but it must be tied to an end to Israel's long-term closure and blockade, which lies at the core of Gaza's economic misery. Without the unencumbered movement of people and goods, Gaza will be condemned to continued ruination. The UN states it thus: "The question … is not whether Gaza is livable, but how much longer can it exist on the life support that the UN and international partners are providing."[113] Is Gaza now in a state of post-collapse?

Israel claims it must maintain the blockade against an enemy that threatens it. This claim should not remain unchallenged as it long has. It should be critically examined and clarified legally. This matter cannot be left ambiguous for political expedience but must come under rigorous scrutiny by the international community, especially the European Union. Dispossession is not a past event, but a continuous and unceasing one. Yet, although the international community has long provided needed humanitarian assistance and some measure of protection to Palestinians, the humanitarian response is a double-edged sword; by helping Palestinians survive, it also creates dependency and facilitates and empowers Israeli violations, absolving Israel, in effect, of any responsibility and accountability for its actions. However, this lack of accountability also applies to the international community.

According to Michael Lynk, the UN Special Rapporteur:

The … Israeli occupation of the Palestinian territory—Gaza and the West Bank, including East Jerusalem—is a bitter illustration of the absence of international accountability in the face of the systemic violations of Palestinian rights under human rights and humanitarian law … Israel, a relatively small country in terms of geography and population and with a particular dependence on the international community for both trade and investment and diplomatic cooperation, could not have sustained such a prolonged and repressive occupation in clear violation of international law without the active support and malign neglect of many in the industrialized world. While the international community has issued numerous resolutions and declarations critical of the unending occupation by Israel and its steady designs for annexation, such criticisms have rarely been matched with any meaningful consequences ... It is therefore necessary to ask whether it is simply to be accepted that, with this occupation, international law is closer to power than it is to justice.[114]

Hence, in the absence of meaningful political and *economic* action by the international community designed to stop Israeli violations, little will change.

Israel's struggle against the Palestinian people is fundamentally about their presence and their representation to the world. It is about diminishing if not removing their certainty by depriving them of agency and capacity and condemning them for their own privation. Palestinians have resisted. Yet, their resistance is not enough. Palestinians, like all people in the Middle East, must be seen and understood far beyond the negative and motionless characterizations imposed upon them. They must be seen as a civil society with aspirations no different from ours. They must be seen as *the* solution to the problems of their region, far more effective than authoritarian rulers or military interventions.

Palestinians want to live their lives in peace, work, take care of their children, move freely and create. If Israel continues to deny these basic human rights and if the West continues to support Israel in that denial, there will be no resolution to the conflict and no possibility of regional peace, no matter how many agreements Israel signs with Arab states. As my late friend and activist, Mary Khass, told me long ago, "There is no freedom if you are an occupier."

Epilogue: On the Falseness of Distinctions—"We are no different than you"*

I know that my father was not a mule and not a thing.

James Baldwin
Address
University of California, Berkeley
January 15, 1979

For myself, I cannot live without my art. But I have never placed it above everything. If, on the other hand, I need it, it is because it cannot be separated from my fellow men, and it allows me to live, such as I am, on one level with them. It is a means of stirring the greatest number of people by offering them a privileged picture of common joys and sufferings. It obliges the artist not to keep himself apart; it subjects him to the most humble and the most universal truth. And often he who has chosen the fate of the artist because he felt himself to be different soon realizes that he can maintain neither his art nor his difference unless he admits that he is like the others.

Albert Camus
Nobel Prize Acceptance Speech
December 10, 1957

In another distressing email to me, Sami recounted the following: "I am barely sleeping from utter worry and fear, a new kind I haven't had [since] 2008/09. Stories of civilian targeting on the streets and at home are [terrifying]. Unbelievable. So often, I spend my time running from one place to the other around the house fearing what may come. I started mistaking the sound of boiling water on the

---

* Originally published in the "Prologue," *Hamas and Civil Society in Gaza: Engaging the Islamist Social Sector* (Princeton, NJ: Princeton University Press, 2011, 2014), pp. xv–xvii. Printed in full here.

stove as though it is something descending from the sky ... You don't know when it will start, where, for what reason or how long it will [last]. Sheer paranoia."

As I pictured Sami running from one room to another trying desperately to find a place of safety, a family story from the Holocaust immediately forced its way into my memory, a story I try hard not to recall because of the pain it always inflicts. The Nazis came to the *shtetl* where my grandparents lived. All of their nine children—my mother, aunts and uncles—were adults and no longer lived at home except for my aunt Frania (who told me this story) and my aunt Sophie who was only 12 years old. Before emptying the town of its Jewish inhabitants, the Nazis decided to take their children first. On the day they came for Sophie, my grandfather and grandmother frantically ran through the rooms of their home searching for a place—a closet, a chest, a cupboard—to hide Sophie from the destruction that ultimately claimed her. My grandparents succeeded at first but eventually she was taken—as they were—and never seen again.

How can I not think of those innocents murdered in Gaza last summer [2014]—among them over 500 children—alongside my grandfather, grandmother and Sophie?

Sara Roy
"No se puede mirar—One cannot look: A Brief Reflection"
in *Gaza as Metaphor*

It is never easy to end a book because there is always so much more to say, especially after 35 years of academic and personal engagement with Palestinians and Israelis. Nearly four decades after my first visit to Gaza in 1985, it is still necessary to argue for the humanity of Palestinians, even after everything they have endured and we know to be true. The conceptual diminishing of Palestinians from a people with rights and claims to a people living in a state of exception speaks to a reality where evidence, no matter how accurate or compelling, is never enough.

Gaza is not only treated as an exception but is also made irrelevant and inconsequential, where human life is wholly vulnerable without, in effect, any legal or juridical status, recourse, or appeal, while Israel remains distanced from the violence it inflicts. In this state of exception, Gazans are stripped of culture and accomplishment, existing not as human beings but as abstractions voided of "substance and specificity,"[1] without names and with needs that are only biological, unable to resist the "deaths [they] are expected to live."[2] They cease to inhabit space that has any meaning or promise, where they "cannot be seen and can be seen through."[3]

Yet, this must not be the last word for, as this book has also shown, there are many examples of purpose and ingenuity and active, constructive and creative resistance among the people of Gaza.[4] There is also vibrancy and imagination in Gaza, as there always has been, a continuation of the once-important position Gaza held in Palestine's cultural and intellectual past.

I want to end with a description of an encounter that had a profound impact on me and one that I have never forgotten. This story is excerpted from my book examining the work of the Islamist social sector and speaks to what is perhaps the most vilified and misunderstood part of the Palestinian community: religious Muslims and Islamists (not always the same). With this story and its concluding message, I close this book.

*   *   *

On a warm, sunny day in the spring of 1999, I was touring an Islamic kindergarten in the Gaza Strip with my friend Ramadan, who would sometimes translate for me. After viewing a class in session, we were escorted into the school courtyard, a large, clean space that was serenely, yet surprisingly, silent. As we stood in this empty expanse, a bell rang. Within seconds, scores of children poured into the vast silence, filling it with laughter and play, their joy utterly infectious. The teachers, all women, also laughed at the children's apparent insuppressible excitement.

Our guide, the school director, invited us back inside to continue the conversation. He led us into a room where three men and a woman were sitting at a long rectangular table. "This is our board of directors, and they would like to speak with you." I was surprised and delighted, because I did not expect to have such easy access. With Ramadan translating, I began by thanking them for this unexpected opportunity. The exchange that followed proved to be a critically important experience in my research on Hamas and the Islamic movement.

The conversation turned to the school's operations, curriculum and pedagogy, teachers and their backgrounds, and from there branched out to the local community, the demographic composition of the student body, and family life in Gaza. As we talked, a young woman knocked at the door. She was a student's mother searching for someone, and she abashedly apologized for intruding. Instead of sending her away, one board member, Dr. Ahmad, invited her to enter and join the discussion.

Pointing to me, Dr. Ahmad addressed the young mother and said, "This is *Doctora* Sara from America. She is here to learn about our school and what we teach our children. Would you be willing to answer some of her questions?" In an instant, this young, soft-spoken wisp of a girl transformed into a self-possessed powerhouse of a woman, and it stunned me.

Although she was speaking before the board, she did not seem at all intimidated. She described the school's many strengths. I then asked her to address its weaknesses. Unhesitatingly, she took my question as an opportunity to voice her concern: "I would like more help with taking care of my children after school; I mean programs after school that would keep them busy in more creative ways, and [provide] more ways for me as a parent to be involved with the school." Concerned that I might have somehow compromised her by my question, I looked at the board members to gauge their reaction. All but one were smiling. They thanked her, and she then excused herself and left with a certain confidence she had not visibly possessed when she entered.

"In America, people think that Palestinians are terrorists and that we are backward, that we prefer the gun to the computer," said Dr. Ahmad. "We as a people have always valued education, like the Jews, and like your people, *Doctora* Sara. You are a Christian?" The question was asked more as a formality that aimed to restate the obvious than as an inquiry. Suddenly, the conundrum I had assiduously and, for the most part, successfully avoided in my research with the Islamic community confronted me without escape: Do I admit I am Jewish and possibly risk my ability to work with that community—or do I lie?

Understandably, most Palestinians assume that the (non-Israeli) foreigners among them are Christian, for what Jew would want to befriend Palestinians or live in Gaza, let alone learn about the Islamic movement? Before the first Palestinian uprising in 1987, one of the first questions I was inevitably asked in Gaza was, are you a Christian? I always told the truth. When people learned I was Jewish, there was concern, curiosity and some suspicion, but rarely, if ever, hostility. Once I explained why I was in Gaza—to learn about Palestinians and their lives—and gained their trust, which surprisingly did not take very long, my being Jewish became invaluable. In fact, it opened many doors that usually remained shut to outsiders. However, as the occupation grew increasingly repressive, beginning with the first Intifada … the question of my religious and ethnic background was *never* again raised, not once. The answer was simply too inconceivable.

Turning to Dr. Ahmad who had so gently asked the question, I answered, "I am not Christian, I am Jewish." The room instantly fell silent. The board members were clearly surprised, even shocked. Ramadan (who himself was not an Islamist but a member of the main nationalist secular movement, Fatah) turned to me and asked incredulously, "You are *Jewish*?!" Tension rose and the air in the room became thick and stagnant.

I had imagined this moment many times—how I might respond, how others might respond to me, and what I would do if the situation became difficult or hostile. What followed, however, was altogether unexpected. I began:

I understand why you are surprised. But you should know that within the Jewish community there are many people who oppose Israel's occupation and who support the right of Palestinians to live in their own state as free people. Many Jews in Israel, in America, and elsewhere speak out against Israeli policies in Gaza and the West Bank. Jews are not all the same, just as Palestinians and Muslims are not all the same. I am here doing this work not only as a scholar and researcher but as a Jew, as an American, and as a human being. I want to learn more than I have been taught and I am hoping you will help me. That is why I am here.

After a moment, Dr. Ahmad quietly asked, "What are you hoping to learn and leave here with?"

"Knowledge. And perhaps a deeper understanding of your community, your lives and what you are trying to achieve."
"And how will you use what you have learned here?"
"I shall use it to educate others, or at least try."
"Americans think all Palestinians are terrorists, especially those of us who are religious Muslims. We are not human beings to them, just people who kill Jews. Do you really think you can change that?"
"At a larger level, no, I cannot change that, but at an individual or community level, perhaps I can. What I have always tried to do through my work is give others a different way of understanding this conflict, to challenge the ways of thinking that have been created for us."

I could feel the tension abating and myself relaxing. The one woman on the board, Um Mohammad, then asked me, *"Doctora* Sara, do you have children?"

"Yes, I have one child, a little girl. Her name is Annie."
"When you look at your child, what do you feel?" I looked at Um Mohammad and hesitated.
"I feel indescribable love and joy," I answered.
"Can you imagine that it is different for a Palestinian mother?"
"No, Um Mohammad, I cannot."
"This is what you must teach others. That we are no different than you."

Silence for Gaza
(excerpts)
Mahmoud Darwish

Gaza is not the most beautiful city.

Its shore is not bluer than the shores of Arab cities.

Its oranges are not the most beautiful in the Mediterranean basin.

Gaza is not the richest city.

It is not the most elegant or the biggest, but it equals the history of an entire homeland, because it is more ugly, impoverished, miserable, and vicious in the eyes of enemies. Because it is the most capable, among us, of disturbing the enemy's mood and his comfort. Because it is his nightmare. Because it is oranges hollowed into booby traps, children without a childhood, old men without old age and women without desires. Because of all this it is the most beautiful, the purest and richest among us and the one most worthy of love.

What is beautiful about Gaza is that our voices do not reach it. Nothing distracts it; nothing takes its fist away from the enemy's face. Not the forms of the Palestinian state we will establish whether on the eastern side of the moon, or the western side of Mars when it is explored. Gaza is devoted to rejection ... hunger and rejection, thirst and rejection, displacement and rejection, torture and rejection, siege and rejection, death and rejection.

Enemies might triumph over Gaza (the storming sea might triumph over an island ... they might chop down all its trees).

They might break its bones.

They might implant tanks on the insides of its children and women. They might throw it into the sea, sand, or blood.

But it will not repeat lies and say "Yes" to invaders.

It will continue to explode.

It is neither death, nor suicide. It is Gaza's way of declaring that it deserves to live. It will continue to explode.

It is neither death, nor suicide. It is Gaza's way of declaring that it deserves to live.

Notes

INTRODUCTION: "I CAN'T EAT MY LIGHTS"

1. A similar agreement was signed with Morocco. Also in October 2020, Israel and Sudan agreed to normalize relations.

2. In fact, according to the Israeli journalist Amira Hass, these agreements represented the "confirmation of a process that began over 25 years ago under Oslo with Israeli businessmen." Historically, this process was always kept quiet and unseen in order not to humiliate the Palestinians. This has now changed: Lecture, WCFIA-CMES, Middle East Seminar, Harvard University, November 19, 2020.

3. Noa Landau, "Israel Suspends West Bank Annexation in Deal to Normalize Relations with the UAE," *Haaretz*, August 13, 2020, online: www.haaretz.com/israel-news/with-trump-s-help-israel-and-the-uae-reach-historic-deal-to-normalize-relations-1.9070687. Also see Anshel Pfeffer, "In UAE Deal, Netanyahu Trades Imaginary Annexation for Real Life Diplomacy Win," *Haaretz*, August 14, 2020, online: www.haaretz.com/israel-news/.premium-in-uae-deal-netanyahu-trades-imaginary-annexation-for-real-life-diplomacy-win-1.9071474; Jonathan Cook, "How the Israel-UAE Deal put the Bogus Peace Industry Back in Business," *Middle East Eye*, August 15, 2020, online: www.middleeasteye.net/opinion/how-israel-uae-deal-put-bogus-peace-industry-back-business, and Henry Siegman, "Israel Will Have to Reckon with the Occupation One Way or Another," *Responsible Statecraft*, August 16, 2020, online: https://responsiblestatecraft.org/2020/08/16/israel-will-have-to-reckon-with-the-occupation/.

4. GISHA—Legal Center for Freedom of Movement, "Israel Reverses Punitive Restrictions Imposed in Recent Weeks, Including its Ban on Entry of Fuel into Gaza but Leaves the 'Regular' Closure in Place," September 1, 2020, online: https://gisha.org/updates/11509, and Amir Rotem, "Israel's Disproportionate and Cynical 'Coronavirus Lockdown' on Gaza," *Haaretz*, August 18, 2020, online: www.haaretz.com/opinion/.premium-israel-s-sweeping-disproportionate-and-cynical-coronavirus-lockdown-on-gaza-1.9080095.

5. See "James Baldwin vs William F. Buckley: A Legendary Debate from 1965," online: www.youtube.com/watch?v=5Tek9h3a5wQ.

6. In the interest of full disclosure, I sit on the Board of Directors of the Gaza Mental Health Foundation, which was founded to support the provision of mental health services to the Gaza Strip. As such,

the Foundation is a strong supporter of the Gaza Community Mental Health Programme, largely through fundraising and educational awareness.

7. Edward Said, "The Public Role of Writers and Intellectuals," in Sandra Berman and Michael Wood (eds.), *Nation, Language and the Ethics of Translation* (Princeton, NJ: Princeton University Press, 2005), p. 28. Also see Edward Said, *Humanism and Democratic Criticism* (New York: Columbia University Press, 2004).

8. I borrow this phrase from Toni Morrison, *Playing in the Dark: Whiteness and the Literary Imagination* (New York: Vintage Books, 1992), p. xii.

2   US FOREIGN POLICY AND THE ISRAELI–PALESTINIAN CONFLICT: A VIEW FROM PALESTINE

1. This article is excerpted in part from the new conclusion to the third edition of my book, *The Gaza Strip: The Political Economy of De-development* (Washington, DC: Institute for Palestine Studies, 2016).

2. Dr. Husam Zomlot, "A Paradigm Shift: The Arab-Israeli Conflict and Regional Transformation," Lecture, Center for Middle Eastern Studies, Harvard University, March 23, 2011, Cambridge, MA.

3. Ibid.

4. Ethan Bronner and Isabel Kershner, "Fatah and Hamas Announce Outline of Deal," *New York Times*, April 27, 2011.

5. Joel Beinin, *Fatah-Hamas Reconciliation and Palestinian-Israeli Peace*, May 11, 2011, http://jewishvoiceforpeace.org.

6. Yousef Munayyer, "Will a Palestinian Autumn Follow an Arab Spring?" *Palestine Center Brief* No. 211, Washington, DC, April 22, 2011.

7. Mushtaq H. Khan, "Learning the Lessons of Oslo: State Building and Freedoms in Palestine," Paper presented at a closed meeting, Jerusalem, December 2010, and Zomlot, "A Paradigm Shift." With regard to the last point about engaging Israelis—an approach with a long history but one that seems to have renewed emphasis—growing numbers of Palestinians are aiming, through more directed, structured and coordinated action, to identify and work directly with those groups in Israel—across all sectors—who support the Palestinian struggle. As one official put it, "We will fight only with those Israelis [who want] to end the structures that hurt both peoples."

8. Karl Vick, "Palestinian Border Protests: The Arab Spring Model for Confronting Israel," *Time Magazine*, May 16, 2011. See also "Here comes your non-violent resistance," *The Economist*, May 17, 2011, and Rami G. Khouri, "A New Palestinian Strategy Unfolds," *Agence Global*, June 29, 2011. Even the Palestinian Authority in Ramallah, which

never officially embraced non-violent resistance as a policy (nor has the Hamas-led Authority in Gaza), has now adopted non-violence as part of its state-building efforts, arguing that the promotion of internal Palestinian security and calm is linked to security for Israelis, which serves the Palestinian national cause.

9. Munayyer, "Will a Palestinian Autumn Follow an Arab Spring?"

10. Khan, "Learning the Lessons of Oslo."

11. Mahmoud Abbas, "The Long Overdue Palestinian State," *New York Times*, May 16, 2011. There is some confusion over the actual request to be made to the UN, what is in fact possible and the appropriate legal strategy. See for example, Camille Mansour, "Palestinian Options at the United Nations," Institute for Palestine Studies, http://palestine-studies.org/columndetails.aspx?t=2&id=34; Akiva Eldar, "The Battle for September," *Haaretz*, June 5, 2011; Lamis Andoni, "Palestinian Statehood and Bypassing Israel," *AlJazeera.net*, June 16, 2011, and Rema Rahman, "Palestinian Leaders Weigh U.N. Options," *United Press International*, July 13, 2011.

12. Ahmad Khalidi, "A West Bank Anachronism," *The Guardian*, April 19, 2011.

13. Abbas, "The Long Overdue Palestinian State."

14. Michael Sfard, "The Legal Tsunami is on its way," *Haaretz*, April 29, 2011.

15. See, for example, Ron Kampeas, "Jewish Groups Debate Ways to Thwart U.N. Recognition of 'Palestine,'" *Jewish Telegraphic Agency*, April 15, 2011.

16. Barak Ravid, "Netanyahu Mulling West Bank Pullout to Stave Off 'Diplomatic Tsunami,'" *Haaretz*, April 12, 2011.

17. Ami Isseroff, "Unilateral Palestinian State Declaration—More Important than Settlement Freeze," September 14, 2009, www.zionism-israel.com/log/archives/00000713.html.

18. Bronner and Kershner, "Fatah and Hamas Announce Outline of Deal."

19. Ravid, "Netanyahu Mulling West Bank Pullout."

20. For example, see Ali Abunimah, "Recognising Palestine?" *Al Jazeera*, April 13, 2011, www.aljazeera.com/opinions/2011/4/13/recognising-palestine, and Dr. Salman Abu Sitta, "The PLO is to 'Liberate' not to Legalise Partition," http://australiansforpalestine.com, July 2011.

21. Abunimah, "Recognising Palestine?"

22. Aaron David Miller, "The Palestinians' Mistake in Seeking Statehood from the U.N.," *Washington Post*, April 14, 2011, www.washingtonpost.com/opinions/the-palestinians-mistake-in-seeking-statehood-from-the-un/2011/04/12/AFlW08eD_story.html.

23. Abunimah, "Recognising Palestine?"

24. Beinin, *Fatah-Hamas Reconciliation and Palestinian-Israeli Peace.*

25. More specifically, this includes a technocratic government representing all factions, security arrangements, reconstitution and revitalization

of the PLO to allow Hamas membership, a tribunal for general elections, and a date for elections within a year of the signing of the final agreement.

26. See Palestinian National Authority, *National Development Plan 2011–13: Establishing the State, Building our Future*, April 2011; Office of the UN Special Coordinator for the Middle East Peace Process, *Palestinian State-Building: A Decisive Period*, Brussels, April 13, 2011; The World Bank, *Towards a Palestinian State: Reforms for Fiscal Strengthening*, Washington, DC, April 13, 2010; *idem, The Underpinnings of the Future Palestinian State: Sustainable Growth and Institutions*, Washington, DC, September 21, 2010; International Monetary Fund, *Macroeconomic and Fiscal Framework for the West Bank and Gaza: Seventh Review of Progress*, Staff Report for the Meeting of the Ad Hoc Liaison Committee, Brussels, April 13, 2011, and Reuters, "Palestinians Ready for Statehood Now, says Fayyad," *Haaretz* , April 11, 2011.

27. Analyst, Gaza, email communication, April 28, 2011.

28. Political official, Ramallah, telephone communication, May 18, 2011.

29. Analyst, Gaza, email communication, May 17, 2011.

30. Political official, Ramallah, telephone communication, May 18, 2011.

31. Analyst, Gaza, email communication, May 1, 2011.

32. Ibid., May 17, 2011.

33. Analyst, Gaza, email communication, May 11, 2011.

34. Zomlot, "A Paradigm Shift."

35. Ibid.

36. Jamil Hilal, "Palestinian Answers in the Arab Spring," *Al Shabaka Policy Brief,* May 2011. See also Jeff Halper, *The Palestinian Authority's Historic Mistake—and Opportunity*, June 24, 2011, http://icahdusa.org/2011/06/the-palestinian-authority's-historic-mistake-and-opportunity, and Khalidi, "A West Bank Anachronism."

37. Noura Erakat, "Palestinian Youth: New Movement, New Borders," *Al Jazeera*, May 4, 2011, http://english.aljazeera.net/indepth/features/201 1/05/2011531012311834961.html.

38. Nadia Hijab, "Just as well that Obama had No Details about Middle East Peace," *The Hill's Congress Blog*, May 19, 2011, http://thehill.com/blogs/congress-blog/foreignpolicy/162395.

39. Erakat, "Palestinian Youth."

40. Ibid.

41. Khalidi, "A West Bank Anachronism."

42. Rahman, "Palestinian Leaders Weigh U.N. Options."

43. Geoffrey Aronson, "Back to Square One—The Obama Administration Resets U.S. Policy," *Report on Israeli Settlement in the Occupied Territories*, Volume 20, No. 6, November–December 2010, p. 1.

44. Ibid., p. 4.

45. Ibid.

46. Ibid.

47. Interview with Professor Shibley Telhami and Robert Malley, National Public Radio, May 19(?), 2011.

48. Ibid.

49. Phyllis Bennis, *On the Eve of Obama's Middle East Speech*, Institute for Policy Studies, www.ipsdc.org/blog/on_the_eve_of_obamas_middle_east_speech.

50. Josh Ruebner, "The Two Speeches of Barack Obama," *The Hill's Congress Blog*, May 20, 2011, http://thehill.com/blogs/congress-blog/foreignpolicy/162387.

51. Ibid.

52. Not only does the US face the declaration of a Palestinian state on 1967 borders and its admission to the UN in some legal form, it must respond to the end of Fayyad's two-year development/economic/institution building plan, in which the US has made enormous financial and political investments.

53. Based on interviews with this individual, Spring 2011.

54. Interview, telephone communication, May 2011.

55. Transcript & Video: House Majority Leader Eric Cantor AIPAC Speech May 22, 2011 [Update: "Cantor Expresses Disappointment in Obama's Mideast Speech-Text"], http://ironicsurrealism.com/2011/05/22/transcript-house-majority-leader-eric-cantor-speech-at-aipac-may-22-2011, and Lamis Andoni, "Kindly Remain Seated," *AlJazeera.net*, May 27, 2011. Former US president Jimmy Carter offers a different view in Jimmy Carter, "Support the Palestinian Unity," *Washington Post*, May 3, 2011.

56. Netanyahu described his foreign policy position as follows: "The demand that Palestinians recognize Israel as the national homeland of the Jewish people; a commitment to end the conflict; a solution to the Palestinian refugee issue that did not require absorption within Israel's borders; the establishment of a Palestinian state only in accordance with a peace deal that did not infringe on Israel's security; that said Palestinian state be demilitarized; the preservation of large settlement blocs within the West Bank; and the insistence that Jerusalem remain the undivided capital of Israel." "Netanyahu: Israel Willing to 'Cede Parts of Our Homeland' for True Peace," *Haaretz*, May 16, 2011.

57. J.J. Goldberg, "Israel's Security Elite Joins the Opposition," *The Forward*, May 11, 2011 (issue of May 20, 2011), http://forward.com/articles/137697.

58. Ibid.

59. Barak Ravid, "While Netanyahu met Merkel in Berlin, Envoys Pushed in U.S. for European Peace Conference," *Haaretz*, April 12, 2011.

60. Miller, "The Palestinians' Mistake in Seeking Statehood from the U.N."

61. Analyst, Gaza, email communication, April 13, 2011.

62. Ibid, May 11, 2011.
63. Lahav Harkov, "Poll: Most Egyptians Favor Annulling Peace with Israel," *The Jerusalem Post*, April 26, 2011, and Amira Hass, "Palestinian Reconciliation May Lead to Israel's Palestinian Separation," *Haaretz*, May 2, 2011. In May 2011, thousands of Palestinian flags commemorating the Nakba were flown in Tahrir Square.
64. Internal document from a US institution involved in the reconciliation efforts that I am not at liberty to cite. The document is a draft outline of comments dated May 10, 2011. Although the Egyptians are credited with the success of the reconciliation agreement, the Egyptian Foreign Minister had asked Turkey to participate in reconciliation efforts, which apparently played an important role. Hamas had met with the Turkish Foreign Minister Davutoğlu in Damascus prior. Furthermore, President Abdullah Gul's opinion piece in the New York Times telling Israel about the necessity of peace with the Palestinians if Israel is to deal with emerging changes in the Middle East and Turkey's willingness to assist, suggests a potentially stronger role for Turkey together with Egypt in resolving the Israeli–Palestinian conflict and beyond. See Abdullah Gul, "The Revolution's Missing Peace," *New York Times*, April 20, 2011.
65. NPR Interview with Telhami and Malley (n. 47).
66. In this regard, see "Clinton's Remarks at the U.S.-Islamic World Forum," *Essential Documents*, Council on Foreign Relations, Washington, DC, April 12, 2011.

4   ENDGAME IN THE GAZA WAR?

1. Intelligence and Terrorism Information Center at the Israel Intelligence Heritage & Commemoration Center, *The Six Months of the Lull Arrangement*, December 2008, p. 2. I was told that this report was removed not long after being posted.
2. The original report from which this quote is drawn is no longer available online. See United Nations Office for the Coordination of Humanitarian Affairs (UNOCHA), *Gaza Humanitarian Situation Report, January 2, 2009 as of 14:30*, which contains some of the information in this quote.

6   GAZA AFTER THE REVOLUTION

1. Physicians for Human Rights – *Israel, "Humanitarian Minimum" – Israel's Role in Creating Food and Water Insecurity in the Gaza Strip*, December 2010, p. 10, online: https://reliefweb.int/sites/reliefweb.int/files/resources/file.pdf.

7 IT'S WORTH PUTTING HAMAS TO THE TEST

1. Shlomo Ben-Ami, "Internationalizing the Solution: Multilateralism and International Legitimacy," *Palestine-Israel Journal*, Volume 13, Number 4, 2007, online: https://pij.org/articles/969/internationalizing-the-solution-multilateralism-and-international-legitimacy.

2. David Miliband, "Remembering Gaza," *Al Jazeera*, October 17, 2011, online: www.aljazeera.com/opinions/2011/10/17/remembering-gaza.

8 BEFORE GAZA, AFTER GAZA

1. This chapter is an abbreviated version of the (revised) "Introduction" to the third edition of my book, *The Gaza Strip: The Political Economy of De-development*, which was published by the Institute for Palestine Studies in 2016.

2. Joseph Massad, "Resisting the Nakba," *Al-Ahram Weekly*, Issue 897, May 15–21, 2008, www.ahram.org.eg/2008/897/op8.htm.

3. United Nations Office for the Coordination of Humanitarian Affairs (UNOCHA), *The Humanitarian Impact on Palestinians of Israeli Settlements and Other Infrastructure in the West Bank*, July 2007. This figure has gone as high as 50+ percent but the more conservative one is used here. See, for example, The World Bank, *Movement and Access Restrictions in the West Bank: Uncertainty and Inefficiency in the Palestinian Economy*, May 9, 2007, pp. 1–2 and 5–6.

4. Amira Hass, "An Israeli Achievement," www.Bitterlemons.org, April 20, 2009.

5. Shir Hever, *The Political Economy of Israel's Occupation: Beyond Mere Exploitation* (London: Pluto Press, 2010).

6. By 2008, the Israeli shekel was one of the 15 strongest currencies in the world. See Jeff Halper, *Rethinking Israel after 60 Years*, Israel Committee Against Home Demolitions (ICAHD), 2008.

7. George Bisharat, "Changing Rules of War," *San Francisco Chronicle*, April 1, 2009, www.sfgate.com/cgi-bin/article.cgi?f=/c/a/2009/03/31/EDKP16PF6S.DTL.

8. Correspondence with John Whitbeck.

9. See Virginia Tilley, "A Beacon of Hope: Apartheid Israel," *Counterpunch*, December 5, 2006, and Bashir Abu-Manneh, "In Palestine, a Dream Deferred," *The Nation*, December 18, 2006, www.thenation.com/doc/20061218/abumanneh.

10. Saree Makdisi, "The Strangulation of Gaza," *The Nation*, February 3, 2008.

11. Karen Abu Zayd, *Palestine Refugees: Exile, Isolation and Prospects*, Edward Said Lecture, Princeton University, Princeton, NJ, May 6, 2008.

12. Presentation by Mouin Rabbani, *Symposium on Palestine and the Palestinians Today*, Center for Contemporary Arab Studies, Georgetown University, Washington, DC, April 2, 2009.

13. Neve Gordon and Erez Tzfadia, "Privatising Zionism," *Palestine Chronicle.com*, http://palestinechronicle.com/story-121807172249.htm, and Daniel Levy, "A More Private Occupation," *Haaretz*, April 11, 2008, www.haaretz.com/hasen/pages/ShArt.jhtml?itemNo=973974.

14. Presentation (via phone) by Sami Abdel Shafi, *Symposium on Gaza*, Harvard Law School, March 31, 2009. Also see Ilana Feldman, "Gaza's Humanitarianism Problem," *Journal of Palestine Studies*, Volume 38, No. 3 (Spring 2009): pp. 22–37.

15. See Atif Kubursi and Fadle Naqib, "The Palestinian Economy Under Occupation: The Economics of Subjugation and Dynamics of Dependency," Paper presented at the University of London School of Oriental and African Studies, London, January 27–28, 2007.

16. The World Bank Group, "Palestinian Economic Prospects: Gaza Recovery and West Bank Revival," *Relief Web*, June 4, 2009, www.reliefweb.int/rw/rwb.nsf/db900sid/SNAA-7SPA46?OpenDocument&rc=3D=3&emid=3DACOS-635PFR.

17. Catholic Agency for Overseas Development, Amnesty International, Christian Aid et al., *The Gaza Strip: A Humanitarian Implosion*, Jerusalem, 2008, p. 4 ftn 6. Also see Ian Black, "Sanctions Cause Gaza to Implode, Says Rights Group," *The Guardian*, March 6, 2008, www.guardian.co.uk/world/2008/mar/06/israelandthepalestinians.humanrights.

18. For example, USAID policy changes after Hamas's legislative (and municipal) election victories.

19. The Grassroots Palestinian Anti-Apartheid Wall Campaign, *The Occupation's "Convergence Plan": Legitimizing Palestinian Bantustans*, *Analysis*, May 17, 2006.

20. The World Bank, *Palestinian Economic Prospects: Aid, Access and Reform* (Washington, DC: World Bank, September 22, 2008), pp. 7, 22.

21. Ibid., p. 22.

22. Ibid.

23. The World Bank Group, "Palestinian Economic Prospects: Gaza Recovery and West Bank Revival."

24. World Bank, *Palestinian Economic Prospects: Aid, Access and Reform*, p. 22.

25. For an examination of the economic costs of the occupation on Israel, see Shlomo Swirski, *The Cost of Occupation: The Burden of the Israeli-Palestinian Conflict, 2008 Report* (Tel Aviv: Information of Equality and Social Justice in Israel, ADVA, June 2008).

26. Darryl Li, "From Prison to Zoo: Israel's 'Humanitarian' Control of Gaza," *Adalah's Newsletter*, Volume 44, January 2008. Also see: *HCJ 9132/07, Jaber al-Basyouni Ahmed v. The Prime Minister*, www.adalah.org.

27. Ibid.
28. Ibid.
29. Ibid.
30. Ibid.
31. The World Bank Group, "Palestinian Economic Prospects: Gaza Recovery and West Bank Revival."
32. Ibid.
33. Interview, Fall 2007, Washington, DC.
34. World Bank, *Palestinian Economic Prospects: Aid, Access and Reform*, p. 21, and Palestinian Central Bureau of Statistics (PCBS), *Youth in Palestinian Territory, Statistical Indicators* (On the occasion of the International Youth Day, August 12, 2008).
35. Lecture by Dr. Paul Beran, Center for Middle Eastern Studies, Harvard University, Cambridge, MA, July 18, 2008.
36. Lisa Taraki, "Enclave Micropolis: The Paradoxical Case of Ramallah/ Al Bireh," *Journal of Palestine Studies*, Volume 37, No. 4 (Summer 2008), p. 17 (see pp. 6–20).
37. In this regard see Raja Shehadah, *Palestinian Walks: Forays into a Vanishing Landscape* (New York: Scribner, 2008).
38. Amos Harel, "IDF Probe: Cannot Defend Destruction of Gaza Homes," *Haaretz*, February 15, 2009.
39. There are by now many sources documenting the damage and statistics vary. See: United Nations, *Report of the United Nations Fact Finding Mission on the Gaza Conflict*, September 25, 2009 (The Goldstone Report); Physicians for Human Rights—Israel, and Dan Magen, *"Ill Morals": Grave Violations of the Right to Health during the Israeli Assault on Gaza*, Israel, March 2009; various reports by the United Nations Office for the Coordination of Humanitarian Affairs; Oxfam International, *Situation Report*, May 10–16, 2009, Jerusalem (internal document); Defense for Children International, www.dci-pal.org/english/display.cfm?DocId=1056&CategoryID=1; Israeli Committee Against Home Demolitions, *Statistics on House Demolitions During Operation Cast Lead* (Jerusalem: ICAHD, April 2009); Palestinian National Authority—Ramallah, *The Palestinian National Early Recovery and Reconstruction Plan for Gaza 2009–2010*, International Conference in Support of the Palestinian Economy for the Reconstruction of Gaza, Sharm Al-Sheikh, March 2, 2009; Jan McGirk "Gaza's Health and Humanitarian Situation Remains Fragile," *The Lancet*, February 4, 2009; Amnesty International, *Fueling Conflict: Foreign Arms Supplies to Israel/Gaza*, London, February 23, 2009; Human Rights Watch, *Rain of Fire: Israel's Unlawful Use of White Phosphorus in Gaza*, New York, March 2009, and National Lawyers Guild, *Onslaught: Israel's Attack on Gaza and the Rule of Law*, New York, February 2009. For an excellent review of the 2008 offensive and its impact, see Norman G. Finkelstein,

This Time We Went Too Far: Truth & Consequences of the Gaza Invasion (New York: OR Books, 2010).

40. Sara Flounders, "An Underground Economy and Resistance Symbol: The Tunnels of Gaza," www.workers.org/2009/world/gaza_0212, February 8, 2009.

41. Internal documents from donor NGOs and other aid agencies make this clear. Also see UN Office for the Coordination of Humanitarian Affairs (UNOCHA), "Israel-OPT: Gaza Children "Afraid to Return to School," *IRIN*, www.irinnews.org/Report.aspx?ReportID=83088, February 23, 2009; Dion Nissenbaum, "Israeli Ban on Sending Pasta to Gaza Illustrates Frictions," *McClatchy Washington Bureau*, February 25, 2009, and Ma'an News Agency, "Israel Opens Gaza Crossings for Aid, Fuel, Grain," May 11, 2009, www.maannews.net/en/index. php?opr=3DShowDetails@ID=3D37723.

42. Amira Hass, "Israel Bans Books, Music and Clothes from Entering Gaza," *Haaretz*, May 17, 2009, www.haaretz.com/hasen/objects/pages/PrintArticleEn.jhtml?itemNo=1086045.

43. "Running Short of Concrete, Gazans Build Mud Homes: Gazans Build Mud-Brick Homes as Israel Refuses to Allow Materials into Blockaded Strip, *Associated Press*, May 7, 2009, www.cbsnews.com/stories/2009/05/07/ap/world/main4997452.shtml, and UNOCHA, "OPT: Gaza Building Project Experiments With Clay, Rubble," *Relief Web*, June 4, 2009, www.reliefweb.int/rw/rwb.nsf/db900sid/PSLG-7SPC3E?OpenDocument&rc=3&emid=ACOS-635PFR.

44. United Nations Population Fund, Programme of Assistance to the Palestinian People, *Gaza Crisis—Impact on Reproductive Health, Especially Maternal and Newborn Health and Obstetric Care*, Draft Report, Jerusalem, February 10, 2009, p. 1.

45. UNOCHA, "Israel-OPT: Gaza Children "Afraid to Return to School."

46. The World Bank Group, "Palestinian Economic Prospects: Gaza Recovery and West Bank Revival."

47. See Sara Roy, *Hamas and Civil Society in Gaza: Engaging the Islamist Social Sector* (Princeton, NJ: Princeton University Press, 2011), p. 236.

13   FLOATING IN AN INCH OF WATER: A LETTER FROM GAZA

1. Shlomi Eldar, "Will Abbas Stop Paying Gaza Employees' Salaries?" *Al-Monitor* (March 9, 2017). According to reports in February 2017, donor governments are reevaluating their contributions to these salaries and to the PA overall, with potentially ominous consequences. See Adnan Abu Amer, "What EU Shift in Financial Support Means for Gaza," *Al-Monitor* (February 20, 2017).

2. Email exchange with the author (May 31, 2017). See also Ahmad Melhem, "PA Faces Backlash after Slashing Gaza Salaries," *Al-Monitor* (April 20, 2017); Jack Khoury, "PA Workers in Gaza Take to Streets to Protest 30-percent Cut in Salaries," *Haaretz* (April 9, 2017).

3. United Nations Office for the Coordination of Humanitarian Affairs (UNOCHA OPT), "The Gaza Strip: The Humanitarian Impact of the Blockade," *ochaopt.org* (November 2016); UNOCHA OPT, "Gaza: Two Years after the 2014 Hostilities," *ochaopt.org* (August 2016).

4. Sara Roy, "Introduction to the Third Edition: De-development Completed: Making Gaza Unviable," *The Gaza Strip: The Political Economy of De-development* (Washington, DC: Institute for Palestine Studies, 2016).

5. Palestinian Central Bureau of Statistics, "Indicators—Population," *pcbs.gov.ps* (n.d.).

6. Fares Akram, "Gazans Excited over Territory's New Indoor Mall," *Associated Press* (February 22, 2017).

7. As of December 2016, Israel stated its "willingness to grant hundreds of work permits to laborers from the Gaza Strip." See Moath Al-Amoudi, "How Serious is Israel About Allowing Return of Gaza Workers?" *Al-Monitor* (December 2, 2016).

8. Noam Rabinovich, "Groundhog Day in Gaza," *Haaretz* (March 7, 2017); Ben Caspit, "Israel Has No Gaza Policy," *Al-Monitor* (March 1, 2017).

9. Ben Caspit, "Why Some in Israel are Wary of Hamas's New Gaza Boss," *Al-Monitor* (February 15, 2017).

10. According to Ben Caspit, Israeli officials share this belief: "The state comptroller's report points to many other warnings coming from Dangot and the office of the COGAT [Coordinator of Government Activities in the Territories] and Maj. Gen. Yoav Mordechai, who replaced Dangot in January 2014. Both of them said that the situation in Gaza was like a bubbling pressure cooker about to explode. The bottom line is clear: If nothing is done, it will end in an explosion" (Caspit, "Israel Has No Gaza Policy"). See also Dov Lieber, "Open Up Gaza or it Will Explode, Hamas Threatens Israel," *Times of Israel* (March 13, 2017).

11. The steady reduction in electricity in Gaza reached crisis levels in June 2017, leaving Gazans with only 3–4 hours of electricity per day. See, for example, United Nations, "Humanitarian Impact of the Gaza Electricity Crisis," *reliefweb.int* (May 2017); GISHA, "Gisha in an Urgent Letter to Minister of Defense Avigdor Lieberman: Reducing Israel's Electricity Supply to Gaza is a Red Line that Must Not Be Crossed," *gisha.org* (June 11, 2017); Edo Konrad, "Humanitarian Crisis Looms as Israel Cuts Gaza's Electricity," *+972 Mag* (June 19, 2017).

12. Frances Fitzgerald, *Fire in the Lake: The Vietnamese and the Americans in Vietnam* (Boston, MA: Little Brown & Company, 1972), p. 5.

13. "Ministry of Interior: 24,138 Babies Born in Gaza during the Last 6 Months," *Palestine Chronicle* (March 12, 2017).

14. Data provided by a Gaza-based journalist.

1. Cited in Philip Rizk, "Colonizing the Gaza Strip: Two Phases of Governance—A Critique of the Idea of Sate," M.A. Thesis, Middle East Studies Center, The American University in Cairo, 2010, p. 27, http://dar.aucegypt.edu/bitstream/handle/10526/688/2010mesphiliprizk.pdf?sequence=1.

2. Ann Laura Stoler, *Duress: Imperial Durabilities in Our Times* (Durham, NC: Duke University Press, 2016), pp. 336–79.

3. Ibid., p. 374.

4. Sara Roy, "Introduction to the Third Edition—De-development Completed: Making Gaza Unviable," in *The Gaza Strip: The Political Economy of De-development* (Washington, DC: Institute for Palestine Studies, 2016), p. xix.

5. Stoler, *Duress*, p. 357.

6. Sara Roy, "Preface: Humanism, Scholarship and Politics: Writing on the Palestinian-Israeli Conflict," in *Failing Peace: Gaza and the Palestinian-Israeli Conflict* (London: Pluto Press, 2007), p. xxi.

7. Ariella Azoulay and Adi Ophir, "Abandoning Gaza," in Marcelo Svirsky and Simone Bignall (eds.), *Agamben and Colonialism* (Edinburgh, UK: Edinburgh University Press, 2012), p. 195.

8. Cited in Rizk, "Colonizing the Gaza Strip," title page.

9. Echoing the negative reaction Stoler received from her French colleagues in researching the *Front National* and their fear that she might conclude: "that they were not monsters."

10. Stoler, *Duress*, p. 371.

11. The decision was never President Trump's alone but one that enjoys considerable Congressional support including from many Democrats and from certain Arab and Western countries.

12. Sara Roy, "There is a Life Behind Every Statistic," *London Review of Books Blog* (June 4, 2018).

13. Grant Farred, "Rightlessness: The Case of Basil D'Oliveira," *Levinas Studies* 7 (2012), p. 208.

14. See Rosemary Sayigh's seminal work, *The Palestinians: From Peasants to Revolutionaries* (London: Zed Books, 1979, 2007).

15. Farred, "Rightlessness," pp. 197–218.

16. Roy, "There is a Life."

17. Ibid.

18. Ibid.

19. Stoler, *Duress*, p. 327.

20. Ibid., pp. 327–28.

21. Ibid., p. 329.

22. Roy, 'Introduction to the Third Edition', p. lxviii.

23. Sara Roy, "Floating in an Inch of Water: A Letter from Gaza," in Jamie Stern-Weiner (ed.), *Moment of Truth: Tackling Israel-Palestine's Toughest Questions* (New York: OR Books, 2018), p. 217. See also idem, "If Israel Were Smart," *London Review of Books*, June 15, 2017.

24. Roy, "Floating in an Inch of Water"; Roy, "If Israel Were Smart."

25. Roy, "Introduction to the Third Edition," pp. lx–lxi. Original source: Rajaie Batniji, "Searching for Dignity," *The Lancet* 380 (August 4, 2012), p. 466.

26. Roy, "Introduction to the Third Edition," p. lxi. Original source: Save the Children Sweden and the East Jerusalem YCA Rehabilitation Program, *The Impact of Child Detention: Occupied Palestinian Territory 2012*, 2012, p. 9, http://resourcecentre.savethechildren.se/sites/default/files/documents/5720.pdf.

27. Roy, "Preface: Humanism, Scholarship and Politics: Writing on the Palestinian-Israeli Conflict," p. xv.

28. Roy, "There is a Life."

29. Sara Roy, "Gaza: No se puede mirar—'One cannot look': A Brief Reflection," in Helga Tawil-Souri and Dina Matar (eds.), *Gaza as Metaphor* (London: Hurst & Company, 2016), p. 221.

30. Ibid., pp. 220–21.

31. Donald MacIntyre, *Gaza: Preparing for Dawn* (London: Oneworld Publications, 2017), p. 316 and Chapter 3, pp. 45–63; Ishaan Tharoor and Adam Taylor, "10 Quotes that Explain the History of the Gaza Conflict," *Washington Post*, July 18, 2014, www.washingtonpost.com/news/worldviews/wp/2014/07/18/10-quotes-that-explain-the-history-of-the-gaza-conflict/?utm_term=.f1921b34f670.

15   A JEWISH PLEA

1. Edward Said's favorite poem by Constantine Cavafy, "Waiting for the Barbarians," says, "they were, those people, a kind of solution." See Aliki Barnstone (trans.), *The Collected Poems of C.P. Cavafy: A New Translation* (New York: W.W. Norton, 2006).

2. Jacqueline Rose, "Continuing the Dialogue – on Edward Said," *The Last Resistance* (London: Verso, 2007), p. 194.

3. Parts of this introduction, which are slightly rewritten, first appeared in "Preface: Humanism, Scholarship and Politics: Writing on the Palestinian-Israeli Conflict," in Sara Roy, *Failing Peace: Gaza and the Palestinian-Israeli Conflict* (London: Pluto Press, 2007), xi–xxiii.

4. Ze'ev Schiff, "Analysis: For Israel, the Conflict in Lebanon is a Must-win Situation," *Haaretz*, July 26, 2006 and July 30, 2006.

5. Harry de Quetteville, "You're All Targets, Israel Tells Lebanese in South," *Telegraph.co.uk*, July 28, 2006.

6. Gideon Levy, "Days of Darkness," *Haaretz*, July 30, 2006.

7. The advertisement was placed by Israeli neocons in *Haaretz*, July 30, 2006.

8. Yesha Rabbinical Council, *During Time of War, Enemy Has No Innocents*, July 30, 2006.

9. Rabbinical Council of America, "RCA Solidarity Mission to Israel Expresses View of 'Tohar Haneshek' in Light of the Unprecedented Realities of Recent War with Hezbollah," August 17, 2006, www.rabbis.org.

10. Leonard Fein, "Was There Really No Other Way?" *Forward.com*, August 11, 2006.

11. Cited in Maxwell Taylor Kennedy, *Make Gentle the Life of This World: The Vision of Robert F. Kennedy* (New York: Harcourt Brace, 1998), pp. 74–5.

12. Jacqueline Rose, "Displacement in Zion," *The Last Resistance*, pp. 55–6.

13. Letter to the author from a colleague and friend, July 2006.

14. Silvia Tennenbaum, "Why Doesn't Israel Work for Peace?" *Newsday.com*, August 4, 2006.

15. "After Bomb Kills Loved Ones, Life Turns Ghostly in Lebanon," *New York Times*, August 8, 2006.

16. Anthony Shadid, "Survivors Rise From Rubble of Battered Lebanese Village," *Washington Post Foreign Service*, August 1, 2006.

20   TEARS OF SALT: A BRIEF REFLECTION ON ISRAEL, PALESTINE AND THE CORONAVIRUS

1. The Israeli Information Center for Human Rights in the Occupied Territories (B'Tselem), *During the Coronavirus Crisis, Israel Confiscates Tents Designated for Clinic in the Northern West Bank*, March 26, 2020, www.btselem.org/press_release/20200326_israel_confiscates_clinic_tents_during_coronavirus_crisis.

2. Nir Hasson, "Israel Shuts Palestinian Coronavirus Testing Clinic in East Jerusalem," *Haaretz*, April 15, 2020, www.haaretz.com/israel-news/.premium-israeli-police-raid-palestinian-coronavirus-testing-clinic-in-east-jerusalem-1.8767788?fbclid=IwAR3mZDlBlfGh8hbfHwCJg2LZcYkMa4fOIShwQHh4eUc-mRnCLgN_62Fxiko.

3. Yumna Patel, "Landowner says Israeli Authorities Demolished COVID-19 Testing Site on Donated Plot," *Mondoweiss*, July 23, 2020, https://mondoweiss.net/2020/07/israel-destroys-covid-19-testing-clinic-in-hebron-as-cases-soar/.

4. UNOCHA (United Nations Office for the Coordination of Humanitarian Affairs), *West Bank Demolitions and Displacement: An Overview*, October 2020, www.ochaopt.org/sites/default/files/demolition_monthly_report-october-2020.pdf.

5. Amira Hass, "The Latest in Jewish Morality: House Demolitions, Displacement, Settlement Construction," *Haaretz*, November 1, 2020, www.haaretz.com/opinion/.premium-here-s-the-news-about-jewish-morality-1.9280265.

6. UNOCHA, *West Bank Demolitions and Displacement*.

7. David Mills, Bram Wispelwey, Rania Muhareb and Mads Gilbert, "Structural Violence in the Era of a New Pandemic: The Case of the Gaza Strip," *The Lancet*, March 26, 2020, https://doi.org/10.1016/S0140-6736(20)30730-3. (This page no longer exists on *The Lancet* website and was removed soon after it was posted.)

8. UNRWA (United Nations Relief and Works Agency for Palestine Refugees in the Near East), Jabalia Camp, www.unrwa.org/where-we-work/gaza-strip/jabalia-camp.

9. "Israel Links Coronavirus Aid for Gaza to Recovering Soldiers," *Reuters*, April 1, 2020, www.reuters.com/article/us-health-coronavirus-israel-gaza/israel-links-coronavirus-aid-for-gaza-to-recovering-soldiers-idUSKBN21J5ZC; Motasem A. Dalloul, "Israel Blocks Coronavirus Respirators, Aid, to Gaza until Remains of 2 Israeli Invaders are Returned," *Middle East Monitor*, April 6, 2020, www.juancole.com/2020/04/coronavirus-respirators-invaders.html, and Gideon Levy, "Israel Trading in Ventilators for Helpless Gazans Is Inhumane," *Haaretz*, April 15, 2020, www.haaretz.cm/opinion/.premium-israel-trading-in-ventilators-for-helpless-gazans-is-inhumane-1.8768709. It also should be noted that in business arrangements with Israeli companies, Gazan sewing factories are now providing "Israel with millions of medical face masks [and 50,000 protective suits], while it faces an increasing outbreak of the coronavirus": Dalloul, "Israel Blocks Coronavirus Respirators."

10. Timothy Snyder, *On Tyranny: Twenty Lessons from the Twentieth Century* (New York: Tim Duggan Books, 2017), p. 118.

11. Ibid., p. 120.

12. See Sara Roy, "Introduction to the Third Edition: De-development Completed: Making Gaza Unviable," in *The Gaza Strip: The Political Economy of De-development*, Third Edition (Washington, DC: Institute for Palestine Studies, 2016), p. lxix. Based on a poem by the Israeli poet and author, Almog Behar, which he wrote to Mahmoud Darwish. See Nurit Peled-Elhanan, "The 45th Birthday of the Occupation," *Occupation Magazine*, June 9, 2012, www.kibush.co.il/show_file.asp?num=53383.

13. See Nadine Fresco, "Remembering the Unknown," *International Review of Psychoanalysis*, Volume 11 (1984).

14. Jeremy Sharon and Maayan Jaffe-Hoffman, "Holocaust Memorial Ceremony Staged Without Crowd in Shadow of Pandemic," *Jerusalem Post*, April 22, 2020, https://m.jpost.com/israel-news/holocaust-

memorial-day-official-ceremony-begins-watch-live-625251/
amp.

21   A TRIBUTE TO EYAD EL-SARRAJ

1. Sara Roy, *The Gaza Strip Survey* (Jerusalem: The West Bank Data Base Project and the Jerusalem Post Press, 1986), p. 109.

23   GAZA: OUT OF SIGHT

1. This essay was written nearly 35 years ago. The original English version published here was accompanied by several pages of endnotes citing sources. However, over time these pages were lost. When I found this essay in my archive—I thought it, too, was lost—I could not find the pages with the endnotes. The published French version contains no references, which, as I recall, is what the editors preferred. Hence, the absence of sources, for which I apologize.

24   WHEN A LOAF OF BREAD WAS NOT ENOUGH

1. "A Loaf of Bread is Not Enough" (*Ragheef al-Khubz La Yakfii*) was a slogan of the first Intifada.
2. See Sara Roy, "If Israel were Smart," *London Review of Books*, Volume 39, Number 12, June 15, 2017; Sara Roy, "Floating in an Inch of Water: A Letter from Gaza," in Jamie Stern-Weiner (ed.), *Moment of Truth: Tacking Israel-Palestine's Toughest Questions* (New York: OR Books, 2018), pp. 203–22.
3. Roy, "If Israel were Smart."
4. Cited in David Harrold, "From Sumud to Intifada: Supporting Non-violent Action to Enhance Mental Health," *International Journal of Applied Psychoanalytic Studies*, Volume 17 (2020), p. 165. Original source: Mary Elizabeth King, *A Quiet Revolution: The First Palestinian Intifada and Nonviolent Resistance* (New York: Nation Books, 2007).
5. Children engaged in their own forms of non-violence: "Children throw Palestinian flags tied to shoes and other weighty objects over electrical wires. This drives the soldiers mad because they cannot touch it." Through my many sources at the time, I was told that there were considerable arms in Gaza; in fact, I was offered access to the arms trade (on the Gaza side) between Israeli suppliers and local buyers, which I declined.
6. This is a complex issue far beyond the scope of this essay and is addressed in literature on the Intifada.
7. I wrote about this visit in Sara Roy, *A Land Diminished: Reflections on Gaza's Landscape*, in Mehrene Laurudee (ed.), *Gaza—Palestine: Out of*

the Margins (Birzeit, West Bank: Ibrahim Abu-Lughod Institute for International Studies, Bir Zeit University, 2011), p. 18. Most names have been changed.

8. In a separate visit to Jabalya camp, I was staying with a family when the Israeli military placed the camp under curfew. The windows to our shelter were shuttered and everyone inside sat on the floor in silence. Unthinkingly, I stood up and tried to peer through some cracks in the shutter to see what was going on outside not realizing that by doing so, I was placing the family in jeopardy. Suddenly, a shoe hit the side of my head and nearly knocked me over! When I turned to look, the elderly grandmother of the family, who was sitting in an adjacent room, motioned for me to sit down and threatened me with another shoe, which she held menacingly in her hand! Given the accuracy of her throw—and from the next room(!)—I took her seriously. My head ached but my embarrassment and regret hurt more. I later apologized profusely for my insensitivity.

9. Excerpts of this trip first appeared in Sara Roy, "Black Milk," *Women's Review of Books*, Volume 10, Number 10/11, July 1993, pp. 13–15.

10. Another example of local resistance and the failure to get people to submit is this excerpt from my field notes: "December 1988: Hatem told us that Gaza is getting a new military governor. The old one, Yossi Zeev, reportedly had a nervous breakdown. According to someone in the governor's office, during his first day in Gaza, the new governor got pelted with stones."

11. I told this story in part in Sara Roy, *Hamas and Civil Society in Gaza: Engaging the Islamist Social Sector* (Princeton, NJ: Princeton University Press, 2011/2014), pp. 27–8.

12. Capturing this sentiment, an Israeli officer speaking to my friend who was the Refugee Affairs Officer said, "We used to shoot airplanes, now we shoot Palestinians."

13. My notes are unclear but appear to indicate that this story was published in the *Jerusalem Post*, January 25, 1989.

14. Personal communication, March 2019.

15. Based on the fieldwork research of Dr. Caitlin Proctor, Gaza, March 2019.

16. Interview with Professor Deena Hurwitz, who was then working for the Resource Center on Nonviolence, Santa Cruz, CA, 1989.

17. Glenn Frankel, "Hidden Beneath the Surface, Intifada Spreads Its Roots," *International Herald Tribune*, March 27, 1989.

18. Personal conversation, Cambridge, MA, June 2020.

19. Anton Shammas, "The Reality of Palestine," *New York Times*, January 24, 1996.

20. The Hebrew name for Ansar 3 was *Ktzi'ot*.

21. This statement can be challenged and reflects a misreading or misunderstanding of the history of Jewish-Arab relations in Israel-Palestine but it is nonetheless striking and important.

22. See Sebastian Junger, *Tribe: On Homecoming and Belonging* (New York: Twelve Books, 2016).

23. See Sara Roy, "Preface," in Michael Sorkin and Deen Sharp (eds.), *Open Gaza* (Cairo and New York: The American University in Cairo Press and Terreform, 2021).

24. See, for example, Human Rights Watch, *Two Authorities, One Way, Zero Dissent: Arbitrary Arrest and Torture Under the Palestinian Authority and Hamas*, October 23, 2018, and Alaa Tartir, "Palestinians Have Been Abandoned By Their Leaders," *ForeignPolicy.com*, May 24, 2018.

25. Here I borrow and paraphrase from the writer Mark Danner who said something similar about torture after Abu Ghraib.

25 AN UNACCEPTABLE ABSENCE:
COUNTERING GAZA'S EXCEPTIONALISM

1. These airstrikes are partly in retaliation for incendiary balloons. But they are also meant as a message to Hamas to better control the border. According to one analyst, these airstrikes have increased with regard to the degree of destruction they inflict. They began by targeting empty, open spaces near the border area. This was followed by airstrikes against Hamas training grounds in less populated areas. Starting in August 2020, Israeli airstrikes targeted Hamas's underground infrastructure (without civilian casualties), including an elaborate tunnel and transportation system, telecommunication networks, and weapons and ammunition storage facilities. These strikes continued into November.

2. GISHA-Legal Center for Freedom of Movement, *Incursion of Israeli Bulldozers into the Strip Destroys Crops*, October 18, 2020, https://gisha.org/updates/11612.

3. Parts of this section are drawn from Sara Roy, "Existiert noch eine Wirtshaft? [Is there still an economy?], *der Freitag*, Issue 34, August 25, 2019, www.freitag.de/autoren/der-freitag/existiert-noch-eine-wirtschaft. Reprinted with permission.

4. The World Bank, "Cash-Strapped Gaza and an Economy in Collapse Put Palestinian Basic Needs at Risk," *Press Release*, September 25, 2018, www.worldbank.org/en/news/press-release/2018/09/25/cash-strapped-gaza-and-an-economy-in-collapse-put-palestinian-basic-needs-at-risk.

5. See, for example, Danny Zaken, "Israel Punishes Hamas, but also Advances Gaza Development Programs," *Al-Monitor*, September 9, 2020, www.al-monitor.com/pulse/originals/2020/09/israel-gaza-strip-hamas-benjamin-netanyahu-benny-gantz.html.

6. Tariq Dana, "Between Domination and Pacification: A Political Economy Analysis of Israeli Strategies in the oPt since 1967," Draft, in Alaa Tartir, Tariq Dana and Timothy Seidel (eds.), *Political Economy of Palestine: Critical, Interdisciplinary and Decolonial Perspectives* (New York: Palgrave Macmillan, Forthcoming, 2021).

7. Hugh Lovatt, "Israel's West Bank Annexation: Preparing EU Policy for the Day After," *European Council on Foreign Relations*, May 14, 2020, www.ecfr.eu/article/commentary_israels_west_bank_annexation_preparing_eu_policy_for_the_day_aft; and Gideon Levy, "Europe's Disappointing Response to Israel's Annexation of the West Bank," *Haaretz*, May 15, 2020, www.haaretz.com/opinion/.premium-europe-s-disappointing-response-to-israeli-annexation-of-the-west-bank-1.8850785.

8. See Steven A. Cook, "How to End the Special Relationship With Israel," *Foreign Policy*, May 20, 2020, https://foreignpolicy.com/2020/05/20/israel-palestine-annexation-west-bank-ending-special-relationship/, where he clearly articulates US core interests in this regard.

9. Anas Iqtait, *Economic Desperation and Dependence are Driving the Palestinian Authority's Political Decisions*, Middle East Institute, December 2, 2020, www.mei.edu/publications/economic-desperation-and-dependence-are-driving-palestinian-authoritys-political.

10. See GISHA – The Legal Center for Freedom of Movement, *Area G; From Separation to Annexation – Israel's Isolation of the Gaza Strip and how it Serves Annexationist Goals in the West Bank*, Tel Aviv, June 2020.

11. The World Bank, *Palestine's Economic Outlook*—October 2018, October 3, 2018, www.worldbank.org/en/country/westbankandgaza/publication/economic-outlook-october-2018.

12. United Nations Conference on Trade and Development (UNCTAD), *Report on UNCTAD Assistance to the Palestinian People: Developments in the Economy of the Occupied Palestinian Territory*, Geneva, August 7, 2009, p. 7, https://undocs.org/en/TD/B/56/3.

13. UNCTAD, *Economic Costs of the Israeli Occupation for the Palestinian People: The Gaza Strip Under Closure and Restrictions*, Geneva, August 13, 2020, p. 12, https://unctad.org/system/files/official-document/a75d310_en_1.pdf.

14. Mohammed Samhouri, *Three Years After the 2014 Gaza Hostilities—Beyond Survival: Challenges to Economic Recovery and Long Term Development*, United Nations Development Program (UNDP), May 2017, p. 26, www.undp.org/content/dam/papp/docs/Publications/UNDP-papp-research-Gazaeconomy072017-2022.pdf. UNCTAD, *Economic Costs of the Israeli Occupation*, p. 12, indicates the damage incurred as a result of the 2014 operation was "equivalent to 85 per cent of [Gaza's] capital stock that existed after the 2008–2009 strike."

15. United Nations Conference on Trade and Development (UNCTAD), *Report on UNCTAD Assistance to the Palestinian People: Developments*

in the Economy of the Occupied Palestinian Territory, Geneva, July 22, 2019, p. 8, https://unctad.org/meetings/en/SessionalDocuments/tdbex68d4_en.pdf?user=46.

16. UNCTAD, *Economic Costs of the Israeli Occupation*, p. 12.

17. The World Bank, "Cash-Strapped Gaza and an Economy in Collapse."

18. GISHA, *Unemployment in the First Quarter of 2020: Further Rise in Gaza's Unemployment Rate; 26,500 People Lost Their Jobs Even Before The Pandemic*, Tel Aviv, June 10, 2020, https://gisha.org/updates/11275. Also see GISHA, *Increase in Gaza's unemployment rate in 2019*, March 5, 2020, https://gisha.org/updates/10993#:~:text=March%205%2C%20 2020.,compared%20to%2043.1%25%20in%202018. It states: "Gaza's unemployment rate averaged 45.1% in 2019 overall, compared to 43.1% in 2018. The gap between unemployment in Gaza and the West Bank remains staggering; Gaza's unemployment rate in the fourth quarter, 42.7%, was more than triple that of the West Bank in the same period, 13.7%. The main increase in jobs in the fourth quarter of 2019 can be seen in services, farming and fishing, while jobs in construction and industry fell compared to the previous quarter. From June to December, funds from Qatar supported a United Nations-led project for temporary employment of university graduates. Another project designed to provide temporary jobs for university graduates in the health and education fields was launched in October with World Bank funding and is slated to continue until June 2020." Higher unemployment figures for 2018 were reported in United Nations Office for the Coordination of Humanitarian Affairs (UNOCHA) Occupied Palestinian Territory, *Humanitarian Needs Overview 2019*, December 2018, pp. 7–8, www.ochaopt.org/content/humanitarian-needs-overview-2019.

19. GISHA, *Gaza Unemployment Rate in the Second Quarter of 2020: 49.1%*, September 21, 2020, https://gisha.org/updates/11544.

20. UNOCHA, *Humanitarian Needs Overview 2019*, pp. 7, 24 and 25.

21. UNCTAD, *Economic Costs of the Israeli Occupation*, pp. 2 and 11.

22. UNOCHA, *Humanitarian Needs Overview 2019*, p. 4. Also see United Nations Relief and Works Agency (UNRWA), *2019 oPt Emergency Appeal*, 2019, Amman, Jordan, www.unrwa.org/sites/default/files/content/resources/2019_opt_ea_final.pdf.

23. UNOCHA, *Humanitarian Needs Overview 2019*, p. 4. For example, as of spring 2019, Qatar was funding social payments to 55,000 poor families who received the second installment of $100; 10,000 cash-for-work jobs for eight months through UNDP and UNRWA ($20 million); tens of millions in fuel payments; and millions of dollars in salary payments to the Hamas government.

24. Oliver Holmes, "People in Gaza Sifting Through Rubbish to Find Food, UN Head Says," *The Guardian*, October 12, 2020, www.

theguardian.com/world/2020/oct/12/people-in-gaza-sifting-through-rubbish-for-food-un-head-says.

25. The consequences for health are clear and made more concerning given the crippled state of healthcare delivery in Gaza. Much has been written about Gaza's crumbling healthcare system and the reasons for it. One issue, the longer-term impact of the continued use of munitions on the population, notably infants, children and their mothers, requires further research as this article strongly demonstrates: Nabil al Baraqoni, Samir R. Qouta, Mervi Vanska, Safwat Y. Diab, Raija-Leena Punamaki and Paola Manduca, "It Takes Time to Unravel the Ecology of War in Gaza, Palestine: Long-Term Changes in Maternal, Newborn and Toddlers' Heavy Metal Loads, and Infant and Toddler Developmental Milestones in the Aftermath of the 2014 Military Attacks," *International Journal of Environmental Research and Public Health*, Volume 17, Number 6,698, September 14, 2020. The water and sanitation situation also remains dire and has serious implications for dealing with the coronavirus. See Al Mezan Center for Human Rights et al., *Palestinian and Regional Human Rights Organizations Submit Joint Urgent Appeal to UN Special Procedures on the Escalating Water and Sanitation Crisis in the Gaza Strip*, oPt, November 10, 2020.

26. UNCTAD, *Economic Costs of the Israeli Occupation*, p. 2.

27. Ibid., p. 7.

28. Internal EU document, March 2019, Source asked not to be identified.

29. UNRWA, *2019 oPt Emergency Appeal*, p. 4.

30. Al Mezan, *Press Release: Al Mezan Condemns the Escalating Violence Between Disputing Families in Gaza, and Calls on Local Authorities to Uphold the Rule of Law*, Gaza, September 26, 2020, www.mezan.org/en/post/23810.

31. In 2017, the US pledged $364 million; in 2018 this fell to $60m, and by 2019 $0. Since 1950, soon after UNRWA's establishment, the US has contributed over $6 billion to the agency. See for example, Hady Amr, "In One Move, Trump Eliminated US funding for UNRWA and the US Role as Mideast Peacemaker," *Brookings*, September 7, 2018, www.brookings.edu/blog/order-from-chaos/2018/09/07/in-one-move-trump-eliminated-us-funding-for-unrwa-and-the-us-role-as-mideast-peacemaker; UNRWA, *2018 Confirmed Pledges to UNRWA's Programmes as of 31 December 2018*, www.unrwa.org/sites/default/files/list_of_2018_pledges_by_all_donors.pdf; UNRWA, *2017 Pledges to UNRWA's Programmes (Cash and In-kind) – Overall Donor Ranking as of 31 December 2017*, www.unrwa.org/sites/default/files/overalldonor_ranking.pdf; David Brunnstrom, "Trump Cuts More Than $200 Million in U.S. Aid to Palestinians," *Reuters*, August 24, 2018, www.reuters.com/article/us-usa-palestinians/trump-cuts-more-than-200-million-in-u-s-aid-to-palestinians-idUSKCN1L923C; Peter Beaumont and Oliver Holmes, "US Confirms End to Funding

for UN Palestinian Refugees," *The Guardian*, August 31, 2018, www. theguardian.com/world/2018/aug/31/trump-to-cut-all-us-funding-for-uns-main-palestinian-refugee-programme.

32. UNRWA, *2019 oPt Emergency Appeal*, p. 1.

33. Ibid.

34. Interview, Analyst, Gaza, May 2020, and Oliver Holmes, "People in Gaza Sifting Through Rubbish."

35. Dalal Yassine, "Trump's Aid Cuts Mean Harsh Winter for Palestine's Refugees," *Electronic Intifada*, December 4, 2020, https:// electronicintifada.net/content/trumps-aid-cuts-mean-harsh-winter-palestines-refugees/31856.

36. Brunnstrom, "Trump Cuts More Than $200 Million in U.S. Aid."

37. "H.R. 1164 – Taylor Force Act," December 5, 2017, *Congress.Gov*, www.congress.gov/bill/115th-congress/house-bill/1164; for the text of the bill see: www.congress.gov/bill/115th-congress/house-bill/1164/ text. Also see Amir Tibon, "U.S. Officially Cuts Funding to Palestinian Authority Over Payments to Terrorists and Their Families," *Haaretz*, March 24, 2018, www.haaretz.com/us-news/.premium-u-s-cuts-funding-to-pa-over-payments-to-terrorists-families-1.5937745.

38. Jim Zanotti, *Anti-Terrorism Clarification Act of 2018 (P.L. 115-253) and U.S. Aid for the Palestinians*, Congressional Research Service, February 5, 2019, https://fas.org/sgp/crs/mideast/IN11025.pdf. Also see Harry Graver and Scott R. Anderson, "Shedding Light on the Anti-Terrorism Clarification Act of 2018," *Lawfare*, October 25, 2018, www.lawfareblog. com/shedding-light-anti-terrorism-clarification-act-2018.

39. Evan Gottesman, "The Palestinians and the Anti-Terrorism Clarification Act: FAQ," *Israel Policy Forum*, January 24, 2019, https://israelpolicyforum.org/2019/01/24/the-palestinians-and-the-anti-terrorism-clarification-act-faq/, and Daniel Estrin, "U.S. Ends Funding for Palestinian Security Forces that Counter Militants," *NPR*, February 1, 2019, www.npr.org/2019/02/01/690356547/u-s-ends-funding-for-palestinian-security-forces-that-counter-militants.

40. Ruth Levush, *Israel: Law on Freezing Revenues Designated for the Palestinian Authority*, Law Library, Library of Congress, March 2019, www.loc.gov/law/help/freezing-revenues/israel.php.

41. Shibley Telhami, "Why the Discourse About Palestinian Payments to Prisoners' Families is Distorted and Misleading," *Brookings Institution*, December 7, 2020, www.brookings.edu/blog/ order-from-chaos/2020/12/07/why-the-discourse-about-palestinian-payments-to-prisoners-families-is-distorted-and-misleading/. The article examines the context in which this issue is so often misrepresented.

42. Noa Landau and Jack Khoury, "Israel Freezes Transfer of 500 Million Shekels of Palestinian Authority Taxes," *Haaretz*, February 17, 2019, www.haaretz.com/israel-news/israel-freezes-transfer-of-500-million-

shekels-of-palestinian-authority-taxes-1.6941078. Also see Jonathan Lis, "Israel Passes Law Freezing Funds to Palestinian Authority Over Payments to Security Prisoners," *Haaretz*, July 3, 2018, www.haaretz. com/israel-news/.premium-israel-law-freezes-funds-for-palestinian-security-prisoners-families-1.6240586.

43. Telhami, "Why the Discourse About Palestinian Payments to Prisoners' Families is Distorted and Misleading."

44. Noa Landau and Jack Khoury, "Israel Freezes Transfer of 500 Million Shekels," and "Israel to Withhold $138m from Palestinians Over Prisoner Payments," *Middle East Eye*, February 18, 2019, www.middleeasteye. net/news/israel-withhold-138m-palestinians-over-prisoner-payments.

45. Anas Iqtait, "The Palestinian Authority Political Economy: The Architecture of Fiscal Control," Draft, in Tartir, Dana and Seidel (eds.), *Political Economy of Palestine*.

46. Khaled Abu Toameh, "Palestinian Authority: "We'll Continue to Pay Prisoners and Their Families," *Jerusalem Post*, July 4, 2018, www.jpost. com/arab-israeli-conflict/palestinian-authority-well-continue-to-pay-prisoners-and-their-families-561486. Since Oslo, the provisions for deduction in the Paris Protocol were limited to service-orientated deductions; in contrast, Israel's more recent legislation regarding deductions is clearly politically motivated.

47. Shatha Hammad, "What did the PA Gain for Resuming Security Coordination with Israel?" *Middle East Eye*, November 24, 2020, www.middleeasteye.net/news/israel-palestinian-authority-security-coordination-what-gain.

48. Iqtait, *Economic Desperation and Dependence are Driving the Palestinian Authority's Political Decisions.*

49. David M. Halbfinger and Adam Rasgon, "Reassured by Biden Win, Palestinians Will Resume Cooperation With Israel," *New York Times*, November 19, 2020, www.nytimes.com/2020/11/17/world/middleeast/israel-palestinians-security-annexation.html.

50. Ibid.

51. "Israel Transfers Palestinian Authority $1.14 Billion in Tax Revenues," *Jewish News Syndicate*, December 3, 2020, www.jns.org/israel-transfers-palestinian-authority-1-14-billion-in-tax-revenues, and "Israel Transfers $1.14Bn in Tax Revenues to PA," *Middle East Monitor*, December 3, 2020, www.middleeastmonitor.com/20201203-israel-transfers-1-14bn-in-tax-revenues-to-pa. Also see, Ramona Wadi, "The EU Reaction to Settlements and Security Coordination Reflects the PA Betrayal of Palestine," *Middle East Monitor*, November 26, 2020, www. middleeastmonitor.com/20201126-the-eu-reaction-to-settlements-and-security-coordination-reflects-the-pa-betrayal-of-palestine/.

52. The World Bank, "Cash-Strapped Gaza and an Economy in Collapse."

53. Internal EU document, May 2020.

54. The World Bank, "Cash-Strapped Gaza and an Economy in Collapse."

55. UNOCHA, *Humanitarian Snapshot: Casualties in the Context of Demonstrations and Hostilities in Gaza 30 March 2018—30 September 2019*, Jerusalem, October 15, 2019, https://reliefweb.int/sites/reliefweb.int/files/resources/gaza_snapshot_15_10_2019.pdf. For more general information on casualties since 2008, see UNOCHA, *Data on Casualties*, www.ochaopt.org/data/casualties.

56. Desmond Travers, *War Crimes Post-Nuremburg: Investigation Insights— Reflections on War Crime Investigation Experiences*, Lecture, Town Hall, Naas, Co. Kildare, Ireland, February 26, 2019.

57. According to the UN, "One of the areas affected by this precarious situation is maternal health ... So far in 2019, as many maternal deaths have been reported than in all of 2018. Continued shortages of essential life-saving maternal and child health pharmaceuticals have increased the risk of disability and death among pregnant women and newborns. The percentage of essential medicines with less than a month's supply increased from 38 per cent in 2017 to 46 per cent in 2018, reaching 50 per cent in August 2019." UNOCHA, *Overview— September 2019*, September 2019, www.ochaopt.org/content/overview-september-2019. Also see Michael Lynk, *Report of the Special Rapporteur on the Situation of Human Rights in the Palestinian Territories Occupied Since 1967 (A/74/507)*, United Nations General Assembly, October 21, 2019, https://reliefweb.int/sites/reliefweb.int/files/resources/A_74_507_E.pdf, p. 5.

58. UNOCHA, *Humanitarian Snapshot*.

59. "Gaza: Life 'Extraordinarily Difficult' for People with Disability," *Al Jazeera*, December 3, 2020, www.aljazeera.com/news/2020/12/3/life-in-gaza-extraordinarily-difficult-for-disabled-hrw. Also see International Committee of the Red Cross, *Young Amputees in Gaza are striving to put their lives back on track*, July 8, 2019, www.icrc.org/en/document/young-amputees-gaza-are-striving-put-their-lives-back-track#:~:text=Due%20to%20a%20series%20of,the%20job%20market%20is%20fierce.

60. Travers, *War Crimes Post-Nuremburg*.

61. Interview, Analyst, Gaza, May 2020.

62. Khaled Abu Toameh, "Is Hamas Facing a New Mutiny?" *Jerusalem Post,* July 5, 2020, www.jpost.com/middle-east/is-hamas-facing-a-new-mutiny-633940, and Hamza Abu Al-Tarabeesh, "This Summer has Revealed a Sharp Rise in Suicides in Gaza," *Mondoweiss*, September 11, 2020, https://mondoweiss.net/2020/09/this-summer-has-revealed-a-sharp-rise-in-suicides-in-gaza/.

63. See, for example, Bram Wispelwey and Yasser Abu Jamei, "The Great March of Return: Lessons from Gaza on Mass Resistance and Mental Health," *Health and Human Rights Journal*, Volume 22, Number 1, June 2020; Entsar Abu Jahal, "Gaza Women Use Social Media to Reveal Domestic Abuse," *Al-Monitor*, October 2, 2020, www.al-monitor.com/

pulse/originals/2020/09/gaza-women-domestic-abuse-social-media-campaigns.html, and Save the Children, *A Decade of Distress: The Harsh and Unchanging Reality for Children Living in the Gaza Strip*, 2019, https://resourcecentre.savethechildren.net/library/decade-distress-harsh-and-unchanging-reality-children-living-gaza-strip.

64. Also see Sara Roy, "Afterword: The Wars on Gaza—A Reflection," in Sara Roy, *The Gaza Strip: The Political Economy of De-development, third edition* (Washington, DC: Institute for Palestine Studies, 2016), pp. 395–423.

65. Lynk, *Report of the Special Rapporteur*, pp. 5–6, and Oliver Holmes, "Hamas Violently Suppresses Gaza Economic Protests," *The Guardian*, March 21, 2019, www.theguardian.com/world/2019/mar/21/hamas-violently-suppresses-gaza-economic-israeli-border-protests.

66. Interview, Analyst, Gaza, May 2019.

67. Lynk, *Report of the Special Rapporteur*, pp. 6–7.

68. Interview, Analyst, Gaza, Spring 2020.

69. Lynk, *Report of the Special Rapporteur*, p. 5, and Khaled Abu Toameh, "Is Hamas Facing a New Mutiny?"

70. Interview, Analyst, Gaza, Fall 2019.

71. Ibid.

72. Amira Hass, "Islamic Jihad Reminds Gazans that Hamas Disappoints and Israel Aims to Cut Them Off," *Haaretz*, November 16, 2019, www.haaretz.com/israel-news/.premium-islamic-jihad-reminds-gazans-that-hamas-disappoints-and-israel-aims-to-cut-them-off-1.8131434.

73. "Gaza After the War: A Sea of Despair—Desperate Palestinians Become Boat People," *The Economist*, October 4, 2014, www.economist.com/middle-east-and-africa/2014/10/04/a-sea-of-despair.

74. Interview, Analyst, Gaza, Summer 2019.

75. Ibid.

76. *The Economist*, "Gaza After the War."

77. Interview, Analyst, Gaza, Summer 2019.

78. Al Mezan Center for Human Rights, *Water Shortage in the Gaza Strip Amid Covid-19 Outbreak*, Gaza, September 2020, http://mezan.org/en/uploads/files/1599648780765.pdf.

79. For example, see Sondeep Sen, "The Pandemic Under Siege: A View from the Gaza Strip," *World Development*, Volume 135 (November 2020). A letter from Yasser Abu Jamei, the director of the Gaza Community Mental Health Programme, succinctly captures the problem: "The reality of the underdeveloped health system paralyzed by the Palestinian division and the continuous pressure caused by the attacks on Gaza, the casualties from the Great March of Return and the lack of staffing. The reality is that 2 million people live in a small geographical area of 365 square kilometers (141 sq mi) with two thirds of the population being refugees. The reality is that the poverty rate among this population is 53% and the unemployment rate is 54%. That

more than 95% of water is not potable and electricity is available for 8 hours per day in its best circumstances," Email correspondence, Gaza Strip, September 2020.

80. By mid-October 2020, the obligatory 21-day quarantine had been relaxed to one week at a quarantine site and 14 days at home. Those breaking the home quarantine are subject to arrest by the police and Ministry of the Interior.

81. Interview, Analyst, Gaza, May 2020.

82. *BBC Radio News* (on National Public Radio, Boston, MA), November 25, 2020, and "Coronavirus Test Kits Run Out in Gaza as 'Collapse' Fears Grow," *Al Jazeera*, December 7, 2020, www.aljazeera.com/news/2020/12/7/coronavirus-test-kits-run-out-in-gaza-as-collapse-fears-grow.

83. Interview, Analyst, Gaza, May 2020.

84. Palestinian National Authority Ministry of Health, *Daily Report for COVID 19 Virus*, August 17, 2020, Ramallah, Palestine. Also see "Coronavirus Live: Palestinian Authority Locks Down Hebron, Nablus as Cases Rise," *Haaretz*, June 21, 2020, www.haaretz.com/israel-news/coronavirus-israel-live-new-hot-spots-emerging-in-south-tel-aviv-jaffa-1.8921483, and Adam Rasgon and Iyad Abuheweila, "Covid-19 Spares Gaza, But Travel Restrictions Prove Less Forgiving," *New York Times*, August 8, 2020, www.nytimes.com/2020/08/08/world/middleeast/coronavirus-gaza.html.

85. It should be mentioned that the Israeli security establishment was "quite happy with the way the Hamas authorities [were] handling the crisis." Interview with former security official now based in Europe, May 2020. This individual further pointed out that the Hamas authorities were also working well with UNRWA and the WHO.

86. This last point about training in Israel could not be verified.

87. Ministry of Health, Gaza, Palestine, *Cumulative Statistics: Covid-19 in Gaza Strip*, September 10, 2020; Ministry of Health, Gaza, Palestine, *Covid Gaza, 26 August–14 September,* September 14, 2020; International Crisis Group, *Gaza's New Coronavirus Fears*, Middle East Briefing no. 78, September 9, 2020, and Osaid Alser, Shaymaa AlWaheidi, Khamis Elessi and Hamza Meghari, "COVID-19 in Gaza: A Pandemic Spreading in a Place Already Under Protracted Lockdown," *Eastern Mediterranean Health Journal*, Volume 26, 2020.

88. Ministry of Health, Gaza, Palestine, *Cumulative Statistics: Covid-19 in Gaza Strip*, October 12, 2020 and October 30, 2020. Community spread was facilitated by the lifting of certain closure measures, the laxity of mask wearing, and infighting between the Ministries of Health and Interior over policy.

89. "Covid: Gaza Health System 'Days from Being Overwhelmed,'" *BBC News*, November 22, 2020, www.bbc.com/news/world-middle-east-55035955, and Correspondence, Omar Shaban, Economist, Gaza,

November 16, 2020 who reported over 10,000 infected people just a few days before.

90. Ministry of Health, Gaza, Palestine, *Covid-19 Daily Updates in Gaza Strip*, December 15, 2020.

91. Interview, Analyst, Gaza, October 2020. According to this individual, the number of people requiring hospitalization had not exceeded hospital resources, and this remained the case throughout the fall of 2020. However, given that majority of new active cases in the oPt are in Gaza and given Gaza's fragile healthcare system and the lack of vaccines, the healthcare system is under enormous pressure, and the chances of survival for Covid patients with chronic diseases is low.

92. Ahmed Abu Artema, "Gaza Holds Its Breath as the Threat of Coronavirus Looms," *The Nation*, May 15, 2020, www.thenation.com/article/world/coronavirus-gaza-crisis/.

93. BBC News, "Covid: Gaza Health System 'Days from Being Overwhelmed.'"

94. Alice Rothchild, MD, *Jewish Voice for Peace Health Advisory Council Weekly Covid 19 Timeline in Israel/Palestine*, December 13, 2020, www.jvphealth.org/covid-19. This publication also indicates that the number of families in Israel living in poverty increased from one-fifth to nearly one-third since the outbreak of the virus earlier in 2020.

95. Mosques were opened for the first time on Friday, May 29, 2020, at 30 percent capacity after being cleaned and disinfected.

96. Internal memo, email correspondence, December 3, 2020, and Al Jazeera, "Coronavirus Test Kits Run Out in Gaza."

97. GISHA, *The Rights of Gaza's Civilian Population Must Be Protected*, June 14, 2020, https://gisha.org/updates/11278, and Office of the United Nations Special Coordinator For The Middle East Peace Process, *Paper to the Ad-Hoc Liaison Committee*, June 2, 2020, https://unsco.unmissions.org/sites/default/files/unsco_ahlc_paper_-_june_2020_0.pdf?mc_cid=0546c05582&mc_eid=dc60fbdf23.

98. Internal document, European NGO, May 2020. The West Bank economy also was negatively impacted with a near-doubling of unemployment among other consequences.

99. GISHA, *Gaza Unemployment Rate in the Second Quarter of 2020*.

100. Islamic Relief Worldwide, *New Study Shows Shocking Economic and Psychological Toll of Covid-19 In Gaza*, November 2020, www.islamic-relief.org/new-study-shows-shocking-economic-and-psychological-toll-of-covid-19-in-gaza/.

101. "Gaza Workers Union: The Unemployment Rate has Exceeded 70% as a Result of the Blockade and Corona," *Al-Quds Al-Arabi*, October 28, 2020.

102. Internal document, European NGO, May 2020. Another area of concern (that is beyond the scope of this chapter to examine in any detail) is the impact of the pandemic on a society where social solidarity

is critical to addressing and mediating crises and conflicts. Combined with a weakened economy, virus-based restrictions such as quarantine, have led to alarming increases in crime, among other serious problems. See Talal Abu Rukbah, *Impact of Corona Pandemic on Social Relations in Gaza Strip\Palestine,* Palestinian NGOs Network (PNGO) and the Friedrich Ebert Stiftung, Palestine, June 2020.

103. In this regard, see Ghassan Abu-Sittah, "The Virus, the Settler and the Siege: Gaza in the Age of Corona," *Journal of Palestine Studies,* Volume XLIX, No. 4 (Summer 2020), pp. 65–76.

104. Interview with a colleague in Gaza, Summer 2020.

105. This sense of insecurity and instability was also seen in Israel's assassination of a senior leader of the Palestinian Islamic Jihad in November 2019, which provoked a violent response by the Islamist group in Gaza (who fired over 450 rockets into Israel) and Israeli retaliation that left 34 Palestinians dead, including eight members of one family and 111 injured including 46 children and 20 women. In addition, five Israelis were injured and 63 required medical treatment. This assault attests to the continuing lack of accountability and impunity with which Israel continues to act toward Gaza. See Yaniv Kubovich and Jack Khoury, "Israeli Army Admits to Killing Eight Gaza Family Members: We Thought the House Was Empty," *Haaretz,* November 15, 2019, www.haaretz.com/middle-east-news/palestinians/.premium-israeli-army-admits-strike-that-killed-palestinian-family-intended-for-empty-house-1.8129435; Gideon Levy, "No One in Israel Knew They Were Committing a Massacre, and They Didn't Care," *Haaretz,* November 17, 2019, www.haaretz.com/opinion/.premium-no-one-in-the-israel-knew-they-were-committing-a-massacre-and-they-didn-t-care-1.8133763.

106. Hamza Abu Al-Tarabeesh, "This Summer has Revealed a Sharp Rise in Suicides in Gaza," *Mondoweiss,* September 11, 2020, https://mondoweiss.net/2020/09/this-summer-has-revealed-a-sharp-rise-in-suicides-in-gaza/.

107. Interview, Analyst, Gaza, Summer 2019. This same analyst made another disturbing point regarding Palestinians in East Jerusalem, stating that there is a "general lack of national identity [which] is becoming more acute. On the one hand, they are integrated into the Israeli economy with ... the benefits that brings; on the other, they are so disconnected from [other] Palestinians ... they don't share the same understanding of what it means to be Palestinian with those in the West Bank and Gaza."

108. Ibid. This is why the announcement in September 2020 of a Fatah-Hamas agreement to hold legislative and presidential elections in 2021—the first time in 15 years—did little to mitigate popular despair.

109. Tweet from @JoeBiden in "Joe Biden declares 'Israel has a right to defend itself' after it kills scores in Gaza," *The New Arab,* November 14,

2019, https://english.alaraby.co.uk/english/news/2019/11/14/biden-okays-israels-killing-of-palestinian-children-civilians. Also see *Remarks by Vice President Joe Biden to the 2014 Saban Forum*, The Willard Hotel, Washington, DC, December 7, 2014, https://obamawhitehouse.archives.gov/the-press-office/2014/12/07/remarks-vice-president-joe-biden-2014-saban-forum.

110. Internal memo, EU, December 2020. The author and institution asked not to be identified. Also see, "Joe Biden and the Jewish Community: A Record and a Plan of Friendship, Support and Action," Biden/Harris 2020 Website, https://joebiden.com/joe-biden-and-the-jewish-community-a-record-and-a-plan-of-friendship-support-and-action/#, and Sumaya Awad and Hadas Their, "Be Ready to Fight President Joe Biden on Israel-Palestine," *Jacobin*, November 12, 2020, https://jacobinmag.com/2020/11/president-joe-biden-israel-palestine-foreign-policy.

111. Internal EU memo, December 2020.

112. George T. Abed, "The Economic Viability of a Palestinian State," *Journal of Palestine Studies*, No. 2, Volume 19 (1989/90), p. 23. Original source: The Jewish Agency for Palestine, *The Jewish Case Before the Anglo-American Committee of Inquiry on Palestine* (Jerusalem, 1947), p. 495.

113. UNOCHA, *Overview—September 2019*.

114. Lynk, *Report of the Special Rapporteur*, pp. 10 and 21.

EPILOGUE "WE ARE NO DIFFERENT THAN YOU"

1. Here I quote from the literary critic, Shoshana Felman, writing about the Nazi treatment of Jews. In doing so, I am not drawing any equivalency between the Holocaust and Israel's treatment of the Palestinians, but to certain parallels that do exist. See Shoshana Felman, "The Return of the Voice: Claude Lanzmann's *Shoah*," in Shoshana Felman and Dori Laub, *Testimony: Crises of Witnessing in Literature, Psychoanalysis and History* (New York: Routledge, 1992), pp. 209–10.

2. Audre Lorde, *Poetry Is Not A Luxury*, 1985, https://makinglearning.files.wordpress.com/2014/01/poetry-is-not-a-luxury-audre-lorde.pdf.

3. Felman, "The Return of the Voice," pp. 209–10.

4. See Brian K. Barber, "Contrasting Portraits of War: Youths' Varied Experiences with Political Violence in Bosnia and Palestine," *International Journal of Behavioural Development*, Volume 32, No. 4 (July 2008), pp. 298–309, and Brian K. Barber et al., "Whither the "Children of the Stone"? An Entire Life Under Occupation," *Journal of Palestine Studies*, Volume 45, Issue 2 (Winter 2016), pp. 77–108. Also see, for example, *The Palestine Writes Literature Festival (A Virtual Event)*, December 2–6, 2020, www.palestinewrites.org; Atef Abu

Saif (ed.), *The Book of Gaza: A City in Short Fiction (Reading the City)* (Manchester, UK: Comma Press, July 3, 2014); Basma Galayini (ed.), *Palestine +100: Stories from a Century After the Nakba* (Manchester, UK: Comma Press, August 27, 2019); Ibtisam Azem, *The Book of Disappearance: A Novel* (Syracuse, NY: Syracuse University Press, 2019), and Michael Sorkin and Deen Sharp (eds.) *Open Gaza: Architectures of Hope* (Cairo and New York: The American University in Cairo Press and Terreform, 2021).

Index

The Pluto Press Newsletter

Hello friend of Pluto!

Want to stay on top of the best radical books we publish?

Then sign up to be the first to hear about our new books, as well as special events, podcasts and videos.

You'll also get 50% off your first order with us when you sign up.

Come and join us!

Go to bit.ly/PlutoNewsletter